# REALMS *of* GOLD

A
CORE KNOWLEDGE®
READER

VOLUME TWO

# Realms of Gold

## A Core Knowledge® Reader

## Volume Two

editor: Michael J. Marshall

general editor: E. D. Hirsch, Jr.

library of congress card catalog number: 00-100085

isbn 1-89-0517-23-2 trade paperback



printed in canada

design:

Bill Womack Incorporated, free union, virginia

cover illustration:

detail from *The Milkmaid* by Maxfield Parrish, 1901

4th printing, october 2004

Core Knowledge® Foundation

801 east high street, charlottesville, virginia 22902

www.coreknowledge.org

## ABOUT THIS BOOK

THE THREE-VOLUME *Realms of Gold* series brings together all the shorter literary works taught in the Core Knowledge Sequence for the middle school grades. Volume Two includes those for grade seven. Each volume also offers additional classic works in every genre for teachers and students interested in supplementary readings. Speeches and autobiographical excerpts were selected partly for their pertinence to historical topics taught in the Sequence at each grade level.

The Core Knowledge Sequence outlines a core curriculum in English/language arts, history and geography, math, science, the fine arts and music for preschool through grade eight. It is designed to ensure that children are exposed to the essential knowledge that establishes cultural literacy as they also acquire a broad, firm foundation for higher-level schooling. Its first version, covering grades one through six, was developed in 1990 at a convention of teachers and subject matter experts in Charlottesville, Virginia, and embodied the best guidance of cognitive scientists and international educational research. It was revised in 1995 to reflect the classroom experience of Core Knowledge teachers, and subsequently content outlines for preschool, kindergarten, and grades seven and eight were prepared. The Sequence is now used in more than a thousand schools across America. Its content is also offered through the Core Knowledge Series of books, *What Your Kindergartner-Sixth Grader Needs to Know.*

# CONTENTS

## POEMS

CONTENTS

THE SELECTIONS BELOW ARE FOR ADDITIONAL READING



STORIES



THE SELECTIONS BELOW ARE FOR ADDITIONAL READING

CONTENTS



## ESSAYS



## SPEECHES



THE SELECTIONS BELOW ARE FOR ADDITIONAL READING



## AUTOBIOGRAPHY

THE SELECTIONS BELOW ARE FOR ADDITIONAL READING

# POEMS

# William Blake

## *The Chimney Sweeper*

–From *Songs of Innocence*

WHEN MY mother died I was very young,
And my father sold me while yet my tongue
Could scarcely cry "weep! 'weep! 'weep! 'weep!"
So your chimneys I sweep, & in soot I sleep.

There's little Tom Dacre, who cried when his head,
That curled like a lamb's back, was shav'd; so I said,
"Hush, Tom! never mind it, for when your bead's bare,
You know that the soot cannot spoil your white hair."

And so he was quiet, & that very night,
As Tom was asleeping he had such a sight—
That thousands of sweepers, Dick, Joe, Ned & Jack,
Were all of them locked up in coffins of black;

And by came an Angel who had a bright key,
And he opened the coffins & set them all free;
Then down a green plain leaping, laughing they run,
And wash in a river and shine in the sun.

Then naked & white, all their bags left behind,
They rise upon clouds, and sport in the wind.
And the angel told Tom, if he'd be a good boy,
He'd have God for his father & never want joy.

And so Tom awoke, and we rose in the dark,
And got with our bags & our brushes to work.
Though the morning was cold, Tom was happy & warm;
So if all do their duty, they need not fear harm.

## *The Chimney Sweeper*

—From *Songs of Experience*

A LITTLE black thing among the snow
Crying " 'weep, 'weep," in notes of woe!
"Where are thy father & mother? say?"
"They are both gone up to the church to pray.

"Because I was happy upon the heath,
And smil'd among the winter's snow;
They clothed me in the clothes of death,
And taught me to sing the notes of woe.

"And because I am happy, & dance & sing,
They think they have done me no injury,
And are gone to praise God & his Priest & King,
Who make up a heaven of our misery."

# Robert Burns

## *Auld Lang Syne*

SHOULD AULD acquaintance be forgot,
And never brought to min'?
Should auld acquaintance be forgot,
And days o' **lang syne** ?

*Chorus*
*For auld lang syne, my dear,*
*For auld lang syne,*
*We'll tak a cup o' kindness yet,*
*For auld lang syne.*

We twa hae run about the **braes**,
And pu'd the **gowans** fine,
But we've wandered mony a weary foot,
Sin' auld lang syne.

[*Chorus*]

We twa hae paidled i' the **burn**,
From morning sun till **dine**,
But seas between us **braid** hae roared,
Sin' auld lang syne.

[*Chorus*] »

---

**Lang syne:** Long ago. **Braes:** Slopes. **Gowans:** Daisies.
**Burn:** Stream. **Dine:** Dinner, noon. **Braid:** Broad.

And there's a hand, my trusty **fiere**,
And gie's a hand o' thine;
And we'll tak a right gude-**willie waught**,
For auld lang syne.

[*Chorus*]

And surely ye'll **be your pint-stowp**,
And surely I'll be mine;
And we'll tak a cup o' kindness yet,
For auld lang syne.

[*Chorus*]

---

**Fiere:** Friend. **Willie waught:** Deep drink.
**Be your pint-stowp:** Pay for your pint-cup.

# Countee Cullen

## *Heritage*

For Harold Jackman

What is Africa to me:
Copper sun or scarlet sea,
Jungle star or jungle track,
Strong bronzed men, or regal black
Women from whose loins I sprang
When the birds of Eden sang?
*One three centuries removed*
*From the scenes his fathers loved,*
*Spicy grove, cinnamon tree,*
*What is Africa to me?*

So I lie, who all day long
Want no sound except the song
Sung by wild barbaric birds
Goading massive jungle herds,
Juggernauts of flesh that pass
Trampling tall defiant grass
Where young forest lovers lie,
Plighting troth beneath the sky.
So I lie, who always hear,
Though I cram against my ear
Both my thumbs, and keep them there,
Great drums throbbing through the air.
So I lie, whose fount of pride,
Dear distress, and joy allied,
Is my somber flesh and skin,
With the dark blood dammed within »

Like great pulsing tides of wine
That, I fear, must burst the fine
Channels of the chafing net
Where they surge and foam and fret.

Africa? A book one thumbs
Listlessly, till slumber comes.
Unremembered are her bats
Circling through the night, her cats
Crouching in the river reeds,
Stalking gentle flesh that feeds
By the river brink; no more
Does the bugle-throated roar
Cry that monarch claws have leapt
From the scabbards where they slept.
Silver snakes that once a year
Doff the lovely coats you wear,
Seek no covert in your fear
Lest a mortal eye should see;
What's your nakedness to me?
Here no leprous flowers rear
Fierce corollas in the air;
Here no bodies sleek and wet,
Dripping mingled rain and sweat,
Tread the savage measures of
Jungle boys and girls in love.
What is last year's snow to me,
Last year's anything? The tree

Budding yearly must forget
How its past arose or set—
Bough and blossom, flower, fruit,

Even what shy bird with mute
Wonder at her travail there,
Meekly labored in its hair.
*One three centuries removed*
*From the scenes his fathers loved,*
*Spicy grove, cinnamon tree,*
*What is Africa to me?*

So I lie, who find no peace
Night or day, no slight release
From the unremittent beat
Made by cruel padded feet
Walking through my body's street.
Up and down they go, and back,
Treading out a jungle track.
So I lie, who never quite
Safely sleep from rain at night—
I can never rest at all
When the rain begins to fall;
Like a soul gone mad with pain
I must match its weird refrain;
Ever must I twist and squirm,
Writhing like a baited worm,
While its primal measures drip
Through my body, crying, "Strip!
Doff this new exuberance.
Come and dance the Lover's Dance!"
In an old remembered way
Rain works on me night and day.

Quaint, outlandish heathen gods
Black men fashion out of rods, »

Clay, and brittle bits of stone,
In a likeness like their own,
My conversion came high-priced;
I belong to Jesus Christ,
Preacher of humility;
Heathen gods are naught to me.

Father, Son, and Holy Ghost,
So I make an idle boast;
Jesus of the twice-turned cheek,
Lamb of God, although I speak
With my mouth thus, in my heart
Do I play a double part.
Ever at Thy glowing altar
Must my heart grow sick and falter,
Wishing He I served were black,
Thinking then it would not lack
Precedent of pain to guide it,
Let who would or might deride it;

Surely then this flesh would know
Yours had borne a kindred woe.
Lord, I fashion dark gods, too,
Daring even to give You
Dark despairing features where,
Crowned with dark rebellious hair,
Patience wavers just so much as
Mortal grief compels, while touches
Quick and hot, of anger, rise
To smitten cheek and weary eyes.
Lord, forgive me if my need
Sometimes shapes a human creed.

*All day long and all night through,*
*One thing only must I do:*
*Quench my pride and cool my blood,*
*Lest I perish in the flood.*
*Lest a hidden ember set*
*Timber that I thought was wet*
*Burning like the driest flax,*
*Melting like the merest wax,*
*Lest the grave restore its dead.*
*Not yet has my heart or head*
*In the least way realized*
*They and I are civilized.*

## Emily Dickinson

### *Because I could not stop for Death*

BECAUSE I could not stop for Death—
He kindly stopped for me—
The Carriage held but just Ourselves—
And Immortality.

We slowly drove—He knew no haste
And I had put away
My labor and my leisure too,
For His Civility—

We passed the School, where Children strove
At Recess—in the Ring—
We passed the Fields of Gazing Grain—
We passed the Setting Sun—

Or rather—He passed Us—
The Dews drew quivering and chill—
For only Gossamer, my Gown—
My Tippet—only Tulle—

We paused before a House that seemed
A Swelling of the Ground—
The Roof was scarcely visible—
The Cornice—in the Ground—

Since then—'tis Centuries—and yet
Feels shorter than the Day
I first surmised the Horses' Heads
Were toward Eternity—

# T. S. Eliot

## *Macavity: The Mystery Cat*

MACAVITY'S A Mystery Cat: he's called the Hidden Paw—
For he's the master criminal who can defy the Law.
He's the bafflement of Scotland Yard, the Flying Squad's despair:
For when they reach the scene of crime—*Macavity's not there!*

Macavity, Macavity, there's no one like Macavity,
He's broken every human law, he breaks the law of gravity.
His powers of levitation would make a fakir stare,
And when you reach the scene of crime—*Macavity's not there!*
You may seek him in the basement, you may look up in the air—
But I tell you once and once again, *Macavity's not there!*

Macavity's a ginger cat, he's very tall and thin;
You would know him if you saw him, for his eyes are sunken in.
His brow is deeply lined with thought, his head is highly domed;
His coat is dusty from neglect, his whiskers are uncombed.
He sways his head from side to side, with movements like a
snake;
And when you think he's half asleep, he's always wide awake.

Macavity, Macavity, there's no one like Macavity,
For he's a fiend in feline shape, a monster of depravity.
You may meet him in a by-street, you may see him in the
square—
But when a crime's discovered, then *Macavity's not there!*

He's outwardly respectable (They say he cheats at cards.)
And his footprints are not found in any file of Scotland Yard's.
And when the larder's looted, or the jewel-case is rifled, »

Or when the milk is missing, or another **Peke's** been stifled,
Or the greenhouse glass is broken, and the trellis past repair—
Ay, there's the wonder of the thing! *Macavity's not there!*

And when the Foreign Office find a Treaty's gone astray,
Or the Admiralty lose some plans and drawings by the way,
There may be a scrap of paper in the hall or on the stair—
But it's useless to investigate—*Macavity's not there!*
And when the loss has been disclosed, the Secret Service say:
'It must have been Macavity!'—but he's a mile away.
You'll be sure to find him resting, or a-licking of his thumbs,
Or engaged in doing complicated long division sums.

Macavity, Macavity, there's no one like Macavity,
There never was a Cat of such deceitfulness and suavity.
He always has an alibi, and one or two to spare:
At whatever time the deed took place—Macavity wasn't there!
And they say that all the Cats whose wicked deeds are widely
known
(I might mention Mungojerrie, I might mention Griddlebone)
Are nothing more than agents for the Cat who all the time
Just controls their operations: the Napoleon of Crime!

---

**Peke:** A Pekingese dog.

# Robert Frost

## *Fire and Ice*

SOME SAY the world will end in fire,
Some say in ice.
From what I've tasted of desire
I hold with those who favor fire,
But if it had to perish twice,
I think I know enough of hate
To say that for destruction ice
Is also great
And would suffice.

## *Nothing Gold Can Stay*

NATURE'S FIRST green is gold,
Her hardest hue to hold.
Her early leaf's a flower;
But only so an hour.
Then leaf subsides to leaf.
So Eden sank to grief,
So dawn goes down to day.
Nothing gold can stay.

# Langston Hughes

## *The Negro Speaks of Rivers*

I'VE KNOWN rivers:
I've known rivers ancient as the world and older than the flow
of human blood in human veins.

My soul has grown deep like the rivers.

I bathed in the Euphrates when dawns were young.
I built my hut near the Congo and it lulled me to sleep.

I looked upon the Nile and raised the pyramids above it.
I heard the singing of the Mississippi when Abe Lincoln went
down to New Orleans, and I've seen its muddy bosom turn
all golden in the sunset.

I've known rivers:
Ancient, dusky rivers.

My soul has grown deep like the rivers.

## *Life Is Fine*

I WENT down to the river,
I set down on the bank.
I tried to think but couldn't,
So I jumped in and sank.

I came up once and hollered!
I came up twice and cried!
If that water hadn't a-been so cold
I might've sunk and died.

*But it was*
*Cold in that water!*
*It was cold!*

I took the elevator
Sixteen floors above the ground.
I thought about my baby
And thought I would jump down.

I stood there and I hollered!
I stood there and I cried!
If it hadn't a-been so high
I might've jumped and died.

*But it was*
*High up there*
*It was high!*

So since I'm still here livin',
I guess I will live on.
I could've died for love—
But for livin' I was born.

Though you may hear me holler,
And you may see me cry—
I'll be dogged, sweet baby,
If you gonna see me die.

*Life is fine!*
*Fine as wine!*
*Life is fine!*

## *Harlem* [2]

WHAT HAPPENS to a dream deferred?

Does it dry up
like a raisin in the sun?
Or fester like a sore—
And then run?
Does it stink like rotten meat?
Or crust and sugar over—
like a syrupy sweet?

Maybe it just sags
like a heavy load.

*Or does it explode?*

# Wilfred Owen

## *Dulce et Decorum Est*

BENT DOUBLE, like old beggars under sacks,
Knock-kneed, coughing like hags, we cursed through sludge,
Till on the haunting flares we turned our backs
And towards our distant rest began to trudge.
Men marched asleep. Many had lost their boots
But limped on, blood-shod. All went lame; all blind;
Drunk with fatigue; deaf even to the hoots
Of tired, outstripped **Five-Nines** that dropped behind.

Gas! Gas! Quick, boys—An ecstasy of fumbling,
Fitting the clumsy helmets just in time;
But someone still was yelling out and stumbling
And flound'ring like a man in fire or lime...
Dim, through the misty **panes** and thick green light,
As under a green sea, I saw him drowning.
In all my dreams, before my helpless sight,
He plunges at me, guttering, choking, drowning.

If in some smothering dreams you too could pace
Behind the wagon that we flung him in,
And watch the white eyes writhing in his face,
His hanging face, like a devil's sick of sin;
If you could hear, at every jolt, the blood
Come gargling from the froth-corrupted lungs, »

---

**Five-Nines:** Shells with a caliber of 5.9 inches.

**Panes:** The window of the gas mask.

Obscene as cancer, bitter as the cud
Of vile, incurable sores on innocent tongues,—
My friend, you would not tell with such high zest
To children ardent for some desperate glory,
The old Lie: **Dulce et decorum est**
**Pro patria mori.**

---

**Dulce et decorum est pro patria mori:** "Sweet and fitting it is to die for one's country, " —From the Roman poet Horace's *Odes*, Book III, Number 2, "Call to Youth."

# Edgar Allan Poe

## *Annabel Lee*

IT WAS many and many a year ago,
In a kingdom by the sea,
That a maiden there lived whom you may know
By the name of Annabel Lee;
And this maiden she lived with no other thought
Than to love and be loved by me.

*She* was a child and *I* was a child,
In this kingdom by the sea,
But we loved with a love that was more than love—
I and my Annabel Lee—
With a love that the winged seraphs of Heaven
Coveted her and me.

And this was the reason that, long ago,
In this kingdom by the sea,
A wind blew out of a cloud by night
Chilling my Annabel Lee;
So that her high-born kinsmen came
And bore her away from me,
To shut her up in a sepulchre
In this kingdom by the sea.

The angels, not half so happy in Heaven,
Went envying her and me:—
Yes! that was the reason (as all men know,
In this kingdom by the sea)
That the wind came out of the cloud chilling
And killing my Annabel Lee. »

But our love it was stronger by far than the love
Of those who were older than we—
Of many far wiser than we—
And neither the angels in Heaven above
Nor the demons down under the sea
Can ever dissever my soul from the soul
Of the beautiful Annabel Lee:—

For the moon never beams without bringing me dreams
Of the beautiful Annabel Lee;
And the stars never rise but I feel the bright eyes
Of the beautiful Annabel Lee:
And so all the night-tide, I lie down by the side
Of my darling, my darling, my life and my bride
In her sepulchre there by the sea—
In her tomb by the side of the sea.

# Robert Service

## *The Cremation of Sam McGee*

*THERE ARE strange things done in the midnight sun*
*By the men who moil for gold;*
*The Arctic trails have their secret tales*
*That would make your blood run cold;*
*The Northern Lights have seen queer sights,*
*But the queerest they ever did see*
*Was that night on the marge of Lake Lebarge*
*I cremated Sam McGee.*

Now Sam McGee was from Tennessee,
where the cotton blooms and blows.
Why he left his home in the South to roam
'round the Pole, God only knows.
He was always cold, but the land of gold
seemed to hold him like a spell;
Though he'd often say in his homely way
that he'd "sooner live in Hell."

On a Christmas Day we were mushing our way
over the Dawson trail.
Talk of your cold! through the parka's fold
it stabbed like a driven nail.
If our eyes we'd close, then the lashes froze
till sometimes we couldn't see,
It wasn't much fun, but the only one
to whimper was Sam McGee. »

And that very night, as we lay packed tight
in our robes beneath the snow,
And the dogs were fed, and the stars o'erhead
were dancing heel and toe,
He turned to me, and "Cap," says he,
"I'll cash in this trip, I guess;
And if I do, I'm asking that you
won't refuse my last request."

Well, he seemed so low that I couldn't say no;
then he says with a sort of moan,
"It's the cursed cold, and it's got right hold
till I'm chilled clean through to the bone.
Yet 'taint being dead—it's my awful dread
of the icy grave that pains;
So I want you to swear that, foul or fair,
you'll cremate my last remains."

A pal's last need is a thing to heed,
so I swore I would not fail;
And we started on at the streak of dawn;
but God! he looked ghastly pale.
He crouched on the sleigh, and he raved all day
of his home in Tennessee;
And before nightfall a corpse was all
that was left of Sam McGee.

There wasn't a breath in that land of death,
and I hurried, horror-driven,
With a corpse half hid that I couldn't get rid,
because of a promise given;

It was lashed to the sleigh, and it seemed to say:
"You may tax your brawn and brains,
But you promised true, and it's up to you
to cremate these last remains."

Now a promise made is a debt unpaid,
and the trail has its own stern code.
In the days to come, though my lips were dumb,
in my heart how I cursed that load!
In the long, long night, by the lone firelight,
while the huskies, round in a ring,
Howled out their woes to the homeless snows—
Oh God, how I loathed the thing!

And every day that quiet clay
seemed to heavy and heavier grow;
And on I went, though the dogs were spent
and the grub was getting low.
The trail was bad, and I felt half mad,
but I swore I would not give in;
And I'd often sing to the hateful thing,
and it hearkened with a grin.

Till I came to the marge of Lake Lebarge,
and a derelict there lay;
It was jammed in the ice, but I saw in a trice
it was called the *Alice May*.
And I looked at it, and I thought a bit,
and I looked at my frozen chum;
Then "Here," said I, with a sudden cry,
"is my cre-ma-tor-eum!" »

Some planks I tore from the cabin floor,
and I lit the boiler fire;
Some coal I found that was lying around,
and I heaped the fuel higher;
The flames just soared, and the furnace roared—
such a blaze you seldom see,
And I burrowed a hole in the glowing coal,
and I stuffed in Sam McGee.

Then I made a hike, for I didn't like
to hear him sizzle so;
And the heavens scowled, and the huskies howled,
and the wind began to blow.
It was icy cold, but the hot sweat rolled
down my cheeks, and I don't know why;
And the greasy smoke in an inky cloak
went streaking down the sky.

I do not know how long in the snow
I wrestled with grisly fear;
But the stars came out and they danced about
ere again I ventured near;
I was sick with dread, but I bravely said,
"I'll just take a peep inside.
I guess he's cooked, and it's time I looked."
Then the door I opened wide.

And there sat Sam, looking cool and calm,
in the heart of the furnace roar;
And he wore a smile you could see a mile,
and he said, "Please close that door.
It's fine in here, but I greatly fear
you'll let in the cold and storm—
Since I left Plumtree, down in Tennessee,
it's the first time I've been warm."

*There are strange things done in the midnight sun*
*By the men who moil for gold;*
*The Arctic trails have their secret tales*
*That would make your blood run cold;*
*The Northern Lights have seen queer sights,*
*But the queerest they ever did see*
*Was that night on the marge of Lake Lebarge*
*I cremated Sam McGee.*

# Alfred Lord Tennyson

## *The Charge of the Light Brigade*

I

HALF A league, half a league,
Half a league onward,
All in the valley of Death
Rode the six hundred.
"Forward the Light Brigade!
Charge for the guns!" he said.
Into the valley of Death
Rode the six hundred.

II

"Forward, the Light Brigade!"
Was there a man dismayed?
Not though the soldier knew
Someone had blundered.
Theirs not to make reply,
Theirs not to reason why,
Theirs but to do and die.
Into the valley of Death
Rode the six hundred.

III

Cannon to right of them,
Cannon to left of them,
Cannon in front of them
Volleyed and thundered;
Stormed at with shot and shell,
Boldly they rode and well,
Into the jaws of Death,

Into the mouth of hell
      Rode the six hundred.

IV

Flashed all their sabres bare,
Flashed as they turned in air
Sabring the gunners there,
Charging an army, while
      All the world wondered.
Plunged in the battery-smoke
Right through the line they broke;
Cossack and Russian
Reeled from the sabre-stroke
      Shattered and sundered.
Then they rode back, but not,
      Not the six hundred.

V

Cannon to right of them,
Cannon to left of them,
Cannon behind them
      Volleyed and thundered;
Stormed at with shot and shell,
While horse and hero fell.
They that had fought so well
Came through the jaws of Death,
Back from the mouth of hell,
All that was left of them,
      Left of six hundred. »

VI

When can their glory fade?
O the wild charge they made!
    All the world wondered.
Honor the charge they made!
Honor the Light Brigade,
    Noble six hundred!

# William Carlos Williams

## *The Red Wheelbarrow*

SO MUCH depends
upon

a red wheel
barrow

glazed with rain
water

beside the white
chickens

## *This Is Just To Say*

I HAVE eaten
the plums
that were in
the icebox

and which
you were probably
saving
for breakfast

Forgive me
they were delicious
so sweet
and so cold

# W. H. Auden

## *The Unknown Citizen*

*(To JS/07/M/378 This Marble Monument Is Erected by the State)*

HE WAS found by the Bureau of Statistics to be
One against whom there was no official complaint,
And all the reports on his conduct agree
That, in the modern sense of an old-fashioned word, he was a
saint,
For in everything he did he served the Greater Community.
Except for the War till the day he retired
He worked in a factory and never got fired,
But satisfied his employers, Fudge Motors Inc.
Yet he wasn't a scab or odd in his views,
For his Union reports that he paid his dues,
(Our report on his Union shows it was sound)
And our Social Psychology workers found
That he was popular with his mates and liked a drink.
The Press are convinced that he bought a paper every day
And that his reactions to advertisements were normal in every
way.
Policies taken out in his name prove that he was fully insured.
And his Health-card shows he was once in hospital but left it
cured.
Both Producers Research and High-Grade Living declare
He was fully sensible to the advantages of the Installment Plan
And had everything necessary to the Modern Man,
A phonograph, a radio, a car and a frigidaire.
Our researchers into Public Opinion are content
That he held the proper opinions for the time of year; »

When there was peace, he was for peace; when there was war, he
went.
He was married and added five children to the population,
Which our Eugenist says was the right number for a
parent of his generation,
And our teachers report that he never interfered with their
education.
Was he free? Was he happy? The question is absurd:
Had anything been wrong, we should certainly have heard.

# e. e. cummings

## *next to of course god america i*

"next to of course god america i
love you land of the pilgrims' and so forth oh
say can you see by the dawn's early my
country 'tis of centuries come and go
and are no more what of it we should worry
in every language even deafanddumb
thy sons acclaim your glorious name by gorry
by jingo by gee by gosh by gum
why talk of beauty what could be more beaut-
iful than these heroic happy dead
who rushed like lions to the roaring slaughter
they did not stop to think they died instead
then shall the voice of liberty be mute?"

He spoke. And drank rapidly a glass of water

## Robert Frost

### *Design*

I FOUND a dimpled spider, fat and white,
On a white heal-all, holding up a moth
Like a white piece of rigid satin cloth—
Assorted characters of death and blight
Mixed ready to begin the morning right,
Like the ingredients of a witches' broth—
A snow-drop spider, a flower like a froth,
And dead wings carried like a paper kite.

What had that flower to do with being white,
The wayside blue and innocent heal-all?
What brought the kindred spider to that height,
Then steered the white moth thither in the night?
What but design of darkness to appall?—
If design govern in a thing so small.

# Thomas Hardy

## *Channel Firing*

THAT NIGHT your great guns, unawares,
Shook all our coffins as we lay,
And broke the **chancel** window-squares,
We thought it was the Judgment-day

And sat upright. While drearisome
Arose the howl of wakened hounds:
The mouse let fall the altar-crumb,
The worms drew back into the mounds,

The **glebe** cow drooled. Till God called, "No;
It's gunnery practice out at sea
Just as before you went below;
The world is as it used to be:

"All nations striving strong to make
Red war yet redder. Mad as hatters
They do no more for Christés sake
Than you who are helpless in such matters.

"That this is not the judgment-hour
For some of them's a blessed thing,
For if it were they'd have to scour
Hell's floor for so much threatening.... »

---

**Chancel:** Part of a church near the altar.

**Glebe:** A small field.

"Ha, ha. It will be warmer when
I blow the trumpet (if indeed
I ever do; for you are men,
And rest eternal sorely need)."
So down we lay again. "I wonder,
Will the world ever saner be,"
Said one, "than when He sent us under
In our indifferent century!"

And many a skeleton shook his head.
"Instead of preaching forty year,"
My neighbor Parson Thirdly said,
"I wish I had stuck to pipes and beer."

Again the guns disturbed the hour,
Roaring their readiness to avenge,
As far inland as Stourton Tower,
And Camelot, and starlit Stonehenge.

# Gerard Manley Hopkins

## *Pied Beauty*

GLORY BE to God for dappled things—
For skies of couple-colour as a brinded cow;
For rose-moles all in stipple upon trout that swim;
Fresh-firecoal chestnut-falls; finches' wings;
Landscape plotted and pieced—fold, fallow, and plough;
And áll trádes, their gear and tackle and trim.
All things counter, original, spare, strange;
Whatever is fickle, freckled (who knows how?)
With swift, slow; sweet, sour; adazzle, dim;
He fathers-forth whose beauty is past change:
Praise him.

# Wilfred Owen

## *Anthem for Doomed Youth*

WHAT PASSING-BELLS for these who die as cattle?
    —Only the monstrous anger of the guns.
    Only the stuttering rifles' rapid rattle
Can patter out their hasty orisons.
No mockeries now for them; no prayers nor bells,
    Nor any voice of mourning save the choirs,—
The shrill, demented choirs of wailing shells;
And bugles calling for them from sad shires.

What candles may be held to speed them all?
    Not in the hands of boys but in their eyes
Shall shine the holy glimmers of goodbyes.
    The pallor of girls' brows shall be their pall;
Their flowers the tenderness of patient minds,
And each slow dusk a drawing-down of blinds.

# Ezra Pound

## *In a Station of the Metro*

THE APPARITION of these faces in the crowd;
Petals on a wet, black bough.

## Theodore Roethke

### *My Papa's Waltz*

THE WHISKEY on your breath
Could make a small boy dizzy;
But I hung on like death:
Such waltzing was not easy.

We romped until the pans
Slid from the kitchen shelf;
My mother's countenance
Could not unfrown itself.

The hand that held my wrist
Was battered on one knuckle;
At every step you missed
My right ear scraped a buckle.

You beat time on my head
With a palm caked hard by dirt,
Then waltzed me off to bed
Still clinging to your shirt.

# William Shakespeare

## *Sonnet 29*

WHEN, IN disgrace with fortune and men's eyes,
I all alone beweep my outcast state,
And trouble deaf heaven with my bootless cries,
And look upon myself, and curse my fate,
Wishing me like to one more rich in hope,
Featured like him, like him with friends possessed,
Desiring this man's art, and that man's scope,
With what I most enjoy contented least;
Yet in these thoughts myself almost despising,
Haply I think on thee, and then my state,
Like to the lark at break of day arising
From sullen earth, sings hymns at heaven's gate;
    For thy sweet love remembered such wealth brings
    That then I scorn to change my state with kings.

# Wallace Stevens

## *Anecdote of the Jar*

I PLACED a jar in Tennessee,
And round it was, upon a hill.
It made the slovenly wilderness
Surround that hill.

The wilderness rose up to it,
And sprawled around, no longer wild.
The jar was round upon the ground
And tall and of a port in air.

It took dominion everywhere.
The jar was gray and bare.
It did not give of bird or bush,
Like nothing else in Tennessee.

# Alfred, Lord Tennyson

## *Ulysses*

IT LITTLE profits that an idle king,
By this still hearth, among these barren crags,
Matched with an agèd wife, I mete and dole
Unequal laws unto a savage race
That hoard, and sleep, and feed, and know not me.
I cannot rest from travel; I will drink
Life to the lees. All times I have enjoyed
Greatly, have suffered greatly, both with those
That loved me, and alone; on shore, and when
Through scudding drifts the rainy Hyades
Vexed the dim sea. I am become a name;
For always roaming with a hungry heart
Much have I seen and known—cities of men
And manners, climates, councils, governments,
Myself not least, but honored of them all—
And drunk delight of battle with my peers,
Far on the ringing plains of windy Troy.
I am a part of all that I have met;
Yet all experience is an arch wherethrough
Gleams that untraveled world whose margin fades
Forever and forever when I move.
How dull it is to pause, to make an end,
To rust unburnished, not to shine in use!
As though to breathe were life! Life piled on life
Were all too little, and of one to me
Little remains; but every hour is saved
From that eternal silence, something more,
A bringer of new things; and vile it were
For some three suns to store and hoard myself, »

And this gray spirit yearning in desire
To follow knowledge like a sinking star,
Beyond the utmost bound of human thought.
      This is my son, mine own Telemachus,
To whom I leave the scepter and the isle—
Well-loved of me, discerning to fulfill
This labor, by slow prudence to make mild
A rugged people, and through soft degrees
Subdue them to the useful and the good.
Most blameless is he, centered in the sphere
Of common duties, decent not to fail
In offices of tenderness, a pay
Meet adoration to my household gods,
When I am gone. He works his work, I mine.
      There lies the port; the vessel puffs her sail;
There gloom the dark, broad seas. My mariners,
Souls that have toiled, and wrought, and thought with me—
That ever with a frolic welcome took
The thunder and the sunshine, and opposed
Free hearts, free foreheads—you and I are old;
Old age hath yet his honor and his toil.
Death closes all; but something ere the end,
Some work of noble note, may yet be done,
Not unbecoming men that strove with Gods.
The lights begin to twinkle from the rocks;
The long day wanes, the low moon climbs; the deep
Moans round with many voices. Come, my friends,
'Tis not too late to seek a newer world.
Push off, and sitting well in order smite
The sounding furrows; for my purpose holds
To sail beyond the sunset, and the baths
Of all the western stars, until I die.

It may be that the gulfs will wash us down;
It may be we shall touch the Happy Isles,
And see the great Achilles, whom we knew.
Though much is taken, much abides; and though
We are not now that strength which in old days
Moved earth and heaven, that which we are, we are—
One equal temper of heroic hearts,
Made weak by time and fate, but strong in will
To strive, to seek, to find, and not to yield.

# William Butler Yeats

## *An Irish Airman Foresees His Death*

I KNOW that I shall meet my fate
Somewhere among the clouds above;
Those that I fight I do not hate,
Those that I guard I do not love;
My country is Kiltartan Cross,
My countrymen Kiltartan's poor,
No likely end could bring them loss
Or leave them happier than before.
Nor law, nor duty bade me fight,
Nor public men, nor cheering crowds,
A lonely impulse of delight
Drove to this tumult in the clouds;
I balanced all, brought all to mind,
The years to come seemed waste of breath,
A waste of breath the years behind
In balance with this life, this death.

# STORIES

## Guy De Maupassant

# *The Necklace*

SHE WAS ONE OF THOSE PRETTY, CHARMING YOUNG ladies, born, as if through an error of destiny, into a family of clerks. She had no dowry, no hopes, no means of becoming known, appreciated, loved, and married by a man either rich or distinguished; and she allowed herself to marry a petty clerk in the office of the Board of Education.

She was simple, not being able to adorn herself; but she was unhappy, as one out of her class; for women belong to no caste, no race; their grace, their beauty, and their charm serving them in the place of birth and family. Their inborn finesse, their instinctive elegance, their suppleness of wit are their only aristocracy, making some daughters of the people the equal of great ladies.

She suffered incessantly, feeling herself born for all delicacies and luxuries. She suffered from the poverty of her apartment, the shabby walls, the worn chairs, and the faded stuffs. All these things, which another woman of her station would not have noticed, tortured and angered her. The sight of the little **Breton**, who made this humble home, awoke in her sad regrets and desperate dreams. She thought of quiet antechambers, with their Oriental hangings, lighted by high, bronze torches, and of the two great footmen in short trousers who sleep in the large armchairs, made sleepy by the heavy air from the heating apparatus. She thought of large drawing-rooms, hung in old silks, of graceful pieces of furniture carrying bric-à-brac of inestimable value, and of the little perfumed coquettish apartments, made for five o'clock chats with most intimate friends, men known and sought after, whose attention all women envied and desired.

When she seated herself for dinner, before the round table where the tablecloth had been used three days, opposite her husband who uncovered the tureen with a delighted air, saying: "Oh! the good potpie! I know nothing better than that—" she would think of the elegant dinners, of the shining silver, of the tapestries peopling the walls with ancient personages and rare birds in the midst of fairy forests; she thought of the exquisite food served on marvelous dishes, of the whispered gallantries, listened to with the smile of the sphinx, while eating the rose-colored flesh of the trout or a chicken's wing.

She had neither frocks nor jewels, nothing. And she loved only those things. She felt that she was made for them. She had such a desire to please, to be sought after, to be clever, and courted.

She had a rich friend, a schoolmate at the convent, whom she did not like to visit, she suffered so much when she returned. And she wept for whole days from chagrin, from regret, from despair, and disappointment.

One evening her husband returned elated, bearing in his hand a large envelope.

"Here," said he, "here is something for you."

---

**Breton:** A native of Brittany in northwest France.

She quickly tore open the wrapper and drew out a printed card on which were inscribed these words:

"The Minister of Public Instruction and Madame George Ramponneau ask the honor of Mr. and Mrs. Loisel's company Monday evening, January 18, at the Minister's residence."

Instead of being delighted, as her husband had hoped, she threw the invitation spitefully upon the table murmuring:

"What do you suppose I want with that?"

"But, my dearie, I thought it would make you happy. You never go out, and this is an occasion, and a fine one! I had a great deal of trouble to get it. Everybody wishes one, and it is very select; not many are given to employees. You will see the whole official world there."

She looked at him with an irritated eye and declared impatiently:

"What do you suppose I have to wear to such a thing as that?"

He had not thought of that; he stammered:

"Why, the dress you wear when we go to the theater. It seems very pretty, to me—"

He was silent, stupefied, in dismay, at the sight of his wife weeping. Two great tears fell slowly from the corners of his eyes toward the corners of his mouth; he stammered:

"What is the matter? What is the matter?"

By a violent effort, she had controlled her vexation and responded in a calm voice, wiping her moist cheeks:

"Nothing. Only I have no dress and consequently I cannot go to this affair. Give your card to some colleague whose wife is better fitted out than I."

He was grieved, but answered:

"Let us see, Matilda. How much would a suitable costume cost, something that would serve for other occasions, something very simple?"

She reflected for some seconds, making estimates and thinking of a sum that she could ask for without bringing with it an immediate refusal and a frightened exclamation from the economical clerk.

Finally she said, in a hesitating voice:

"I cannot tell exactly, but it seems to me that four hundred francs ought to cover it."

He turned a little pale, for he had saved just this sum to buy a gun that he might be able to join some hunting parties the next summer, on the plains at Nanterre, with some friends who went to shoot larks up there on Sunday. Nevertheless, he answered:

"Very well. I will give you four hundred francs. But try to have a pretty dress."

The day of the ball approached and Mme. Loisel seemed sad, disturbed, anxious. Nevertheless, her dress was nearly ready. Her husband said to her one evening:

"What is the matter with you? You have acted strangely for two or three days."

And she responded: "I am vexed not to have a jewel, not one stone, nothing to adorn myself with. I shall have such a poverty-laden look. I would prefer not to go to this party."

He replied: "You can wear some natural flowers. At this season they look very *chic*. For ten francs you can have two or three magnificent roses."

She was not convinced. "No," she replied, "there is nothing more humiliating than to have a shabby air in the midst of rich women."

Then her husband cried out: "How stupid we are! Go and find your friend Mrs. Forestier and ask her to lend you her jewels. You are well enough acquainted with her to do this."

She uttered a cry of joy: "It is true!" she said. "I had not thought of that."

The next day she took herself to her friend's house and related her story of distress. Mrs. Forestier went to her closet with the glass doors, took out a large jewelcase, brought it, opened it, and said: "Choose, my dear."

She saw at first some bracelets, then a collar of pearls, then a Venetian cross of gold and jewels and of admirable workmanship. She tried the jewels before the glass, hesitated, but could neither decide to take them nor leave them. Then she asked:

"Have you nothing more?"

"Why, yes. Look for yourself. I do not know what will please you."

Suddenly she discovered, in a black satin box, a superb necklace of diamonds, and her heart beat fast with an immoderate desire. Her hands trembled as she took them up. She placed them about her throat against her dress, and remained in ecstasy before them. Then she asked, in a hesitating voice, full of anxiety:

"Could you lend me this? Only this?"

"Why, yes, certainly."

She fell upon the neck of her friend, embraced her with passion, then went away with her treasure.

The day of the ball arrived. Mme. Loisel was a great success. She was the prettiest of all, elegant, gracious, smiling, and full of joy. All the men noticed her, asked her name, and wanted to be presented. All the members of the Cabinet wished to waltz with her. The Minister of Education paid her some attention.

She danced with enthusiasm, with passion, intoxicated with pleasure, thinking of nothing, in the triumph of her beauty, in the glory of her success, in a kind of cloud of happiness that came of all this homage, and all this admiration, of all these awakened desires, and this victory so complete and sweet to the heart of woman.

She went home toward four o'clock in the morning. Her husband had been half asleep in one of the little salons since midnight, with three other gentlemen whose wives were enjoying themselves very much.

He threw around her shoulders the wraps they had carried for the coming home, modest garments of everyday wear, whose poverty clashed with the elegance of the ball costume. She felt this and wished to hurry away in order not to be noticed by the other women who were wrapping themselves in rich furs.

Loisel retained her: "Wait," said he. "You will catch cold out there. I am going to call a cab."

But she would not listen and descended the steps rapidly. When they were in the street, they found no carriage; and they began to seek one, hailing the coachmen whom they saw at a distance.

They walked along toward the **Seine**, hopeless and shivering. Finally they found on the dock one of those old, nocturnal *coupés* that one sees in Paris after nightfall, as if they were ashamed of their misery by day.

It took them as far as their door in Martyr Street, and they went wearily up to their apartment. It was all over for her. And on his part, he remembered that he would have to be at the office by ten o'clock.

She removed the wraps from her shoulders before the glass, for a final view of herself in her glory. Suddenly she uttered a cry. Her necklace was not around her neck.

Her husband, already half undressed, asked: "What is the matter?"

---

**Seine**: The river flowing through the center of Paris.

She turned toward him excitedly:

"I have—I have—I no longer have Mrs. Forestier's necklace."

He arose in dismay: "What! How is that? It is not possible."

And they looked in the folds of the dress, in the folds of the mantle, in the pockets, everywhere. They could not find it.

He asked: "You are sure you still had it when we left the house?"

"Yes, I felt it in the vestibule as we came out."

"But if you had lost it in the street, we should have heard it fall. It must be in the cab."

"Yes. It is probable. Did you take the number?"

"No. And you, did you notice what it was?"

"No."

They looked at each other utterly cast down. Finally, Loisel dressed himself again.

"I am going," said he, "over the track where we went on foot, to see if I can find it."

And he went. She remained in her evening gown, not having the strength to go to bed, stretched upon a chair, without ambition or thoughts.

Toward seven o'clock her husband returned. He had found nothing.

He went to the police and to the cab offices, and put an advertisement in the newspapers, offering a reward; he did everything that afforded them a suspicion of hope.

She waited all day in a state of bewilderment before this frightful disaster. Loisel returned at evening with his face harrowed and pale; he had discovered nothing.

"It will be necessary," said he, "to write to your friend that you have broken the clasp of the necklace and that you will have it repaired. That will give us time to turn around."

She wrote as he dictated.

At the end of a week, they had lost all hope. And Loisel, older by five years, declared:

"We must take measures to replace this jewel."

The next day they took the box which had inclosed it to the jeweler whose name was on the inside. He consulted his books.

"It is not I, Madame," said he, "who sold this necklace; I only furnished the casket."

Then they went from jeweler to jeweler seeking a necklace like the other one, consulting their memories, and ill, both of them, with chagrin and anxiety.

In a shop of the Palais-Royal, they found a chaplet of diamonds which seemed to them exactly like the one they had lost. It was valued at forty thousand francs. They could get it for thirty-six thousand.

They begged the jeweler not to sell it for three days. And they made an arrangement by which they might return it for thirty-four thousand francs if they found the other one before the end of February.

Loisel possessed eighteen thousand francs which his father had left him. He borrowed the rest.

He borrowed it, asking for a thousand francs of one, five hundred of another, five **louis** of this one, and three louis of that one. He gave notes, made ruinous promises, took money of usurers and the whole race of lenders. He compromised his whole existence, in fact, risked his signature, without even knowing whether he could make it good or not, and, harassed by anxiety for the future, by the black misery which surrounded him, and by the prospect of all physical priva-

---

**Louis** : a French gold coin worth 20 francs.

tions and moral torture, he went to get the new necklace, depositing on the merchant's counter thirty-six thousand francs.

When Mrs. Loisel took back the jewels to Mrs. Forestier, the latter said to her in a frigid tone:

"You should have returned them to me sooner, for I might have needed them."

She did not open the jewel-box as her friend feared she would. If she should perceive the substitution, what would she think? What should she say? Would she take her for a robber?

Mrs. Loisel now knew the horrible life of necessity. She did her part, however, completely, heroically. It was necessary to pay this frightful debt. She would pay it. They sent away the maid; they changed their lodgings; they rented some rooms under a mansard roof.

She learned the heavy cares of a household, the odious work of a kitchen. She washed the dishes, using her rosy nails upon the greasy pots and the bottoms of the stewpans. She washed the soiled linen, the chemises and dishcloths, which she hung on the line to dry; she took down the refuse to the street each morning and brought up the water, stopping at each landing to breathe. And, clothed like a woman of the people, she went to the grocer's, the butcher's, and the fruiterer's with her basket on her arm, shopping, haggling, defending to the last **sou** her miserable money.

Every month it was necessary to renew some notes, thus obtaining time, and to pay others.

The husband worked evenings, putting the books of some merchants in order, and nights he often did copying at five sous a page.

---

**Sou:** A French five-cent coin.

And this life lasted for ten years.

At the end of ten years, they had restored all, all, with interest of the usurer, and accumulated interest besides.

Mrs. Loisel seemed old now. She had become a strong, hard woman, the crude woman of the poor household. Her hair badly dressed, her skirts awry, her hands red, she spoke in a loud tone, and washed the floors, using large pails of water. But sometimes, when her husband was at the office, she would seat herself before the window and think of that evening party of former times, of that ball where she was so beautiful and so flattered.

How would it have been if she had not lost that necklace? Who knows? Who knows? How singular is life, and how full of changes! How small a thing will ruin or save one!

One Sunday, as she was taking a walk in the Champs-Elysées to rid herself of the cares of the week, she suddenly perceived a woman walking with a child. It was Mrs. Forestier, still young, still pretty, still attractive. Mrs. Loisel was affected. Should she speak to her? Yes, certainly. And now that she had paid, she would tell her all. Why not?

She approached her. "Good morning, Jeanne."

Her friend did not recognize her and was astonished to be so familiarly addressed by this common personage. She stammered:

"But, Madame—I do not know—You must be mistaken—"

"No, I am Matilda Loisel."

Her friend uttered a cry of astonishment: "Oh! My poor Matilda! How you have changed—"

"Yes, I have had some hard days since I saw you; and some miserable one—and all because of you—"

"Because of me? How is that?"

"You recall the diamond necklace that you loaned me to

wear to the Commissioner's ball?"

"Yes, very well."

"Well, I lost it."

"How is that, since you returned it to me?"

"I returned another to you exactly like it. And it has taken us ten years to pay for it. You can understand that it was not easy for us who have nothing. But it is finished and I am decently content."

Madame Forestier stopped short. She said:

"You say that you bought a diamond necklace to replace mine?"

"Yes. You did not perceive it then? They were just alike."

And she smiled with a proud and simple joy. Madame Forestier was touched and took both her hands as she replied:

"Oh! My poor Matilda! Mine were false. They were not worth over five hundred francs!"

# Edgar Allan Poe

## *The Tell-tale Heart*

TRUE!—NERVOUS—VERY, VERY DREADFULLY NERvous I had been and am; but why *will* you say that I am mad? The disease had sharpened my senses—not destroyed—not dulled them. Above all was the sense of hearing acute. I heard all things in the heaven and in the earth. I heard many things in hell. How, then, am I mad? Hearken! and observe how healthily—how calmly I can tell you the whole story.

It is impossible to say how first the idea entered my brain; but once conceived, it haunted me day and night. Object there was none. Passion there was none. I loved the old man. He had never wronged me. He had never given me insult. For his gold I had no desire. I think it was his eye! Yes, it was this! He had the eye of a vulture—a pale blue eye, with a film over it. Whenever it fell upon me, my blood ran cold; and so by degrees—very gradually—I made up my mind to take the life of the old man, and thus rid myself of the eye forever.

Now this is the point. You fancy me mad. Madmen know nothing. But you should have seen *me*. You should have seen how wisely I proceeded—with what caution—with what foresight—with what dissimulation I went to work! I was never kinder to the old man than during the whole week before I killed him. And every night, about midnight, I turned the latch of his door and opened it—oh, so gently! And then, when I had made an opening sufficient for my head, I put in a dark lantern, all closed, closed, so that no light shone out, and then I thrust in my head. Oh, you would have laughed to see how cunningly I thrust it in! I moved it slowly—very, very slowly, so that I might not disturb the old man's sleep. It took me an hour to place my whole head within the opening so far that I could see him as he lay upon his bed. Ha!—would a madman have been so wise as this? And then, when my head was well in the room, I undid the lantern cautiously—oh, so cautiously—cautiously (for the hinges creaked)—I undid it just so much that a single thin ray fell upon the vulture eye. And this I did for seven long nights—every night just at midnight—but I found the eye always closed; and so it was impossible to do the work, for it was not the old man who vexed me, but his Evil Eye. And every morning, when the day broke, I went boldly into the chamber, and spoke courageously to him, calling him by name in a hearty tone, and inquiring how he had passed the night. So you see he would have been a very profound old man, indeed, to suspect that every night, just at twelve, I looked in upon him while he slept.

Upon the eighth night I was more than usually cautious in opening the door. A watch's minute hand moves more quickly than did mine. Never before that night, had I *felt* the extent of my own powers—of my sagacity. I could scarcely contain my feelings of triumph. To think that there I was, opening the door, little by little, and he not even to dream of my secret deeds or thoughts. I fairly chuckled at the idea; and perhaps he heard me, for he moved on the bed suddenly, as if startled. Now you may think that I drew back—but no. His room was as black as pitch with the thick darkness (for the shutters were close fastened, through fear of robbers), and so I knew that he could not see the opening of the door, and I kept pushing it on steadily, steadily.

I had my head in, and was about to open the lantern, when my thumb slipped upon the tin fastening, and the old man sprang up in bed, crying out—"Who's there?"

I kept quite still and said nothing. For a whole hour I did not move a muscle, and in the meantime I did not hear him lie down. He was still sitting up in the bed listening—just as I have done, night after night, hearkening to the death watches in the wall.

Presently I heard a slight groan, and I knew it was the groan of mortal terror. It was not a groan of pain or of grief—oh, no!—it was the low stifled sound that arises from the bottom of the soul when overcharged with awe. I knew the sound well. Many a night, just at midnight, when all the world slept, it has welled up from my own bosom, deepening, with its dreadful echo, the terrors that distracted me. I say I knew it well. I knew what the old man felt, and pitied him, although I chuckled at heart. I knew that he had been lying awake ever since the first slight noise, when he had turned in the bed. His fears had been ever since growing upon him. He had been trying to fancy them causeless, but could not. He had been saying to himself—"It is nothing but the wind in the chimney—it is only a mouse crossing the floor," or "It is merely a cricket which has made a single chirp." Yes, he had been trying to comfort himself with these suppositions: but he had found all in vain. *All in vain*; because Death, in approaching him, had stalked with his black shadow before him, and enveloped the victim. And it was the mournful influence of the unperceived shadow that caused him to feel—although he neither saw nor heard—to *feel* the presence of my head within the room.

When I had waited a long time, very patiently, without hearing him lie down, I resolved to open a little—a very, very little—crevice in the lantern. So I opened it—you cannot imagine how stealthily, stealthily—until, at length a single dim ray, like the thread of the spider, shot from out the crevice and fell full upon the vulture eye.

It was open—wide, wide open—and I grew furious as I gazed upon it. I saw it with perfect distinctness—all a dull blue, with a hideous veil over it that chilled the very marrow in my bones; but I could see nothing else of the old man's face or person: for I had directed the ray, as if by instinct, precisely upon the damned spot.

And have I not told you that what you mistake for madness is but over-acuteness of the senses?—Now, I say, there came to my ears a low, dull, quick sound, such as a watch makes when enveloped in cotton. I knew *that* sound well, too. It was the beating of the old man's heart. It increased my fury, as the beating of a drum stimulates the soldier into courage.

But even yet I refrained and kept still. I scarcely breathed. I held the lantern motionless. I tried how steadily I could maintain the ray upon the eye. Meantime the hellish **tattoo** of the heart increased. It grew quicker and quicker, and louder and louder every instant. The old man's terror *must* have been extreme! It grew louder, I say, louder every moment!—Do you mark me well? I have told you that I am nervous: so I am. And now at the dead hour of the night, amid the dreadful silence of that old house, so strange a noise as this excited me to uncontrollable terror. Yet, for some minutes longer I refrained and stood still. But the beating grew louder, louder! I thought the heart must burst. And now a new anxiety

---

**Tattoo**: Rapid rhythmic tapping or drumming.

seized me—the sound would be heard by a neighbor! The old man's hour had come! With a loud yell, I threw open the lantern and leaped into the room. He shrieked once—once only. In an instant I dragged him to the floor, and pulled the heavy bed over him. I then smiled gaily, to find the deed so far done. But, for many minutes, the heart beat on with a muffled sound. This, however, did not vex me; it would not be heard through the wall. At length it ceased. The old man was dead. I removed the bed and examined the corpse. Yes, he was stone, stone dead. I placed my hand upon the heart and held it there many minutes. There was no pulsation. He was stone dead. His eye would trouble me no more.

If still you think me mad, you will think so no longer when I describe the wise precautions I took for the concealment of the body. The night waned, and I worked hastily, but in silence. First of all I dismembered the corpse. I cut off the head and the arms and the legs.

I then took up three planks from the flooring of the chamber and deposited all between the **scantlings**. I then replaced the boards so cleverly, so cunningly, that no human eye—not even *his*— could have detected anything wrong. There was nothing to wash out—no stain of any kind—no bloodspot whatever. I had been too wary for that. A tub had caught all—ha! ha!

When I had made an end of these labors, it was four o'clock—still dark as midnight. As the bell sounded the hour, there came a knocking at the street door. I went down to open it with a light heart—for what had I *now* to fear? There entered three men, who introduced themselves, with perfect suavity, as officers of the police. A shriek had been heard by a neighbor during the night; suspicion of foul play had been

---

**Scantlings:** Small upright pieces of lumber in the framing of a building.

aroused; information had been lodged at the police office, and they (the officers) had been deputed to search the premises.

I smiled—for *what* had I to fear? I bade the gentlemen welcome. The shriek, I said, was my own in a dream. The old man, I mentioned, was absent in the country. I took my visitors all over the house. I bade them search—search *well*. I led them, at length, to *his* chamber. I showed them his treasures, secure, undisturbed. In the enthusiasm of my confidence, I brought chairs into the room, and desired them *here* to rest from their fatigues, while I myself, in the wild audacity of my perfect triumph, placed my own seat upon the very spot beneath which reposed the corpse of the victim.

The officers were satisfied. My *manner* had convinced them. I was singularly at ease. They sat, and while I answered cheerily, they chatted of familiar things. But, ere long, I felt myself getting pale and wished them gone. My head ached, and I fancied a ringing in my ears: but still they sat and still chatted. The ringing became more distinct—it continued and became more distinct. I talked more freely to get rid of the feeling: but it continued and gained definiteness—until, at length, I found that the noise was *not* within my ears.

No doubt I now grew *very* pale—but I talked more fluently, and with a heightened voice. Yet the sound increased—and what could I do? It was *a low, dull, quick sound—much such a sound as a watch makes when enveloped in cotton*. I gasped for breath—and yet the officers heard it not. I talked more quickly—more vehemently, but the noise steadily increased. I arose and argued about trifles, in a high key and with violent gesticulations, but the noise steadily increased. Why *would* they not be gone? I paced the floor to and fro with heavy strides, as if excited to fury by the observations of the men—but the noise steadily increased. Oh God! what *could*

I do? I foamed—I raved—I swore! I swung the chair upon which I had been sitting, and grated it upon the boards, but the noise arose over all and continually increased. It grew louder—louder—*louder!* And still the men chatted pleasantly, and smiled. Was it possible they heard not? Almighty God!—No, no! They heard!—they suspected—they *knew!*—they were making a mockery of my horror!—this I thought, and this I think. But anything was better than this agony! Anything was more tolerable than this derision! I could bear those hypocritical smiles no longer! I felt that I must scream or die! And now—again!—hark! louder! louder! louder! *louder!*

"Villains!" I shrieked, "dissemble no more! I admit the deed!—tear up the planks! here, here!—it is the beating of his hideous heart!"

# Edgar Allan Poe

# *The Purloined Letter*

***Nil sapientiœ odiosius acumine nimio.***

—Seneca

At Paris, just after dark one gusty evening in the autumn of 18—, I was enjoying the twofold luxury of meditation and a **meerschaum**, in company with my friend C. Auguste Dupin, in his little back library, or book-closet, *au troisième, No. 33, Rue Dunôt, Faubourg St. Germain*. For one hour at least we had maintained a profound silence; while each, to any casual observer, might have seemed intently and exclusively occupied with the curling eddies of smoke that oppressed the atmosphere of the chamber. For myself, however, I was mentally discussing certain topics which had formed matter for conversation between us at an earlier period of the evening; I mean the affair of the Rue Morgue, and the mystery attending the murder of Marie Rogêt. I looked upon it, therefore, as something of a coincidence, when the door of our apartment was

---

**Nil sapientioe odiosius acumine nimio**: In Latin, "There is nothing wisdom hates more than cleverness."

**Meerschaum**: A tobacco pipe made of a white, clay-like mineral found mainly in Asia Minor.

thrown open and admitted our old acquaintance, Monsieur G—, the Prefect of the Parisian police.

We gave him a hearty welcome, for there was nearly half as much of the entertaining as of the contemptible about the man, and we had not seen him for several years. We had been sitting in the dark, and Dupin now arose for the purpose of lighting a lamp, but sat down again, without doing so, upon G—'s saying that he had called to consult us, or rather to ask the opinion of my friend, about some official business which had occasioned a great deal of trouble.

"If it is any point requiring reflection," observed Dupin, as he forbore to enkindle the wick, "we shall examine it to better purpose in the dark."

"That is another of your odd notions," said the Prefect, who had a fashion of calling everything "odd" that was beyond his comprehension, and thus lived amid an absolute legion of "oddities."

"Very true," said Dupin, as he supplied his visitor with a pipe and rolled towards him a comfortable chair.

"And what is the difficulty now?" I asked. "Nothing more in the assassination way, I hope?"

"Oh no; nothing of that nature. The fact is, the business is *very* simple indeed, and I make no doubt that we can manage it sufficiently well ourselves; but then I thought Dupin would like to hear the details of it, because it is so excessively *odd*."

"Simple and odd," said Dupin.

"Why, yes; and not exactly that, either. The fact is, we have all been a good deal puzzled because the affair *is* so simple, and yet baffles us altogether."

"Perhaps it is the very simplicity of the thing which puts you at fault," said my friend.

"What nonsense you *do* talk!" replied the Prefect, laughing heartily.

"Perhaps the mystery is a little *too* plain," said Dupin.

"Oh, good heavens! Who ever heard of such an idea?"

"A little *too* self-evident."

"Ha! ha! ha!—ha! ha! ha!—ho! ho! ho!"—roared our visitor, profoundly amused. "Oh, Dupin, you will be the death of me yet!"

"And what, after all, *is* the matter on hand?" I asked.

"Why, I will tell you," replied the Prefect, as he gave a long, steady, and contemplative puff, and settled himself in his chair. "I will tell you in a few words; but, before I begin, let me caution you that this is an affair demanding the greatest secrecy, and that I should most probably lose the position I now hold, were it known that I confided it to any one."

"Proceed," said I.

"Or not," said Dupin.

"Well, then; I have received personal information, from a very high quarter, that a certain document of the last importance has been purloined from the royal apartments. The individual who purloined it is known; this beyond a doubt; he was seen to take it. It is known, also, that it still remains in his possession."

"How is this known?" asked Dupin.

"It is clearly inferred," replied the Prefect, "from the nature of the document, and from the non-appearance of certain results which would at once arise from its passing *out* of the robber's possession—that is to say, from his employing it as he must design in the end to employ it."

"Be a little more explicit," I said.

"Well, I may venture so far as to say that the paper gives its holder a certain power in a certain quarter where such power is immensely valuable." The Prefect was fond of the cant of diplomacy.

"Still I do not quite understand," said Dupin.

"No? Well, the disclosure of the document to a third person, who shall be nameless, would bring in question the honor of a personage of most exalted station; and this fact gives the holder of the document an ascendancy over the illustrious personage whose honor and peace are so jeopardized."

"But this ascendancy," I interposed, "would depend upon the robber's knowledge of the loser's knowledge of the robber. Who would dare—"

"The thief," said G—, "is the Minister D—, who dares all things, those unbecoming as well as those becoming a man. The method of the theft was not less ingenious than bold. The document in question—a letter, to be frank—had been received by the personage robbed while alone in the royal *boudoir*. During its perusal she was suddenly interrupted by the entrance of the other exalted personage from whom especially it was her wish to conceal it. After a hurried and vain endeavor to thrust it in a drawer, she was forced to place it, open as it was, upon a table. The address, however, was uppermost, and, the contents thus unexposed, the letter escaped notice. At this juncture enters the Minister D—. His lynx eye immediately perceives the paper, recognizes the handwriting of the address, observes the confusion of the personage addressed, and fathoms her secret. After some business transactions, hurried through in his ordinary manner, he produces a letter somewhat similar to the one in question, opens it, pretends to read it, and then places it in close juxtaposition to the other. Again he converses, for some fifteen minutes, upon the public affairs. At length, in taking leave, he takes also from the table the letter to which he had no claim. Its rightful owner saw, but, of course, dared not call attention to the act, in the presence of the third personage who stood at her elbow. The minister decamped; leaving his own letter—one of no importance—upon the table."

"Here, then," said Dupin to me, "you have precisely what you demand to make the ascendancy complete—the robber's knowledge of the loser's knowledge of the robber."

"Yes," replied the Prefect, "and the power thus attained has, for some months past, been wielded, for political purposes, to a very dangerous extent. The personage robbed is more thoroughly convinced, every day, of the necessity of reclaiming her letter. But this, of course, cannot be done openly. In fine, driven to despair, she has committed the matter to me."

"Than whom," said Dupin, amid a perfect whirlwind of smoke, "no more sagacious agent could, I suppose, be desired, or even imagined."

"You flatter me," replied the Prefect, "but it is possible that some such opinion may have been entertained."

"It is clear," said I, "as you observe, that the letter is still in possession of the minister; since it is this possession, and not any employment of the letter, which bestows the power. With the employment the power departs."

"True," said G—; "and upon this conviction I proceeded. My first care was to make thorough search of the minister's hotel; and here my chief embarrassment lay in the necessity of searching without his knowledge. Beyond all things, I have been warned of the danger which would result from giving him reason to suspect our design."

"But," said I, "you are quite **au fait** in these investigations. The Parisian police have done this thing often before."

"Oh yes; and for this reason I did not despair. The habits of the minister gave me, too, a great advantage. He is fre-

---

**Au fait**: Fully capable and competent; from French, literally "to the point."

quently absent from home all night. His servants are by no means numerous. They sleep at a distance from their master's apartment, and, being chiefly Neapolitans, are readily made drunk. I have keys, as you know, with which I can open any chamber or cabinet in Paris. For three months a night has not passed, during the greater part of which I have not been engaged, personally, in ransacking the D— hotel. My honor is interested, and, to mention a great secret, the reward is enormous. So I did not abandon the search until I had become fully satisfied that the thief is a more astute man than myself. I fancy that I have investigated every nook and corner of the premises in which it is possible that the paper can be concealed."

"But is it not possible," I suggested, "that although the letter may be in possession of the minister, as it unquestionably is, he may have concealed it elsewhere than upon his own premises?"

"This is barely possible," said Dupin. "The present peculiar condition of affairs at court, and especially of those intrigues in which D— is known to be involved, would render the instant availability of the document—its susceptibility of being produced at a moment's notice—a point of nearly equal importance with its possession."

"Its susceptibility of being produced?" said I.

"That is to say, of being *destroyed*," said Dupin.

"True," I observed; "the paper is clearly then upon the premises. As for its being upon the person of the minister, we may consider that as out of the question."

"Entirely," said the Prefect. "He has been twice waylaid, as if by **footpads**, and his person rigorously searched under my own inspection."

---

**Footpads**: Someone who robs a pedestrian, a mugger.

"You might have spared yourself this trouble," said Dupin. "D—, I presume, is not altogether a fool, and, if not, must have anticipated these waylayings, as a matter of course."

"Not *altogether* a fool," said G—, "but then he's a poet, which I take to be only one remove from a fool."

"True," said Dupin, after a long and thoughtful whiff from his meerschaum, "although I have been guilty of certain doggerel myself."

"Suppose you detail," said I, "the particulars of your search."

"Why, the fact is, we took our time, and we searched *everywhere*. I have had long experience in these affairs. I took the entire building, room by room, devoting the nights of a whole week to each. We examined, first, the furniture of each apartment. We opened every possible drawer; and I presume you know that, to a properly trained police agent, such a thing as a secret *drawer* is impossible. Any man is a dolt who permits a 'secret' drawer to escape him in a search of this kind. The thing is *so* plain. There is a certain amount of bulk—of space—to be accounted for in every cabinet. Then we have accurate rules. The fiftieth part of a line could not escape us. After the cabinets we took the chairs. The cushions we probed with the fine long needles you have seen me employ. From the tables we removed the tops."

"Why so?"

"Sometimes the top of a table, or other similarly arranged piece of furniture, is removed by the person wishing to conceal an article; then the leg is excavated, the article deposited within the cavity, and the top replaced. The bottoms and tops of bedposts are employed in the same way."

"But could not the cavity be detected by sounding?" I asked.

"By no means, if, when the article is deposited, a sufficient wadding of cotton be placed around it. Besides, in our case, we were obliged to proceed without noise."

"But you could not have removed—you could not have taken to pieces *all* articles of furniture in which it would have been possible to make a deposit in the manner you mention. A letter may be compressed into a thin spiral roll, not differing much in shape or bulk from a large knitting-needle, and in this form it might be inserted into the rung of a chair, for example. You did not take to pieces all the chairs?"

"Certainly not; but we did better—we examined the rungs of every chair in the hotel, and, indeed, the jointings of every description of furniture, by the aid of a most powerful microscope. Had there been any traces of recent disturbance we should not have failed to detect it instantly. A single grain of **gimlet**-dust, for example, would have been as obvious as an apple. Any disorder in the gluing—any unusual gaping in the joints—would have sufficed to insure detection."

"I presume you looked to the mirrors, between the boards and the plates, and you probed the beds and the bedclothes, as well as the curtains and carpets."

"That of course; and when we had absolutely completed every particle of the furniture in this way, then we examined the house itself. We divided its entire surface into compartments, which we numbered, so that none might be missed; then we scrutinized each individual square inch throughout the premises, including the two houses immediately adjoining, with the microscope, as before."

"The two houses adjoining!" I exclaimed; "you must have had a great deal of trouble."

"We had, but the reward offered is prodigious."

---

**Gimlet:** A small tool for drilling holes.

"You included the *grounds* about the houses?"

"All the grounds are paved with brick. They gave us comparatively little trouble. We examined the moss between the bricks, and found it undisturbed."

"You looked among D—'s papers, of course, and into the books of the library?"

"Certainly; we opened every package and parcel; we not only opened every book, but we turned over every leaf in each volume, not contenting ourselves with a mere shake, according to the fashion of some of our police officers. We also measured the thickness of every book-*cover*, with the most accurate admeasurement, and applied to each the most jealous scrutiny of the microscope. Had any of the bindings been recently meddled with, it would have been utterly impossible that the fact should have escaped observation. Some five or six volumes, just from the hands of the binder, we carefully probed, longitudinally, with the needles."

"You explored the floors beneath the carpets?"

"Beyond doubt. We removed every carpet, and examined the boards with the microscope."

"And the paper on the walls?"

"Yes."

"You looked into the cellars?"

"We did."

"Then," I said, "you have been making a miscalculation, and the letter is *not* upon the premises, as you suppose."

"I fear you are right there," said the Prefect. "And now, Dupin, what would you advise me to do?"

"To make a thorough re-search of the premises."

"That is absolutely needless," replied G—. "I am not more sure that I breathe than I am that the letter is not at the hotel."

"I have no better advice to give you," said Dupin. "You

have, of course, an accurate description of the letter?"

"Oh yes!"—And here the Prefect, producing a memorandum book, proceeded to read aloud a minute account of the internal, and especially of the external, appearance of the missing document. Soon after finishing the perusal of this description, he took his departure, more entirely depressed in spirits than I had ever known the good gentleman before.

In about a month afterwards he paid us another visit, and found us occupied very nearly as before. He took a pipe and a chair and entered into some ordinary conversation. At length I said, "Well, but, G—, what of the purloined letter? I presume you have at last made up your mind that there is no such thing as overreaching the minister?"

"Confound him, say I—yes; I made the re-examination, however, as Dupin suggested—but it was all labor lost, as I knew it would be."

"How much was the reward offered, did you say?" asked Dupin.

"Why, a very great deal—a *very* liberal reward—I don't like to say how much, precisely; but one thing I *will* say, that I wouldn't mind giving my individual check for fifty thousand francs to any one who could obtain me that letter. The fact is, it is becoming of more and more importance every day; and the reward has been lately doubled. If it were trebled, however, I could do no more than I have done."

"Why, yes," said Dupin, drawlingly, between the whiffs of his meerschaum, "I really—think, G—, you have not exerted yourself—to the utmost in this matter. You might—do a little more, I think, eh?"

"How?—in what way?"

"Why—puff, puff—you might—puff, puff—employ counsel in the matter, eh?—puff, puff, puff. Do you remember the story they tell of Abernethy?"

"No; hang Abernethy!"

"To be sure! Hang him and welcome. But, once upon a time, a certain rich miser conceived the design of sponging upon this Abernethy for a medical opinion. Getting up, for this purpose, an ordinary conversation in a private company, he insinuated his case to the physician as that of an imaginary individual.

"'We will suppose, said the miser, 'that his symptoms are such and such; now, doctor, what would *you* have directed him to take?'"

"'Take!' said Abernethy, 'why, take *advice*, to be sure.'"

"But," said the Prefect, a little discomposed, "I am *perfectly* willing to take advice, and to pay for it. I would *really* give fifty thousand francs to any one who would aid me in the matter."

"In that case," replied Dupin, opening a drawer, and producing a checkbook, "you may as well fill me up a check for the amount mentioned. When you have signed it, I will hand you the letter."

I was astounded. The Prefect appeared absolutely thunderstricken. For some minutes he remained speechless and motionless, looking incredulously at my friend with open mouth, and eyes that seemed starting from their sockets; then, apparently recovering himself in some measure, he seized a pen, and after several pauses and vacant stares, finally filled up and signed a check for fifty thousand francs and handed it across the table to Dupin. The latter examined it carefully and deposited it in his pocket-book; then, unlocking an **escritoire**, took thence a letter and gave it to the Prefect. This functionary grasped it in a perfect agony of joy, opened it with a trembling hand, cast a rapid glance

---

**Escritoire:** A writing desk.

at its contents, and then, scrambling and struggling to the door, rushed at length unceremoniously from the room and from the house, without having uttered a syllable since Dupin had requested him to fill up the check.

When he had gone, my friend entered into some explanations.

"The Parisian police," he said, "are exceedingly able in their way. They are persevering, ingenious, cunning, and thoroughly versed in the knowledge which their duties seem chiefly to demand. Thus, when G— detailed to us his mode of searching the premises at the Hôtel D—, I felt entire confidence in his having made a satisfactory investigation—so far as his labors extended."

"So far as his labors extended?" said I.

"Yes," said Dupin. "The measures adopted were not only the best of their kind, but carried out to absolute perfection. Had the letter been deposited within the range of their search, these fellows would, beyond a question, have found it."

I merely laughed—but he seemed quite serious in all that he said.

"The measures, then," he continued, "were good in their kind, and well executed; their defect lay in their being inapplicable to the case, and to the man. A certain set of highly ingenious resources are, with the Prefect, a sort of **Procrustean bed** to which he forcibly adapts his designs. But he perpetually errs by being too deep or too shallow for the matter in hand; and many a schoolboy is a better reasoner

---

**Procrustean bed:** In Greek mythology, Procrustes was a robber who forced travellers passing his house to fit into one of two beds. The tall were put in a little bed and had their feet cut off, and the short were put in a large bed and their bodies stretched apart.

than he. I knew one about eight years of age whose success at guessing in the game of 'even and odd' attracted universal admiration. This game is simple, and is played with marbles. One player holds in his hand a number of these toys, and demands of another whether that number is even or odd. If the guess is right, the guesser wins one; if wrong, he loses one. The boy to whom I allude won all the marbles of the school. Of course he had some principle of guessing; and this lay in mere observation and admeasurement of the astuteness of his opponents. For example, an arrant simpleton is his opponent, and, holding up his closed hand, asks, 'Are they even or odd?' Our schoolboy replies, 'odd,' and loses; but upon the second trial he wins, for he then says to himself, 'the simpleton had them even upon the first trial, and his amount of cunning is just sufficient to make him have them odd upon the second; I will therefore guess odd':—he guesses odd, and wins. Now, with a simpleton a degree above the first, he would have reasoned thus: 'This fellow finds that in the first instance I guessed odd, and, in the second, he will propose to himself upon the first impulse, a simple variation from even to odd, as did the first simpleton; but then a second thought will suggest that this is too simple a variation, and finally he will decide upon putting it even as before. I will therefore guess even':—he guesses even, and wins. Now this mode of reasoning in the schoolboy, whom his fellows termed 'lucky,'—what, in its last analysis, is it?"

"It is merely," I said, "an identification of the reasoner's intellect with that of his opponent."

"It is," said Dupin; "and, upon inquiring of the boy by what means he effected the *thorough* identification in which his success consisted, I received his answer as follows: 'When I wish to find out how wise, or how stupid, or how good, or how wicked is any one, or what are his thoughts at the moment, I fashion the expression of my face, as accurately as possible, in accordance with the expression of his, and then wait to see what thoughts or sentiments arise in my mind or heart, as if to match or correspond with the expression.' This response of the schoolboy lies at the bottom of all the spurious profundity which has been attributed to **Rochefoucauld** to **La Bougive**, to **Machiavelli**, and to **Campanella**."

"And the identification," I said, "of the reasoner's intellect with that of his opponent, depends, if I understand you aright, upon the accuracy with which the opponent's intellect is admeasured."

"For its practical value it depends upon this," replied Dupin; "and the Prefect and his cohort fail so frequently, first, by default of this identification, and, secondly, by ill-admeasurement, or rather through non-admeasurement, of the intellect with which they are engaged. They consider only their *own* ideas of ingenuity; and, in searching for anything hidden, advert only to the modes in which *they* would have hidden it. They are right in this much—that their own ingenuity is a faithful representative of that of *the mass*; but when the cunning of the individual felon is diverse in character from their own, the felon foils them, of course. This always happens when it is above their own, and very usually when it is below. They have no variation of principle in their investigations; at best, when urged by some unusual emergency—by some extraordinary reward—they extend or exaggerate their old modes of *practice*, without touching their principles.

"What, for example, in this case of D—, has been done to vary the principle of action? What is all this boring, and

---

**Rochefoucauld, La Bougive, Machiavelli and Campanella:** Examples of philosophers and moralists known for wise sayings. La Bougive may be meant to refer to Jean de La Bruyere.

probing, and sounding, and scrutinizing with the microscope, and dividing the surface of the building into registered square inches—what is it all but an exaggeration *of the application* of the one principle or set of principles of search, which are based upon the one set of notions regarding human ingenuity, to which the Prefect, in the long routine of his duty, has been accustomed? Do you not see he has taken it for granted that *all* men proceed to conceal a letter—not exactly in a gimlet-hole bored in a chair-leg—but, at least, in *some* out-of-the-way hole or corner suggested by the same tenor of thought which would urge a man to secret a letter in a gimlet-hole bored in a chair-leg? And do you not see also, that such ***recherchés*** nooks for concealment are adapted only for ordinary occasions, and would be adopted only by ordinary intellects; for, in all cases of concealment, a disposal of the article concealed—a disposal of it in this *recherché* manner,—is, in the very first instance, presumable and presumed; and thus its discovery depends, not at all upon the acumen, but altogether upon the mere care, patience, and determination of the seekers; and where the case is of importance—or, what amounts to the same thing in the policial eyes, when the reward is of magnitude,—the qualities in question have *never* been known to fail.

"You will now understand what I mean in suggesting that, had the purloined letter been hidden anywhere within the limits of the Prefect's examination—in other words, had the principle of its concealment been comprehended within the principles of the Prefect—its discovery would have been a matter altogether beyond question. This functionary, however, has been thoroughly mystified; and the remote source of his defeat lies in the supposition that the minister is a fool,

---

**Recherchés**: Something exotic or rare, perhaps excessively overdone.

because he has acquired renown as a poet. All fools are poets; this the Prefect *feels*; and he is merely guilty of a **non distributio medii** in thence inferring that all poets are fools."

"But is this really the poet?" I asked. "There are two brothers, I know; and both have attained reputation in letters. The minister I believe has written learnedly on the Differential Calculus. He is a mathematician, and no poet."

"You are mistaken; I know him well; he is both. As poet *and* mathematician, he would reason well; as mere mathematician, he could not have reasoned at all, and thus would have been at the mercy of the Prefect."

"You surprise me," I said, "by these opinions, which have been contradicted by the voice of the world. You do not mean to set at naught the well-digested idea of centuries. The mathematical reason has long been regarded as *the* reason *par excellence*."

"'***Il y a à parier***,'" replied Dupin, quoting from Chamfort, "'***que toute idée publique, toute convention reçue, est une sottise, car elle a convenu au plus grand nombre.***' The mathematicians, I grant you, have done their best to promulgate the popular error to which you allude, and which is nonetheless an error for its promulgation as truth. With an art worthy of a better cause, for example, they have insinuated the term 'analysis' into application to algebra. The French are the originators of this particular deception; but if a term is of any importance—if words derive any value from

---

**Non distributio medii:** A type of error in logical reasoning. In this case, Dupin is saying that in fact some poets are not fools.

**Il y a à parier . . . grand nombre:** The chances are that every commonly held idea, every accepted way of doing things, is nonsense precisely because it has suited itself to the majority.

applicability—then 'analysis' conveys 'algebra' about as much as, in Latin, '*ambitus*' implies 'ambition,' '*religio*' 'religion,' or '*homines honesti*,' a set of *honorable* men."

"You have a quarrel on hand, I see," said I, "with some of the algebraists of Paris; but proceed."

"I dispute the availability, and thus the value, of that reason which is cultivated in any special form other than the abstractly logical. I dispute, in particular, the reason educed by mathematical study. The mathematics are the science of form and quantity; mathematical reasoning is merely logic applied to observation upon form and quantity. The great error lies in supposing that even the truths of what is called *pure* algebra are abstract or general truths. And this error is so egregious that I am confounded at the universality with which it has been received. Mathematical axioms are *not* axioms of general truth. What is true of *relation*—of form and quantity—is often grossly false in regard to morals, for example. In this latter science it is very usually *un*true that the aggregated parts are equal to the whole. In chemistry also the axiom fails. In the consideration of motive it fails; for two motives, each of a given value, have not, necessarily, a value when united, equal to the sum of their values apart. There are numerous other mathematical truths which are only truths within the *limits* of relation. But the mathematician argues, from his *finite truths*, through habit, as if they were of an absolutely general applicability—as the world indeed imagines them to be. Bryant, in his very learned *Mythology*, mentions an analogous source of error, when he says that 'although the Pagan fables are not believed, yet we forget ourselves continually, and make inferences from them as existing realities.' With the algebraists, however, who are Pagans themselves, the 'Pagan fables' *are* believed, and the inferences are made, not so much through lapse of memory, as through an unaccountable addling of the brains. In short, I never yet encountered the mere mathematician who could be trusted out of equal roots, or one who did not clandestinely hold it as a point of his faith that $x^2 + px$ was absolutely and unconditionally equal to $q$. Say to one of these gentlemen, by way of experiment, if you please, that you believe occasions may occur where $x^2 + px$ is *not* altogether equal to $q$, and, having made him understand what you mean, get out of his reach as speedily as convenient, for, beyond doubt, he will endeavor to knock you down.

"I mean to say," continued Dupin, while I merely laughed at his last observations, "that if the minister had been no more than a mathematician, the Prefect would have been under no necessity of giving me this check. I knew him, however, as both mathematician and poet, and my measures were adapted to his capacity, with reference to the circumstances by which he was surrounded. I knew him as a courtier, too, and as a bold intriguer. Such a man, I considered, could not fail to be aware of the ordinary police modes of action. He could not have failed to anticipate—and events have proved that he did not fail to anticipate—the waylayings to which he was subjected. He must have foreseen, I reflected, the secret investigations of his premises. His frequent absences from home at night, which were hailed by the Prefect as certain aids to his success, I regarded only as *ruses*, to afford opportunity for thorough search to the police, and thus the sooner to impress them with the conviction to which G—, in fact, did finally arrive—the conviction that the letter was not upon the premises. I felt, also, that the whole train of thought, which I was at some pains in detailing to you just now, concerning the invariable principle of policial action in searches for articles concealed—I felt that this whole train of thought would necessarily pass through the mind of the minister. It would imperatively lead him to despise all the ordinary *nooks* of concealment. *He* could not, I reflected, be so weak as not to see that the most intricate and remote recess of his hotel would be as open as his commonest closets to the eyes, to the probes, to the gimlets, and to the microscopes of the Prefect. I saw, in fine, that he would be driven, as a matter of course, to *simplicity*, if not deliberately induced to it as a matter of choice. You will remember, perhaps, how desperately the Prefect laughed when I suggested, upon our first interview, that it was just possible this mystery troubled him so much on account of its being so *very* self-evident."

"Yes," said I, "I remember his merriment well. I really thought he would have fallen into convulsions."

"The material world," continued Dupin, "abounds with very strict analogies to the immaterial; and thus some color of truth has been given to the rhetorical dogma, that metaphor, or simile, may be made to strengthen an argument, as well as to embellish a description. The principle of the ***vis inertiœ***, for example, seems to be identical in physics and metaphysics. It is not more true in the former, that a large body is with more difficulty set in motion than a smaller one, and that its subsequent *momentum* is commensurate with this difficulty, than it is, in the latter, that intellects of the vaster capacity, while more forcible, more constant, and more eventful in their movements than those of inferior grade, are yet the less readily moved, and more embarrassed and full of hesitation in the first few steps of their progress. Again: have you ever noticed which of the street signs, over

---

**Vis inertiœ:** The power of inertia, the property of matter that causes it to remain at rest or in uniform motion unless acted on by an outside force. Generally, a resistance to change.

the shop doors, are the most attractive of attention?"

"I have never given the matter a thought," I said.

"There is a game of puzzles," he resumed, "which is played upon a map. One party playing requires another to find a given word—the name of town, river, state, or empire—any word, in short, upon the motley and perplexed surface of the chart. A novice in the game generally seeks to embarrass his opponents by giving them the most minutely-lettered names; but the adept selects such words as stretch, in large characters, from one end of the chart to the other. These, like the over-largely lettered signs and placards of the street, escape observation by dint of being excessively obvious; and here the physical oversight is precisely analogous with the moral inapprehension by which the intellect suffers to pass unnoticed those considerations which are too obtrusively and too palpably self-evident. But this is a point, it appears, somewhat above or beneath the understanding of the Prefect. He never once thought it probable, or possible, that the minister had deposited the letter immediately beneath the nose of the whole world, by way of best preventing any portion of that world from perceiving it.

"But the more I reflected upon the daring, dashing, and discriminating ingenuity of D—; upon the fact that the document must always have been *at hand*, if he intended to use it to good purpose; and upon the decisive evidence, obtained by the Prefect, that it was not hidden within the limits of that dignitary's ordinary search—the more satisfied I became that, to conceal this letter, the minister had resorted to the comprehensive and sagacious expedient of not attempting to conceal it at all.

"Full of these ideas, I prepared myself with a pair of green spectacles, and called one fine morning, quite by accident, at the ministerial hotel. I found D— at home, yawning, lounging, and dawdling, as usual, and pretending to be in the last extremity of *ennui*. He is, perhaps, the most really energetic human being now alive—but that is only when nobody sees him.

"To be even with him, I complained of my weak eyes, and lamented the necessity of the spectacles, under cover of which I cautiously and thoroughly surveyed the apartment, while seemingly intent only upon the conversation of my host.

"I paid special attention to a large writing-table near which he sat, and upon which lay confusedly, some miscellaneous letters and other papers, with one or two musical instruments and a few books. Here, however, after a long and very deliberate scrutiny, I saw nothing to excite particular suspicion.

"At length my eyes, in going the circuit of the room, fell upon a trumpery filigree card-rack of paste-board, that hung dangling by a dirty blue ribbon, from a little brass knob just beneath the middle of the mantel-piece. In this rack, which had three or four compartments, were five or six visiting cards and a solitary letter. This last was much soiled and crumpled. It was torn nearly in two, across the middle—as if a design, in the first instance, to tear it entirely up as worthless, had been altered, or stayed, in the second. It had a large black seal, bearing the D— cipher *very* conspicuously, and was addressed, in a diminutive female hand, to D—, the minister, himself. It was thrust carelessly, and even, as it seemed, contemptuously, into one of the upper divisions of the rack.

"No sooner had I glanced at this letter, than I concluded it to be that of which I was in search. To be sure, it was, to all appearance, radically different from the one of which the Perfect had read us so minute a description. Here the seal was large and black, with the D— cipher; there it was small and red, with the ducal arms of the S— family. Here, the address, to the minister, was diminutive and feminine; there the superscription, to a certain royal personage, was markedly bold and decided; the size alone formed a point of correspondence. But, then, the *radicalness* of these differences, which was excessive; the dirt; the soiled and torn condition of the paper, so inconsistent with the *true* methodical habits of D—, and so suggestive of a design to delude the beholder into an idea of the worthlessness of the document; these things, together with the hyperobtrusive situation of this document, full in the view of every visitor, and thus exactly in accordance with the conclusions to which I had previously arrived; these things, I say, were strongly corroborative of suspicion, in one who came with the intention to suspect.

"I protracted my visit as long as possible, and, while I maintained a most animated discussion with the minister, on a topic which I knew well had never failed to interest and excite him, I kept my attention really riveted upon the letter. In this examination, I committed to memory its external appearance and arrangement in the rack; and also fell, at length, upon a discovery which set at rest whatever trivial doubt I might have entertained. In scrutinizing the edges of the paper, I observed them to be more *chafed* than seemed necessary. They presented the *broken* appearance which is manifested when a stiff paper, having been once folded and pressed with a folder, is refolded in a reversed direction, in the same creases or edges which had formed the original fold. This discovery was sufficient. It was clear to me that the letter had been turned, as a glove, inside out, re-directed, and resealed. I bade the minister good morning, and took my departure at once, leaving a gold snuff-box upon the table.

"The next morning I called for the snuff-box, when we

resumed, quite eagerly, the conversation of the preceding day. While thus engaged, however, a loud report, as if of a pistol, was heard immediately beneath the windows of the hotel, and was succeeded by a series of fearful screams, and the shoutings of a mob. D— rushed to a casement, threw it open, and looked out. In the meantime, I stepped to the card-rack, took the letter, put it in my pocket, and replaced it by a *facsimile* (so far as regards externals), which I had carefully prepared at my lodgings; imitating the D— cipher, very readily, by means of a seal formed of bread.

"The disturbance in the street had been occasioned by the frantic behavior of a man with a musket. He had fired it among a crowd of women and children. It proved, however, to have been without ball, and the fellow was suffered to go his way as a lunatic or a drunkard. When he had gone, D— came from the window, whither I had followed him immediately upon securing the object in view. Soon afterwards I bade him farewell. The pretended lunatic was a man in my own pay."

"But what purpose had you," I asked, "in replacing the letter by a facsimile? Would it not have been better, at the first visit, to have seized it openly, and departed?"

"D—," replied Dupin, "is a desperate man, and a man of nerve. His hotel, too, is not without attendants devoted to his interests. Had I made the wild attempt you suggest, I might never have left the ministerial presence alive. The good people of Paris might have heard of me no more. But I had an object apart from these considerations. You know my political pre-possessions. In this matter, I act as a partisan of the lady concerned. For eighteen months the minister has had her in his power. She has now him in hers; since, being unaware that the letter is not in his possession, he will proceed with his exactions as if it was. Thus will he inevitably commit himself, at once, to his political destruction. His downfall, too, will not be more precipitate than awkward. It is all very well to talk about the ***facilis descensus Averni***; but in all kinds of climbing, as Catalani said of singing, it is far more easy to get up than to come down. In the present instance I have no sympathy—at least no pity—for him who descends. He is that ***monstrum horrendum***, an unprincipled man of genius. I confess, however, that I should like very well to know the precise character of his thoughts, when, being defied by her whom the Prefect terms 'a certain personage,' he is reduced to opening the letter which I left for him in the card-rack."

"How? Did you put anything particular in it?"

"Why—it did not seem altogether right to leave the interior blank—that would have been insulting. D—, at Vienna once, did me an evil turn, which I told him, quite good-humoredly, that I should remember. So, as I knew he would feel some curiosity in regard to the identity of the person who had outwitted him, I thought it a pity not to give him a clue. He is well acquainted with my **MS.**, and I just copied into the middle of the blank sheet the words—

**'—Un dessein si funeste,**
**S'il n'est digne d'Atrée, est digne de Thyeste.'**

They are to be found in Crébillon's *Atrée*."

---

**Facilis descensus Averni:** "The descent to Hell is easy" (from Virgil's *Aeneid*, Book VI).

**Monstrum horrendum:** Horrible monstrosity (Virgil's description of Polyphemus, the one-eyed, man-eating giant).

**MS.:** Manuscript; an author's original version, at that time handwritten.

**Un dessein ... de Thyeste:** "Such a wicked scheme, if not worthy of Atreus, is worthy of Thyestes." In Greek mythology, Thyestes seduced his brother Atreus's wife and in revenge Atreus murdered Thyestes' sons and served them to their father at a feast.

## O. Henry

# *The Gift Of The Magi*

ONE DOLLAR AND EIGHTY-SEVEN CENTS. THAT was all. And sixty cents of it was in pennies. Pennies saved one and two at a time by bulldozing the grocer and the vegetable man and the butcher until one's cheeks burned with the silent imputation of parsimony that such close dealing implied. Three times Della counted it. One dollar and eighty-seven cents. And the next day would be Christmas.

There was clearly nothing to do but flop down on the shabby little couch and howl. So Della did it. Which instigates the moral reflection that life is made up of sobs, sniffles, and smiles, with sniffles predominating.

While the mistress of the home is gradually subsiding from the first stage to the second, take a look at the home. A furnished **flat** at $8 per week. It did not exactly beggar description, but it certainly had that word on the lookout for the mendicancy squad.

---

**Magi:** The three wise men of the East who bought gifts to the infant Jesus in Bethlehem.

**Flat:** Apartment.

In the vestibule below was a letter-box into which no letter would go, and an electric button from which no mortal finger could coax a ring. Also appertaining thereunto was a card bearing the name "Mr. James Dillingham Young."

The "Dillingham" had been flung to the breeze during a former period of prosperity when its possessor was being paid $30 per week. Now, when the income was shrunk to $20, the letters of "Dillingham" looked blurred, as though they were thinking seriously of contracting to a modest and unassuming D. But whenever Mr. James Dillingham Young came home and reached his flat above he was called "Jim" and greatly hugged by Mrs. James Dillingham Young, already introduced to you as Della. Which is all very good.

Della finished her cry and attended to her cheeks with the powder rag. She stood by the window and looked out dully at a gray cat walking a gray fence in a gray backyard. Tomorrow would be Christmas Day, and she had only $1.87 with which to buy Jim a present. She had been saving every penny she could for months, with this result. Twenty dollars a week doesn't go far. Expenses had been greater than she had calculated. They always are. Only $1.87 to buy a present for Jim. Her Jim. Many a happy hour she had spent planning for something nice for him. Something fine and rare and sterling—something just a little bit near to being worthy of the honor of being owned by Jim.

There was a **pier-glass** between the windows of the room. Perhaps you have seen a pier-glass in an $8 flat. A very thin and very agile person may, by observing his reflection in a rapid sequence of longitudinal strips, obtain a fairly accurate conception of his looks. Della, being slender, had mastered the art.

---

**Pier-glass:** A large mirror.

Suddenly she whirled from the window and stood before the glass. Her eyes were shining brilliantly, but her face had lost its color within twenty seconds. Rapidly she pulled down her hair and let it fall to its full length.

Now, there were two possessions of the James Dillingham Youngs in which they both took a mighty pride. One was Jim's gold watch that had been his father's and his grandfather's. The other was Della's hair. Had the Queen of Sheba lived in the flat across the airshaft, Della would have let her hair hang out the window some day to dry just to depreciate Her Majesty's jewels and gifts. Had King Solomon been the janitor, with all his treasures piled up in the basement, Jim would have pulled out his watch every time he passed, just to see him pluck at his beard from envy.

So now Della's beautiful hair fell about her, rippling and shining like a cascade of brown waters. It reached below her knee and made itself almost a garment for her. And then she did it up again nervously and quickly. Once she faltered for a minute and stood still while a tear or two splashed on the worn red carpet.

On went her old brown jacket; on went her old brown hat. With a whirl of skirts and with the brilliant sparkle still in her eyes, she fluttered out the door and down the stairs to the street.

Where she stopped the sign read: "Mme. Sofronie. Hair Goods of All Kinds." One flight up Della ran, and collected herself, panting. Madame, large, too white, chilly, hardly looked the "Sofronie."

"Will you buy my hair?" asked Della.

"I buy hair," said Madame. "Take yer hat off and let's have a sight at the looks of it."

Down rippled the brown cascade.

"Twenty dollars," said Madame, lifting the mass with a

practiced hand.

"Give it to me quick," said Della.

Oh, and the next two hours tripped by on rosy wings. Forget the hashed metaphor. She was ransacking the stores for Jim's present.

She found it at last. It surely had been made for Jim and no one else. There was no other like it in any of the stores, and she had turned all of them inside out. It was a platinum **fob** chain simple and chaste in design, properly proclaiming its value by substance alone and not by meretricious ornamentation—as all good things should be. It was even worthy of The Watch. As soon as she saw it she knew that it must be Jim's. It was like him. Quietness and value—the description applied to both. Twenty-one dollars they took from her for it, and she hurried home with the 87 cents. With that chain on his watch Jim might be properly anxious about the time in any company. Grand as the watch was, he sometimes looked at it on the sly on account of the old leather strap that he used in place of a chain.

When Della reached home her intoxication gave way a little to prudence and reason. She got out her curling irons and lighted the gas and went to work repairing the ravages made by generosity added to love. Which is always a tremendous task, dear friends—a mammoth task.

Within forty minutes her head was covered with tiny, close-lying curls that made her look wonderfully like a truant schoolboy. She looked at her reflection in the mirror long, carefully, and critically.

"If Jim doesn't kill me," she said to herself, "before he takes a second look at me, he'll say I look like a **Coney Island** chorus girl. But what could I do—oh! what could I do with a

---

**Fob:** A short strap or ribbon for securing a watch.

dollar and eighty-seven cents?"

At 7 o'clock the coffee was made and the frying pan was on the back of the stove hot and ready to cook the chops.

Jim was never late. Della doubled the fob chain in her hand and sat on the corner of the table near the door that he always entered. Then she heard his step on the stair away down on the first flight, and she turned white for just a moment. She had a habit of saying little silent prayers about the simplest everyday things, and now she whispered: "Please God, make him think I am still pretty."

The door opened and Jim stepped in and closed it. He looked thin and serious. Poor fellow, he was only twenty-two—and to be burdened with a family! He needed a new overcoat and he was without gloves.

Jim stopped inside the door, as immovable as a setter at the scent of quail. His eyes were fixed upon Della, and there was an expression in them that she could not read, and it terrified her. It was not anger, nor surprise, nor disapproval, nor horror, nor any of the sentiments that she had been prepared for. He simply stared at her fixedly with that peculiar expression on his face.

Della wriggled off the table and went for him.

"Jim, darling," she cried, "don't look at me that way. I had my hair cut off and sold it because I couldn't have lived through Christmas without giving you a present. It'll grow out again—you won't mind, will you? I just had to do it. My hair grows awfully fast. Say 'Merry Christmas!' Jim, and let's be happy. You don't know what a nice—what a beautiful, nice gift I've got for you."

---

**Coney Island:** A seaside amusement center in Brooklyn, New York, that was extremely popular in the 19th and early 20th centuries, when more than a million people a day would visit in the summer.

"You've cut off your hair?" asked Jim, laboriously, as if he had not arrived at that patent fact yet even after the hardest mental labor.

"Cut it off and sold it," said Della. "Don't you like me just as well, anyhow? I'm me without my hair, ain't I?" Jim looked about the room curiously.

"You say your hair is gone?" he said, with an air almost of idiocy.

"You needn't look for it," said Della. "It's sold, I tell you—sold and gone, too. It's Christmas Eve, boy. Be good to me, for it went for you. Maybe the hairs of my head were numbered," she went on with a sudden serious sweetness, "but nobody could ever count my love for you. Shall I put the chops on, Jim?"

Out of his trance Jim seemed quickly to wake. He enfolded his Della. For ten seconds let us regard with discreet scrutiny some inconsequential object in the other direction. Eight dollars a week or a million a year—what is the difference? A mathematician or a wit would give you the wrong answer. The magi brought valuable gifts, but that was not among them. This dark assertion will be illuminated later on.

Jim drew a package from his overcoat pocket and threw it upon the table.

"Don't make any mistake, Dell," he said, "about me. I don't think there's anything in the way of a haircut or a shave or a shampoo that could make me like my girl any less. But if you'll unwrap that package you may see why you had me going awhile at first."

White fingers and nimble tore at the string and paper. And then an ecstatic scream of joy; and then, alas! a quick feminine change to hysterical tears and wails, necessitating the immediate employment of all the comforting powers of the lord of the flat.

For there lay The Combs—the set of combs, side and back, that Della had worshipped for long in a Broadway window. Beautiful combs, pure tortoise shell, with jeweled rims—just the shade to wear in the beautiful vanished hair. They were expensive combs, she knew, and her heart had simply craved and yearned over them without the least hope of possession. And now, they were hers, but the tresses that should have adorned the coveted adornments were gone.

But she hugged them to her bosom, and at length she was able to look up with dim eyes and a smile and say: "My hair grows so fast, Jim!"

And then Della leaped up like a little singed cat and cried, "Oh, oh!"

Jim had not yet seen his beautiful present. She held it out to him eagerly upon her open palm. The dull precious metal seemed to flash with a reflection of her bright and ardent spirit.

"Isn't it a dandy, Jim? I hunted all over town to find it. You'll have to look at the time a hundred times a day now. Give me your watch. I want to see how it looks on it."

Instead of obeying, Jim tumbled down on the couch and put his hands under the back of his head and smiled.

"Dell," said he, "let's put our Christmas presents away and keep 'em awhile. They're too nice to use just at present. I sold the watch to get the money to buy your combs. And now suppose you put the chops on."

The magi, as you know, were wise men—wonderfully wise men—who brought gifts to the Babe in the manger. They invented the art of giving Christmas presents. Being wise, their gifts were no doubt wise ones, possibly bearing the privilege of exchange in case of duplication. And here I have lamely related to you the uneventful chronicle of two foolish children in a flat who most unwisely sacrificed for each other the greatest treasures of their house. But in a last word to the wise of these days let it be said that of all who gave gifts, these two were the wisest. Of all who give and receive gifts such as they are wisest. Everywhere they are wisest. They are the magi.

James Thurber

# *The Secret Life of Walter Mitty*

WE'RE GOING THROUGH!" THE COMMANDER'S voice was like thin ice breaking. He wore his full-dress uniform, with the heavily braided white cap pulled down rakishly over one cold gray eye. "We can't made it, sir. It's spoiling for a hurricane, if you ask me." "I'm not asking you, Lieutenant Berg," said the Commander. "Throw on the power lights! Rev her up to 8,500! We're going through!" The pounding of the cylinders increased: ta-pocketa-pocketa-pocketa-*pocketa-pocketa*. The Commander stared at the ice forming on the pilot window. He walked over and twisted a row of complicated dials. "Switch on No. 8 auxiliary!" he shouted. "Switch on No. 8 auxiliary!" repeated Lieutenant Berg. "Full strength in No. 3 turret!" shouted the Commander. "Full strength in No. 3 turret!" The crew, bending to their various tasks in the huge, hurtling eight-engined Navy hydroplane, looked at each other and grinned. "The Old Man'll get us through," they said to one another. "The Old Man ain't afraid of Hell!"...

"Not so fast! You're driving too fast!" said Mrs. Mitty. "What are you driving so fast for?"

"Hmm?" said Walter Mitty. He looked at his wife, in the seat beside him, with shocked astonishment. She seemed grossly unfamiliar, like a strange woman who had yelled at him in a crowd. "You were up to fifty-five," she said. "You know I don't like to go more than forty. You were up to fifty-five." Walter Mitty drove on toward Waterbury in silence, the roaring of the SN202 through the worst storm in twenty years of Navy flying fading in the remote, intimate airways of his mind. "You're tensed up again," said Mrs. Mitty. "It's one of your days. I wish you'd let Dr. Renshaw look you over."

Walter Mitty stopped the car in front of the building where his wife went to have her hair done. "Remember to get those overshoes while I'm having my hair done," she said. "I don't need overshoes," said Mitty. She put her mirror back into her bag. "We've been all through that," she said, getting out of the car. "You're not a young man any longer." He raced the engine a little. "Why don't you wear your gloves? Have you lost your gloves?" Walter Mitty reached in a pocket and brought out the gloves. He put them on, but after she had turned and gone into the building and he had driven on to a red light, he took them off again. "Pick it up, brother!" snapped a cop as the light changed, and Mitty hastily pulled on his gloves and lurched ahead. He drove around the streets aimlessly for a time, and then he drove past the hospital on his way to the parking lot.

... "It's the millionaire banker, Wellington McMillan," said the pretty nurse. "Yes?" said Walter Mitty, removing his gloves slowly. "Who has the case?" "Dr. Renshaw and Dr. Benbow, but there are two specialists here, Dr. Remington from New York and Mr. Pritchard-Mitford from London. He flew over." A door opened down a long, cool corridor and Dr. Renshaw came out. He looked distraught and haggard. "Hello, Mitty," he said. "We're having the devil's own time with McMillan, the millionaire banker and close personal friend of Roosevelt. Obstreosis of the ductal tract. Tertiary. Wish you'd take a look at him." "Glad to," said Mitty.

In the operating room there were whispered introductions: "Dr. Remington, Dr. Mitty. Mr. Pritchard-Mitford, Dr. Mitty." "I've read your book on streptothricosis," said Pritchard-Mitford, shaking hands. "A brilliant performance, sir." "Thank you," said Walter Mitty. "Didn't know you were in the States, Mitty," grumbled Remington. "Coals to Newcastle, bringing Mitford and me up here for a tertiary." "You are very kind," said Mitty. A huge, complicated machine, connected to the operating table, with many tubes and wires, began at this moment to go pocketa-pocketa-pocketa. "The new anesthetizer is giving way!" shouted an intern. "There is no one in the East who knows how to fix it!" "Quiet, man!" said Mitty, in a low, cool voice. He sprang to the machine, which was now going pocketa-pocketa-queep-pocketa-queep. He began fingering delicately a row of glistening dials. "Give me a fountain pen!" he snapped. Someone handed him a fountain pen. He pulled a faulty piston out of the machine and inserted the pen in its place. "That will hold for ten minutes," he said. "Get on with the operation." A nurse hurried over and whispered to Renshaw, and Mitty saw the man turn pale. "Coreopsis has set in," said Renshaw nervously. "If you would take over, Mitty?" Mitty looked at him and at the craven figure of Benbow, who drank, and at the grave, uncertain faces of the two great specialists. "If you wish," he said. They slipped a white gown on him; he adjusted a mask and drew on thin gloves; nurses handed him shining . . .

"Back it up, Mac! Look out for that Buick!" Walter Mitty jammed on the brakes. "Wrong lane, Mac," said the parking-lot attendant, looking at Mitty closely. "Gee. Yeh," muttered Mitty. He began cautiously to back out of the lane marked "Exit Only." "Leave her sit there," said the attendant. "I'll put her away." Mitty got out of the car. "Hey, better leave the key." "Oh," said Mitty, handing the man the ignition key. The attendant vaulted into the car, backed it up with insolent skill, and put it where it belonged.

They're so damn cocky, thought Walter Mitty, walking along Main Street; they think they know everything. Once he had tried to take his chains off, outside New Milford, and he had got them wound around the axles. A man had had to come out in a wrecking car and unwind them, a young, grinning garageman. Since then Mrs. Mitty always made him drive to a garage to have the chains taken off. The next time, he thought, I'll wear my right arm in a sling; they won't grin at me then. I'll have my right arm in a sling and they'll see I couldn't possibly take the chains off myself. He kicked at the slush on the sidewalk. "Overshoes," he said to himself, and he began looking for a shoe store.

When he came out into the street again, with the overshoes in a box under his arm, Walter Mitty began to wonder what the other thing was his wife had told him to get. She had told him, twice, before they set out from their house for Waterbury. In a way he hated these weekly trips to town—he was always getting something wrong. Kleenex, he thought, Squibb's, razor blades? No. Toothpaste, toothbrush, bicarbonate, carborundum, initiative and referendum? He gave it up. But she would remember it. "Where's the what's-its-name?" she would ask. "Don't tell me you forgot the what's-its-name." A newsboy went by shouting something about the Waterbury trial.

... "Perhaps this will refresh your memory." The District Attorney suddenly thrust a heavy automatic at the quiet figure on the witness stand. "Have you ever seen this before?" Walter Mitty took the gun and examined it expertly. "This is my Webley-Vickers 50.80," he said calmly. An excited buzz ran around the courtroom. The Judge rapped for order. "You are a crack shot with any sort of firearms, I believe?" said the District Attorney, insinuatingly. "Objection!" shouted Mitty's attorney. "We have shown that the defendant could not have fired the shot. We have shown that he wore his right arm in a sling on the night of the fourteenth of July." Walter Mitty raised his hand briefly and the bickering attorneys were stilled. "With any known make of gun," he said evenly, "I could have killed Gregory Fitzhurst at three hundred feet *with my left hand*." Pandemonium broke loose in the courtroom. A woman's scream rose above the bedlam and suddenly a lovely, dark-haired girl was in Walter Mitty's arms. The District Attorney struck at her savagely. Without rising from his chair, Mitty let the man have it on the point of the chin. "You miserable cur!"...

"Puppy biscuit," said Walter Mitty. He stopped walking and the buildings of Waterbury rose up out of the misty courtroom and surrounded him again. A woman who was passing laughed. "He said 'puppy biscuit,'" she said to her companion. "That man said 'puppy biscuit' to himself." Walter Mitty hurried on. He went into an A. & P., not the first one he came to but a smaller one farther up the street. "I want some biscuit for small, young dogs," he said to the clerk. "Any special brand, sir?" The greatest pistol shot in the world thought a moment. "It says 'Puppies Bark for It' on the box," said Walter Mitty.

His wife would be through at the hairdresser's in fifteen minutes, Mitty saw in looking at his watch, unless they had trouble drying it; sometimes they had trouble drying it. She didn't like to get to the hotel first; she would want him to be there waiting for her as usual. He found a big leather chair in the lobby, facing a window, and he put the overshoes and the puppy biscuit on the floor beside it. He picked up an old copy of *Liberty* and sank down into the chair. "Can Germany Conquer the World Through the Air?" Walter Mitty looked at the pictures of bombing planes and of ruined streets.

... "The cannonading has got the wind up in young Raleigh, sir," said the sergeant. Captain Mitty looked up at him through touseled hair. "Get him to bed," he said wearily. "With the others. I'll fly alone." "But you can't, sir," said the sergeant anxiously. "It takes two men to handle that bomber and the Archies are pounding hell out of the air. Von Richtman's circus is between here and Saulier." "Somebody's got to get that ammunition dump," said Mitty. "I'm going over. Spot of brandy?" He poured a drink for the sergeant and one for himself. War thundered and whined around the dugout and battered at the door. There was a rending of wood and splinters flew through the room. "A bit of a near thing," said Captain Mitty carelessly. "The box barrage is closing in," said the sergeant. "We only live once, Sergeant," said Mitty, with his faint, fleeting smile. "Or do we?" He poured another brandy and tossed it off. "I never see a man could hold his brandy like you, sir," said the sergeant. "Begging your pardon, sir." Captain Mitty stood up and strapped on his huge Webley-Vickers automatic. "It's forty kilometers through hell, sir," said the sergeant. Mitty finished one last brandy. "After all," he said softly, "what isn't?" The pounding of the cannon increased; there was the rat-tat-tatting of machine guns, and from somewhere came the menacing pocketa-pocketa-pocketa of the new flame-throwers. Walter Mitty walked to the door of the dugout humming

"Auprès de Ma Blonde." He turned and waved to the sergeant. "Cheerio!" he said. . . .

Something struck his shoulder. "I've been looking all over this hotel for you," said Mrs. Mitty. "Why do you have to hide in this old chair? How did you expect me to find you?" "Things close in," said Walter Mitty vaguely. "What?" Mrs. Mitty said. "Did you get the what's-its-name? The puppy biscuit? What's in that box?" "Overshoes," said Mitty. "Couldn't you have put them on in the store?" "I was thinking," said Walter Mitty. "Does it ever occur to you that I am sometimes thinking?" She looked at him. "I'm going to take your temperature when I get you home," she said.

They went out through the revolving doors that made a faintly derisive whistling sound when you pushed them. It was two blocks to the parking lot. At the drugstore on the corner she said, "Wait here for me. I forgot something. I won't be a minute." She was more than a minute. Walter Mitty lighted a cigarette. It began to rain, rain with sleet in it. He stood up against the wall of the drugstore, smoking. . . . He put his shoulders back and his heels together. "To hell with the handkerchief," said Walter Mitty scornfully. He took one last drag on his cigarette and snapped it away. Then, with that faint, fleeting smile playing about his lips, he faced the firing squad; erect and motionless, proud and disdainful, Walter Mitty the Undefeated, inscrutable to the last.

## William Faulkner

# *Barn Burning*

THE STORE IN WHICH THE JUSTICE OF THE PEACE'S court was sitting smelled of cheese. The boy, crouched on his nail keg at the back of the crowded room, knew he smelled cheese, and more: from where he sat he could see the ranked shelves close-packed with the solid, squat, dynamic shapes of tin cans whose labels his stomach read, not from the lettering which meant nothing to his mind but from the scarlet devils and the silver curve of fish—this, the cheese which he knew he smelled and the hermetic meat which his intestines believed he smelled coming in intermittent gusts momentary and brief between the other constant one, the smell and sense just a little of fear because mostly of despair and grief, the old fierce pull of blood. He could not see the table where the Justice sat and before which his father and his father's enemy (*our enemy* he thought in that despair; *ourn! mine and hisn both! He's my father!*) stood, but he could hear them, the two of them that is, because his father had said no word yet:

"But what proof have you, Mr. Harris?"

"I told you. The hog got into my corn. I caught it up and sent it back to him. He had no fence that would hold it. I told him so, warned him. The next time I put the hog in my pen. When he came to get it I gave him enough wire to patch up his pen. The next time I put the hog up and kept it. I rode down to his house and saw the wire I gave him still rolled on to the spool in his yard. I told him he could have the hog when he paid me a dollar pound fee. That evening a Negro came with the dollar and got the hog. He was a strange Negro. He said, 'He say to tell you wood and hay kin burn.' I said, 'What?' 'That whut he say to tell you,' the Negro said. 'Wood and hay kin burn.' That night my barn burned. I got the stock out but I lost the barn."

"Where is the Negro? Have you got him?"

"He was a strange Negro, I tell you. I don't know what became of him."

"But that's not proof. Don't you see that's not proof?"

"Get that boy up here. He knows." For a moment the boy thought too that the man meant his older brother until Harris said, "Not him. The little one. The boy," and, crouching, small for his age, small and wiry like his father, in patched and faded jeans even too small for him, with straight, uncombed, brown hair and eyes gray and wild as storm scud, he saw the men between himself and the table part and become a lane of grim faces, at the end of which he saw the Justice, a shabby, collarless, graying man in spectacles, beckoning him. He felt no floor under his bare feet; he seemed to walk beneath the palpable weight of the grim turning faces. His father, stiff in his black Sunday coat donned not for the trial but for the moving, did not even look at him. *He aims for me to lie*, he thought, again with that frantic grief and despair. *And I will have to do hit*.

"What's your name, boy?" the Justice said.

"Colonel Sartoris Snopes," the boy whispered.

"Hey?" the Justice said. "Talk louder. Colonel Sartoris? I

reckon anybody named for Colonel Sartoris in this country can't help but tell the truth, can they?" The boy said nothing. *Enemy! Enemy!* he thought; for a moment he could not even see, could not see that the Justice's face was kindly nor discern that his voice was troubled when he spoke to the man named Harris: "Do you want me to question this boy?" But he could hear, and during those subsequent long seconds while there was absolutely no sound in the crowded little room save that of quiet and intent breathing it was as if he had swung outward at the end of a grape vine, over a ravine, and at the top of the swing had been caught in a prolonged instant of mesmerized gravity, weightless in time.

"No!" Harris said violently, explosively. "Damnation! Send him out of here!" Now time, the fluid world, rushed beneath him again, the voices coming to him again through the smell of cheese and sealed meat, the fear and despair and the old grief of blood:

"This case is closed. I can't find against you, Snopes, but I can give you advice. Leave this country and don't come back to it."

His father spoke for the first time, his voice cold and harsh, level, without emphasis: "I aim to. I don't figure to stay in a country among people who. . ." he said something unprintable and vile, addressed to no one.

"That'll do," the Justice said. "Take your wagon and get out of this country before dark. Case dismissed."

His father turned, and he followed the stiff black coat, the wiry figure walking a little stiffly from where a Confederate provost's man's musket ball had taken him in the heel on a stolen horse thirty years ago, followed the two backs now, since his older brother had appeared from somewhere in the crowd, no taller than the father but thicker, chewing tobacco steadily, between the two lines of grim-faced men and out of the store and across the worn gallery and down the sagging steps and among the dogs and half-grown boys in the mild May dust, where as he passed a voice hissed:

"Barn burner!"

Again he could not see, whirling; there was a face in a red haze, moonlike, bigger than the full moon, the owner of it half again his size, he leaping in the red haze toward the face, feeling no blow, feeling no shock when his head struck the earth, scrabbling up and leaping again, feeling no blow this time either and tasting no blood, scrabbling up to see the other boy in full flight and himself already leaping into pursuit as his father's hand jerked him back, the harsh, cold voice speaking above him: "Go get in the wagon."

It stood in a grove of locusts and mulberries across the road. His two hulking sisters in their Sunday dresses and his mother and her sister in calico and sunbonnets were already in it, sitting on and among the sorry residue of the dozen and more movings which even the boy could remember—the battered stove, the broken beds and chairs, the clock inlaid with mother-of-pearl, which would not run, stopped at some fourteen minutes past two o'clock of a dead and forgotten day and time, which had been his mother's dowry. She was crying, though when she saw him she drew her sleeve across her face and began to descend from the wagon. "Get back," the father said.

"He's hurt. I got to get some water and wash his..."

"Get back in the wagon," his father said. He got in too, over the tailgate. His father mounted to the seat where the older brother already sat and struck the gaunt mules two savage blows with the peeled willow, but without heat. It was not even sadistic; it was exactly that same quality which in later years would cause his descendants to over-run the engine before putting a motor car into motion, striking and reining back in the same movement. The wagon went on, the store with its quiet crowd of grimly watching men dropped behind; a curve in the road hid it. *Forever* he thought. *Maybe he's done satisfied now, now that he has...* stopping himself, not to say it aloud even to himself. His mother's hand touched his shoulder.

"Does hit hurt?" she said.

"Naw," he said. "Hit don't hurt. Lemme be."

"Can't you wipe some of the blood off before hit dries?"

"I'll wash tonight," he said. "Lemme be, I tell you."

The wagon went on. He did not know where they were going. None of them ever did or ever asked, because it was always somewhere, always a house of sorts waiting for them a day or two days or even three days away. Likely his father had already arranged to make a crop on another farm before he... Again he had to stop himself. He (the father) always did. There was something about his wolflike independence and even courage when the advantage was at least neutral which impressed strangers, as if they got from his latent ravening ferocity not so much a sense of dependability as a feeling that his ferocious conviction in the rightness of his own actions would be of advantage to all whose interest lay with his.

That night they camped, in a grove of oaks and beeches where a spring ran. The nights were still cool and they had a fire against it, of a rail lifted from a nearby fence and cut into lengths—a small fire, neat almost, a shrewd fire; such fires were his father's habit and custom always, even in freezing weather. Older, the boy might have remarked this and wondered why not a big one; why should not a man who had not only seen the waste and extravagance of war, but who had in his blood an inherent voracious prodigality with material not his own, have burned everything in sight? Then he might have gone a step farther and thought that that was the reason: that miserly blaze was the living fruit of nights passed during those four years in the woods hiding from all men, blue or gray, with his strings of horses (captured horses, he called them). And older still, he might have divined the true reason: that the element of fire spoke to some deep mainspring of his father's being, as the element of steel or of powder spoke to other men, as the one weapon for the preservation of integrity, else breath were not worth the breathing, and hence to be regarded with respect and used with discretion.

But he did not think this now and he had seen those same miserly blazes all his life. He merely ate his supper beside it and was already half asleep over his iron plate when his father called him, and once more he followed the stiff back, the stiff and ruthless limp, up the slope and on to the starlit road where, turning, he could see his father against the stars but without face or depth—a shape black, flat, and bloodless as though cut from tin in the iron folds of the frockcoat which had not been made for him, the voice harsh like tin and without heat like tin:

"You were fixing to tell them. You would have told him." He didn't answer. His father struck him with the flat of his hand on the side of the head, hard but without heat, exactly as he had struck the two mules at the store, exactly as he would strike either of them with any stick in order to kill a horse fly, his voice still without heat or anger: "You're getting to be a man. You got to learn. You got to learn to stick to your own blood or you ain't going to have any blood to stick to you. Do you think either of them, any man there this morning, would? Don't you know all they wanted was a chance to get at me because they knew I had them beat? Eh?" Later, twenty years later, he was to tell himself, "If I had said they wanted only truth, justice, he would have hit me again." But now he said nothing. He was not crying. He just stood there. "Answer me," his father said. "Yes," he whispered. His father turned.

"Get on to bed. We'll be there tomorrow."

Tomorrow they were there. In the early afternoon the wagon stopped before a paintless two-room house identical almost with the dozen others it had stopped before even in the boy's ten years, and again, as on the other dozen occasions, his mother and aunt got down and began to unload the wagon, although his two sisters and his father and brother had not moved.

"Likely hit ain't fitten for hawgs," one of the sisters said.

"Nevertheless, fit it will and you'll hog it and like it," his father said. "Get out of them chairs and help your Ma unload."

The two sisters got down, big, bovine, in a flutter of cheap ribbons; one of them drew from the jumbled wagon bed a battered lantern, the other a worn broom. His father handed the reins to the older son and began to climb stiffly over the wheel. "When they get unloaded, take the team to the barn and feed them." Then he said, and at first the boy thought he was still speaking to his brother: "Come with me."

"Me?" he said.

"Yes," his father said. "You."

"Abner," his mother said. His father paused and looked back—the harsh level stare beneath the shaggy, graying, irascible brows.

"I reckon I'll have a word with the man that aims to begin tomorrow owning me body and soul for the next eight months."

They went back up the road. A week ago—or before last night, that is—he would have asked where they were going, but not now. His father had struck him before last night but never before had he paused afterward to explain why; it was as if the blow and the following calm, outrageous voice still rang, repercussed, divulging nothing to him save the terrible handicap of being young, the light weight of his few years, just heavy enough to prevent his soaring free of the world as it seemed to be ordered but not heavy enough to keep him footed solid in it, to resist it and try to change the course of its events.

Presently he could see the grove of oaks and cedars and the other flowering trees and shrubs where the house would be, though not the house yet. They walked beside a fence massed with honeysuckle and Cherokee roses and came to a gate swinging open between two brick pillars, and now, beyond a sweep of drive, he saw the house for the first time and at that instant he forgot his father and the terror and despair both, and even when he remembered his father again (who had not stopped) the terror and despair did not return. Because, for all the twelve movings, they had sojourned until now in a poor country, a land of small farms and fields and houses, and he had never seen a house like this before. *Hit's big as a courthouse* he thought quietly, with a surge of peace and joy whose reason he could not have thought into words, being too young for that: *They are safe from him. People whose lives are a part of this peace and dignity are beyond his touch, he no more to them than a buzzing wasp: capable of stinging for a little moment but that's all; the spell of this peace and dignity rendering even the barns and stable and cribs which belong to it impervious to the puny flames he might contrive...* this, the peace and joy, ebbing for an instant as he looked again at the stiff black back, the stiff and implacable limp of the figure which was not dwarfed by the house, for the reason that it had never looked big anywhere and which now, against the serene columned backdrop, had more than ever that impervious quality of something cut ruthlessly from tin, depthless, as though, sidewise to the sun, it would cast no shadow. Watching him, the boy remarked the absolutely undeviating course which his father held and saw the stiff foot come squarely down in a pile of fresh droppings where a horse had stood in the drive and which his father could have avoided by a simple change of stride. But it ebbed only for a moment, though he could not have thought this into words either, walking on in the spell of the house, which he could even want but without envy, without sorrow, certainly never with that ravening and jealous rage which unknown to him walked in the ironlike black coat before him: *Maybe he will feel it too. Maybe it will even change him now from what maybe he couldn't help but be.*

They crossed the portico. Now he could hear his father's stiff foot as it came down on the boards with clocklike finality, a sound out of all proportion to the displacement of the body it bore and which was not dwarfed either by the white door before it, as though it had attained to a sort of vicious and ravening minimum not to be dwarfed by anything—the flat, wide, black hat, the formal coat of broadcloth which had once been black but which had now that friction-glazed greenish cast of the bodies of old house flies, the lifted sleeve which was too large, the lifted hand like a curled claw. The door opened so promptly that the boy knew the Negro must have been watching them all the time, an old man with neat grizzled hair, in a linen jacket, who stood barring the door with his body, saying, "Wipe yo foots, white man, fo you come in here. Major ain't home nohow."

"Get out of my way," his father said, without heat too,

flinging the door back and the Negro also and entering, his hat still on his head. And now the boy saw the prints of the stiff foot on the doorjamb and saw them appear on the pale rug behind the machinelike deliberation of the foot which seemed to bear (or transmit) twice the weight which the body compassed. The Negro was shouting "Miss Lula! Miss Lula!" somewhere behind them, then the boy, deluged as though by a warm wave by a suave turn of carpeted stair and a pendant glitter of chandeliers and a mute gleam of gold frames, heard the swift feet and saw her too, a lady—perhaps he had never seen her like before either—in a gray, smooth gown with lace at the throat and an apron tied at the waist and the sleeves turned back, wiping cake or biscuit dough from her hands with a towel as she came up the hall, looking not at his father at all but at the tracks on the blond rug with an expression of incredulous amazement.

"I tried," the Negro cried. "I tole him to..."

"Will you please go away?" she said in a shaking voice. "Major de Spain is not at home. Will you please go away?"

His father had not spoken again. He did not speak again. He did not even look at her. He just stood stiff in the center of the rug, in his hat, the shaggy iron-gray brows twitching slightly above the pebble-colored eyes as he appeared to examine the house with brief deliberation. Then with the same deliberation he turned; the boy watched him pivot on the good leg and saw the stiff foot drag round the arc of the turning, leaving a final long and fading smear. His father never looked at it, he never once looked down at the rug. The Negro held the door. It closed behind them, upon the hysteric and indistinguishable woman-wail. His father stopped at the top of the steps and scraped his boot clean on the edge of it. At the gate he stopped again. He stood for a moment, planted stiffly on the stiff foot, looking back at the house.

"Pretty and white, ain't it?" he said. "That's sweat. Black sweat. Maybe it ain't white enough yet to suit him. Maybe he wants to mix some white sweat with it."

Two hours later the boy was chopping wood behind the house within which his mother and aunt and the two sisters (the mother and aunt, not the two girls, he knew that; even at this distance and muffled by walls the flat loud voices of the two girls emanated an incorrigible idle inertia) were setting up the stove to prepare a meal, when he heard the hooves and saw the linen-clad man on a fine sorrel mare, whom he recognized even before he saw the rolled rug in front of the Negro youth following on a fat bay carriage horse—a suffused, angry face vanishing, still at full gallop, beyond the corner of the house where his father and brother were sitting in the two tilted chairs; and a moment later, almost before he could have put the axe down, he heard the hooves again and watched the sorrel mare go back out of the yard, already galloping again. Then his father began to shout one of the sisters' names, who presently emerged backward from the kitchen door dragging the rolled rug along the ground by one end while the other sister walked behind it.

"If you ain't going to tote, go on and set up the wash pot," the first said.

"You, Sarty!" the second shouted. "Set up the wash pot!" His father appeared at the door, framed against that shabbiness, as he had been against that other bland perfection, impervious to either, the mother's anxious face at his shoulder.

"Go on," the father said. "Pick it up." The two sisters stooped, broad, lethargic; stooping, they presented an incredible expanse of pale cloth and a flutter of tawdry ribbons.

"If I thought enough of a rug to have to git hit all the way from France I wouldn't keep hit where folks coming in would have to tromp on hit," the first said. They raised the rug.

"Abner," the mother said. "Let me do it."

"You go back and git dinner," his father said. "I'll tend to this."

From the woodpile through the rest of the afternoon the boy watched them, the rug spread flat in the dust beside the bubbling wash-pot, the two sisters stooping over it with that profound and lethargic reluctance, while the father stood over them in turn, implacable and grim, driving them though never raising his voice again. He could smell the harsh homemade lye they were using; he saw his mother come to the door once and look toward them with an expression not anxious now but very like despair; he saw his father turn, and he fell to with the axe and saw from the corner of his eye his father raise from the ground a flattish fragment of field stone and examine it and return to the pot, and this time his mother actually spoke: "Abner. Abner. Please don't. Please, Abner."

Then he was done too. It was dusk; the whippoorwills had already begun. He could smell coffee from the room where they would presently eat the cold food remaining from the mid-afternoon meal, though when he entered the house he realized they were having coffee again probably because there was a fire on the hearth, before which the rug now lay spread over the backs of the two chairs. The tracks of his father's foot were gone. Where they had been were now long, water-cloudy scoriations resembling the sporadic course of a lilliputian mowing machine.

It still hung there while they ate the cold food and then went to bed, scattered without order or claim up and down the two rooms, his mother in one bed, where his father would later lie, the older brother in the other, himself, the aunt, and the two sisters on pallets on the floor. But his father was not in bed yet. The last thing the boy remembered was the depthless, harsh silhouette of the hat and coat bending over the rug and it seemed to him that he had not even closed his eyes when the silhouette was standing over him, the fire almost dead behind it, the stiff foot prodding him awake. "Catch up the mule," his father said.

When he returned with the mule his father was standing in the black door, the rolled rug over his shoulder. "Ain't you going to ride?" he said.

"No. Give me your foot."

He bent his knee into his father's hand, the wiry, surprising power flowed smoothly, rising, he rising with it, on to the mule's bare back (they had owned a saddle once; the boy could remember it though not when or where) and with the same effortlessness his father swung the rug up in front of him. Now in the starlight they retraced the afternoon's path, up the dusty road rife with honeysuckle, through the gate and up the black tunnel of the drive to the lightless house, where he sat on the mule and felt the rough warp of the rug drag across his thighs and vanish.

"Don't you want me to help?" he whispered. His father did not answer and now he heard again that stiff foot striking the hollow portico with that wooden and clocklike deliberation, that outrageous overstatement of the weight it carried. The rug, hunched, not flung (the boy could tell that even in the darkness) from his father's shoulder struck the angle of wall and floor with a sound unbelievably loud, thunderous, then the foot again, unhurried and enormous; a light came on in the house and the boy sat, tense, breathing steadily and quietly and just a little fast, though the foot itself did not increase its beat at all, descending the steps now; now the boy could see him.

"Don't you want to ride now?" he whispered. "We kin

both ride now," the light within the house altering now, flaring up and sinking. *He's coming down the stairs now*, he thought. He had already ridden the mule up beside the horse block; presently his father was up behind him and he doubled the reins over and slashed the mule across the neck, but before the animal could begin to trot the hard, thin arm came round him, the hard, knotted hand jerking the mule back to a walk.

In the first red rays of the sun they were in the lot, putting plow gear on the mules. This time the sorrel mare was in the lot before he heard it at all, the rider collarless and even bareheaded, trembling, speaking in a shaking voice as the woman in the house had done, his father merely looking up once before stooping again to the **hame** he was buckling, so that the man on the mare spoke to his stooping back:

"You must realize you have ruined that rug. Wasn't there anybody here, any of your women..." he ceased, shaking, the boy watching him, the older brother leaning now in the stable door, chewing, blinking slowly and steadily at nothing apparently. "It cost a hundred dollars. But you never had a hundred dollars. You never will. So I'm going to charge you twenty bushels of corn against your crop. I'll add it in your contract and when you come to the commissary you can sign it. That won't keep Mrs. de Spain quiet but maybe it will teach you to wipe your feet off before you enter her house again."

Then he was gone. The boy looked at his father, who still had not spoken or even looked up again, who was now adjusting the hame.

"Pap," he said. His father looked at him—the inscrutable face, the shaggy brows beneath which the gray eyes glinted

---

**Hame:** A curved wooden support that attaches to the collar of a horse harness.

coldly. Suddenly the boy went toward him, fast, stopping as suddenly. "You done the best you could!" he cried. "If he wanted hit done different why didn't he wait and tell you how? He won't git no twenty bushels! He won't git none! We'll gether hit and hide hit! I kin watch..."

"Did you put the cutter back in that straight stock like I told you?"

"No, sir," he said.

"Then go do it."

That was Wednesday. During the rest of that week he worked steadily, at what was within his scope and some which was beyond it, with an industry that did not need to be driven nor even commanded twice; he had this from his mother, with the difference that some at least of what he did he liked to do, such as splitting wood with the half-size axe which his mother and aunt had earned, or saved money somehow, to present him with at Christmas. In company with the two older women (and on one afternoon, even one of the sisters), he built pens for the shoat and the cow which were a part of his father's contract with the landlord, and one afternoon, his father being absent, gone somewhere on one of the mules, he went to the field.

They were running a middle buster now, his brother holding the plow straight while he handled the reins, and walking beside the straining mule, the rich black soil shearing cool and damp against his bare ankles, he thought *Maybe this is the end of it. Maybe even that twenty bushels that seems hard to have to pay for just a rug will be a cheap price for him to stop forever and always from being what he used to be*; thinking, dreaming now, so that his brother had to speak sharply to him to mind the mule: *Maybe he even won't collect the twenty bushels. Maybe it will all add up and balance and vanish—corn, rug, fire; the terror and grief, the being pulled two ways like between two teams of horses—gone, done with for ever and ever.*

Then it was Saturday; he looked up from beneath the mule he was harnessing and saw his father in the black coat and hat. "Not that," his father said. "The wagon gear." And then, two hours later, sitting in the wagon bed behind his father and brother on the seat, the wagon accomplished a final curve, and he saw the weathered paintless store with its tattered tobacco- and patent-medicine posters and the tethered wagons and saddle animals below the gallery. He mounted the gnawed steps behind his father and brother, and there again was the lane of quiet, watching faces for the three of them to walk through. He saw the man in spectacles sitting at the plank table and he did not need to be told this was a Justice of the Peace; he sent one glare of fierce, exultant, partisan defiance at the man in collar and cravat now, whom he had seen but twice before in his life, and that on a galloping horse, who now wore on his face an expression not of rage but of amazed unbelief which the boy could not have known was at the incredible circumstance of being sued by one of his own tenants, and came and stood against his father and cried at the Justice: "He ain't done it! He ain't burnt..."

"Go back to the wagon," his father said.

"Burnt?" the Justice said. "Do I understand this rug was burned too?"

"Does anybody here claim it was?" his father said. "Go back to the wagon." But he did not, he merely retreated to the rear of the room, crowded as that other had been, but not to sit down this time, instead, to stand pressing among the motionless bodies, listening to the voices:

"And you claim twenty bushels of corn is too high for the damage you did to the rug?"

"He brought the rug to me and said he wanted the tracks

washed out of it. I washed the tracks out and took the rug back to him."

"But you didn't carry the rug back to him in the same condition it was in before you made the tracks on it."

His father did not answer, and now for perhaps half a minute there was no sound at all save that of breathing, the faint, steady suspiration of complete and intent listening.

"You decline to answer that, Mr. Snopes?" Again his father did not answer. "I'm going to find against you, Mr. Snopes. I'm going to find that you were responsible for the injury to Major de Spain's rug and hold you liable for it. But twenty bushels of corn seems a little high for a man in your circumstances to have to pay. Major de Spain claims it cost a hundred dollars. October corn will be worth about fifty cents. I figure that if Major de Spain can stand a ninety-five dollar loss on something he paid cash for, you can stand a five-dollar loss you haven't earned yet. I hold you in damages to Major de Spain to the amount of ten bushels of corn over and above your contract with him, to be paid to him out of your crop at gathering time. Court adjourned."

It had taken no time hardly, the morning was but half begun. He thought they would return home and perhaps back to the field, since they were late, far behind all other farmers. But instead his father passed on behind the wagon, merely indicating with his hand for the older brother to follow with it, and crossed the road toward the blacksmith shop opposite, pressing on after his father, overtaking him, speaking, whispering up at the harsh, calm face beneath the weathered hat: "He won't git no ten bushels neither. He won't git one. We'll. . ." until his father glanced for an instant down at him, the face absolutely calm, the grizzled eyebrows tangled above the cold eyes, the voice almost pleasant, almost gentle:

"You think so? Well, we'll wait till October anyway."

The matter of the wagon—the setting of a spoke or two and the tightening of the tires—did not take long either, the business of the tires accomplished by driving the wagon into the spring branch behind the shop and letting it stand there, the mules nuzzling into the water from time to time, and the boy on the seat with the idle reins, looking up the slope and through the sooty tunnel of the shed where the slow hammer rang and where his father sat on an upended cypress bolt, easily, either talking or listening, still sitting there when the boy brought the dripping wagon up out of the branch and halted it before the door.

"Take them on to the shade and hitch," his father said. He did so and returned. His father and the smith and a third man squatting on his heels inside the door were talking, about crops and animals; the boy, squatting too in the ammoniac dust and hoof-parings and scales of rust, heard his father tell a long and unhurried story out of the time before the birth of the older brother even when he had been a professional horsetrader. And then his father came up beside him where he stood before a tattered last year's circus poster on the other side of the store, gazing rapt and quiet at the scarlet horses, the incredible poisings and convolutions of tulle and tights and the painted leers of comedians, and said, "It's time to eat."

But not at home. Squatting beside his brother against the front wall, he watched his father emerge from the store and produce from a paper sack a segment of cheese and divide it carefully and deliberately into three with his pocket knife and produce crackers from the same sack. They all three squatted on the gallery and ate, slowly, without talking; then in the store again, they drank from a tin dipper tepid water smelling of the cedar bucket and of living beech trees. And still they did not go home. It was a horse lot this time, a tall rail fence upon and along which men stood and sat and out of which one by one horses were led, to be walked and trotted and then cantered back and forth along the road while the slow swapping and buying went on and the sun began to slant westward, they—the three of them—watching and listening, the older brother with his muddy eyes and his steady, inevitable tobacco, the father commenting now and then on certain of the animals, to no one in particular.

It was after sundown when they reached home. They ate supper by lamplight, then, sitting on the doorstep, the boy watched the night fully accomplish, listening to the whippoorwills and the frogs, when he heard his mother's voice: "Abner! No! No! Oh, God. Oh, God. Abner!" and he rose, whirled, and saw the altered light through the door where a candle stub now burned in a bottle neck on the table and his father, still in the hat and coat, at once formal and burlesque as though dressed carefully for some shabby and ceremonial violence, emptying the reservoir of the lamp back into the five-gallon kerosene can from which it had been filled, while the mother tugged at his arm until he shifted the lamp to the other hand and flung her back, not savagely or viciously, just hard, into the wall, her hands flung out against the wall for balance, her mouth open and in her face the same quality of hopeless despair as had been in her voice. Then his father saw him standing in the door.

"Go to the barn and get that can of oil we were oiling the wagon with," he said. The boy did not move. Then he could speak.

"What..." he cried. "What are you..."

"Go get that oil," his father said. "Go."

Then he was moving, running, outside the house, toward the stable: this the old habit, the old blood which he had not been permitted to choose for himself, which had been bequeathed him willy nilly and which had run for so long (and who knew where, battening on what of outrage and savagery and lust) before it came to him. *I could keep on,* he thought. *I could run on and on and never look back, never need to see his face again. Only I can't. I can't,* the rusted can in his hand now, the liquid sploshing in it as he ran back to the house and into it, into the sound of his mother's weeping in the next room, and handed the can to his father.

"Ain't you going to even send a Negro?" he cried. "At least you sent a Negro before!"

This time his father didn't strike him. The hand came even faster than the blow had, the same hand which had set the can on the table with almost excruciating care flashing from the can toward him too quick for him to follow it, gripping him by the back of his shirt and on to tiptoe before he had seen it quit the can, the face stooping at him in breathless and frozen ferocity, the cold, dead voice speaking over him to the older brother who leaned against the table, chewing with that steady, curious, sidewise motion of cows:

"Empty the can into the big one and go on. I'll catch up with you."

"Better tie him up to the bedpost," the brother said.

"Do like I told you," the father said. Then the boy was moving, his bunched shirt and the hard, bony hand between his shoulder-blades, his toes just touching the floor, across the room and into the other one, past the sisters sitting with spread heavy thighs in the two chairs over the cold hearth, and to where his mother and aunt sat side by side on the bed, the aunt's arms about his mother's shoulders.

"Hold him," the father said. The aunt made a startled movement. "Not you," the father said. "Lennie. Take hold of him. I want to see you do it." His mother took him by the wrist. "You'll hold him better than that. If he gets loose don't you know what he is going to do? He will go up yonder." He jerked his head toward the road. "Maybe I'd better tie him."

"I'll hold him," his mother whispered.

"See you do then." Then his father was gone, the stiff foot heavy and measured upon the boards, ceasing at last.

Then he began to struggle. His mother caught him in both arms, he jerking and wrenching at them. He would be stronger in the end, he knew that. But he had no time to wait for it. "Lemme go!" he cried. "I don't want to have to hit you!"

"Let him go!" the aunt said. "If he don't go, before God, I am going up there myself!"

"Don't you see I can't?" his mother cried. "Sarty! Sarty! No! No! Help me, Lizzie!"

Then he was free. His aunt grasped at him but it was too late. He whirled, running, his mother stumbled forward on to her knees behind him, crying to the nearer sister: "Catch him. Net! Catch him!" But that was too late too, the sister (the sisters were twins, born at the same time, yet either of them now gave the impression of being, encompassing as much living meat and volume and weight as any other two of the family) not yet having begun to rise from the chair, her head, face, alone merely turned, presenting to him in the flying instant an astonishing expanse of young female features untroubled by any surprise even, wearing only an expression of bovine interest. Then he was out of the room, out of the house, in the mild dust of the starlit road and the heavy rifeness of honeysuckle, the pale ribbon unspooling with terrific slowness under his running feet, reaching the gate at last and turning in, running, his heart and lungs drumming, on up the drive toward the lighted house, the lighted door. He did not knock, he burst in, sobbing for breath, incapable for the moment of speech; he saw the astonished face of the

Negro in the linen jacket without knowing when the Negro had appeared.

"De Spain!" he cried, panted. "Where's. . ." then he saw the white man too emerging from a white door down the hall. "Barn!" he cried. "Barn!"

"What?" the white man said. "Barn?"

"Yes!" the boy cried. "Barn!"

"Catch him!" the white man shouted.

But it was too late this time too. The Negro grasped his shirt, but the entire sleeve, rotten with washing, carried away, and he was out that door too and in the drive again, and had actually never ceased to run even while he was screaming into the white man's face.

Behind him the white man was shouting, "My horse! Fetch my horse!" and he thought for an instant of cutting across the park and climbing the fence into the road, but he did not know the park nor how high the vine-massed fence might be and he dared not risk it. So he ran on down the drive, blood and breath roaring; presently he was in the road again though he could not see it. He could not hear either: the galloping mare was almost upon him before he heard her, and even then he held his course, as if the very urgency of his wild grief and need must in a moment more find him wings, waiting until the ultimate instant to hurl himself aside and into the weed-choked roadside ditch as the horse thundered past and on, for an instant in furious silhouette against the stars, the tranquil early summer night sky which, even before the shape of the horse and rider vanished, stained abruptly and violently upward: a long, swirling roar incredible and soundless, blotting the stars, and he springing up and into the road again, running again, knowing it was too late yet still running even after he heard the shot and, an instant later, two shots, pausing now without knowing he had ceased to run, crying "Pap! Pap!", running again before he knew he had begun to run, stumbling, tripping over something and scrabbling up again without ceasing to run, looking backward over his shoulder at the glare as he got up, running on among the invisible trees, panting, sobbing, "Father! Father!"

At midnight he was sitting on the crest of a hill. He did not know it was midnight and he did not know how far he had come. But there was no glare behind him now and he sat now, his back toward what he had called home for four days anyhow, his face toward the dark woods which he would enter when breath was strong again, small, shaking steadily in the chill darkness, hugging himself into the remainder of his thin, rotten shirt, the grief and despair now no longer terror and fear but just grief and despair. *Father. My father,* he thought. "He was brave!" he cried suddenly, aloud but not loud, no more than a whisper: "He was! He was in the war! He was in Colonel Sartoris' cav'ry!" not knowing that his father had gone to that war a private in the fine old European sense, wearing no uniform, admitting the authority of and giving fidelity to no man or army or flag, going to war as **Malbrouck** himself did: for booty—it meant nothing and less than nothing to him if it were enemy booty or his own.

The slow constellations wheeled on. It would be dawn and then sun-up after a while and he would be hungry. But that would be tomorrow and now he was only cold, and walking would cure that. His breathing was easier now and he decided to get up and go on, and then he found that he had been asleep because he knew it was almost dawn, the night

---

**Malbrouck:** A character in an 18th century French song based on John Churchill (1650-1722), the first Duke of Marlborough, who is considered one of Britain's greatest military strategists.

almost over. He could tell that from the whippoorwills. They were everywhere now among the dark trees below him, constant and inflectioned and ceaseless, so that, as the instant for giving over to the day birds drew nearer and nearer, there was no interval at all between them. He got up. He was a little stiff, but walking would cure that too as it would the cold, and soon there would be the sun. He went on down the hill, toward the dark woods within which the liquid silver voices of the birds called unceasing—the rapid and urgent beating of the urgent and **quiring** heart of the late spring night. He did not look back.

---

**Quiring:** A variation of choir.

# F. Scott Fitzgerald

# *Bernice Bobs Her Hair*

AFTER DARK ON SATURDAY NIGHT ONE COULD stand on the first tee of the golf course and see the country club windows as a yellow expanse over a very black and wavy ocean. The waves of this ocean, so to speak, were the heads of many curious caddies, a few of the more ingenious chauffeurs, the golf professional's deaf sister—and there were usually several stray, diffident waves who might have rolled inside had they so desired. This was the gallery.

The balcony was inside. It consisted of the circle of wicker chairs that lined the wall of the combination clubroom and ballroom. At these Saturday night dances it was largely feminine; a great babel of middle-aged ladies with sharp eyes and icy hearts behind **lorgnettes** and large bosoms. The main function of the balcony was critical. It occasionally showed grudging admiration, but never approval, for it is well known among ladies over thirty-five that when the younger set dance in the summer-time it is with the very worst intentions in the world, and if they are not bombarded with stony eyes

---

**Lorgnettes:** Eyeglasses or small opera binoculars that have a handle.

stray couples will dance weird barbaric interludes in the corners, and the more popular, more dangerous, girls will sometimes be kissed in the parked limousines of unsuspecting dowagers.

But, after all, this critical circle is not close enough to the stage to see the actors' faces and catch the subtler byplay. It can only frown and lean, ask questions and make satisfactory deductions from its set of postulates, such as the one which states that every young man with a large income leads the life of a hunted partridge. It never really appreciates the drama of the shifting, semicruel world of adolescence. No; boxes, orchestra-circle, principals, and chorus are represented by the medley of faces and voices that sway to the plaintive African rhythm of Dyer's dance orchestra.

From sixteen-year-old Otis Ormonde, who has two more years at Hill School, to G. Reece Stoddard, over whose bureau at home hangs a Harvard law diploma; from little Madeleine Hogue, whose hair still feels strange and uncomfortable on top of her head, to Bessie MacRae, who has been the life of the party a little too long—more than ten years—the medley is not only the center of the stage but contains the only people capable of getting an unobstructed view of it.

With a flourish and a bang the music stops. The couples exchange artificial, effortless smiles, facetiously repeat "*la*-de-*da*-*da* dum-*dum*," and then the clatter of young feminine voices soars over the burst of clapping.

A few disappointed **stags** caught in midfloor as they had been about to cut in subsided listlessly back to the walls, because this was not like the riotous Christmas dances—these summer hops were considered just pleasantly warm and exciting, where even the younger marrieds rose and per-

---

**Stag:** A man at a party or dance without a date.

formed ancient waltzes and terrifying fox trots to the tolerant amusement of their younger brothers and sisters.

Warren McIntyre, who casually attended Yale, being one of the unfortunate stags, felt in his dinner-coat pocket for a cigarette and strolled out onto the wide, semidark veranda, where couples were scattered at tables, filling the lantern-hung night with vague words and hazy laughter. He nodded here and there at the less absorbed, and as he passed each couple some half-forgotten fragment of a story played in his mind, for it was not a large city and every one was Who's Who to every one else's past. There, for example, were Jim Strain and Ethel Demorest, who had been privately engaged for three years. Every one knew that as soon as Jim managed to hold a job for more than two months she would marry him. Yet how bored they both looked, and how wearily Ethel regarded Jim sometimes, as if she wondered why she had trained the vines of her affection on such a wind-shaken poplar.

Warren was nineteen and rather pitying with those of his friends who hadn't gone East to college. But, like most boys, he bragged tremendously about the girls of his city when he was away from it. There was Genevieve Ormonde, who regularly made the rounds of dances, house-parties, and football games at Princeton, Yale, Williams, and Cornell; there was black-eyed Roberta Dillon, who was quite as famous to her own generation as **Hiram Johnson or Ty Cobb**; and, of

**Hiram Johnson or Ty Cobb**: Johnson (1866-1945), who served twice as California's Govenor and five terms in the U.S. Senate, was a well-known political ally of Teddy Roosevelt. Perhaps the greatest baseball player ever, Ty Cobb (1886-1961) set long-standing records for hits and stolen bases while playing for the Detroit Tigers from 1905 to 1926. Nicknamed The Georgia Peach, he was the first player inducted into the Baseball Hall of Fame when it opened in 1936.

course, there was Marjorie Harvey, who besides having a fairylike face and a dazzling, bewildering tongue was already justly celebrated for having turned five cart-wheels in succession during the past pump-and-slipper dance at New Haven.

Warren, who had grown up across the street from Marjorie, had long been "crazy about her." Sometimes she seemed to reciprocate his feeling with a faint gratitude, but she had tried him by her infallible test and informed him gravely that she did not love him. Her test was that when she was away from him she forgot him and had affairs with other boys. Warren found this discouraging, especially as Marjorie had been making little trips all summer, and for the first two or three days after each arrival home he saw great heaps of mail on the Harveys' hall table addressed to her in various masculine handwritings. To make matters worse, all during the month of August she had been visited by her cousin Bernice from Eau Claire, and it seemed impossible to see her alone. It was always necessary to hunt round and find some one to take care of Bernice. As August waned this was becoming more and more difficult.

Much as Warren worshipped Marjorie, he had to admit that Cousin Bernice was sorta dopeless. She was pretty, with dark hair and high color, but she was no fun on a party. Every Saturday night he danced a long arduous duty dance with her to please Marjorie, but he had never been anything but bored in her company.

"Warren"—a soft voice at his elbow broke in upon his thoughts, and he turned to see Marjorie, flushed and radiant as usual. She laid a hand on his shoulder and a glow settled almost imperceptibly over him.

"Warren," she whispered, "do something for me—dance with Bernice. She's been stuck with little Otis Ormonde for almost an hour."

Warren's glow faded.

"Why—sure," he answered half-heartedly.

"You don't mind, do you? I'll see that you don't get stuck."

"'Sall right."

Marjorie smiled—that smile that was thanks enough.

"You're an angel, and I'm obliged loads."

With a sigh the angel glanced round the veranda, but Bernice and Otis were not in sight. He wandered back inside, and there in front of the women's dressing-room he found Otis in the center of a group of young men who were convulsed with laughter. Otis was brandishing a piece of timber he had picked up, and discoursing volubly.

"She's gone in to fix her hair," he announced wildly. "I'm waiting to dance another hour with her."

Their laughter was renewed.

"Why don't some of you cut in?" cried Otis resentfully. "She likes more variety."

"Why, Otis," suggested a friend, "you've just barely got used to her."

"Why the two-by-four, Otis?" inquired Warren, smiling.

"The two-by-four? Oh, this? This is a club. When she comes out I'll hit her on the head and knock her in again."

Warren collapsed on a settee and howled with glee.

"Never mind, Otis," he articulated finally. "I'm relieving you this time."

Otis simulated a sudden fainting attack and handed the stick to Warren.

"If you need it, old man," he said hoarsely.

No matter how beautiful or brilliant a girl may be, the reputation of not being frequently cut in on makes her position at a dance unfortunate. Perhaps boys prefer her company to that of the butterflies with whom they dance a dozen times an evening, but youth in this jazz-nourished generation is temperamentally restless, and the idea of fox-trotting more than one full fox trot with the same girl is distasteful, not to say odious. When it comes to several dances and the intermissions between she can be quite sure that a young man, once relieved, will never tread on her wayward toes again.

Warren danced the next full dance with Bernice, and finally, thankful for the intermission, he led her to a table on the veranda. There was a moment's silence while she did unimpressive things with her fan.

"It's hotter here than in Eau Claire," she said.

Warren stifled a sigh and nodded. It might be for all he knew or cared. He wondered idly whether she was a poor conversationalist because she got no attention or got no attention because she was a poor conversationalist.

"You going to be here much longer?" he asked, and then turned rather red. She might suspect his reasons for asking.

"Another week," she answered, and stared at him as if to lunge at his next remark when it left his lips.

Warren fidgeted. Then with a sudden charitable impulse he decided to try part of his line on her. He turned and looked at her eyes.

"You've got an awfully kissable mouth," he began quietly.

This was a remark that he sometimes made to girls at college proms when they were talking in just such half dark as this. Bernice distinctly jumped. She turned an ungraceful red and became clumsy with her fan. No one had ever made such a remark to her before.

"Fresh!"—the word had slipped out before she realized it, and she bit her lip. Too late she decided to be amused, and offered him a flustered smile.

Warren was annoyed. Though not accustomed to having that remark taken seriously, still it usually provoked a laugh or a paragraph of sentimental banter. And he hated to be called fresh, except in a joking way. His charitable impulse died and he switched the topic.

"Jim Strain and Ethel Demorest sitting out as usual," he commented.

This was more in Bernice's line, but a faint regret mingled with her relief as the subject changed. Men did not talk to her about kissable mouths, but she knew that they talked in some such way to other girls.

"Oh, yes," she said, and laughed. "I hear they've been mooning round for years without a red penny. Isn't it silly?"

Warren's disgust increased. Jim Strain was a close friend of his brother's, and anyway he considered it bad form to sneer at people for not having money. But Bernice had had no intention of sneering. She was merely nervous.

## II

When Marjorie and Bernice reached home at half after midnight they said good night at the top of the stairs. Though cousins, they were not intimates. As a matter of fact Marjorie had no female intimates—she considered girls stupid. Bernice on the contrary all through this parent-arranged visit had rather longed to exchange those confidences flavored with giggles and tears that she considered an indispensable factor in all feminine intercourse. But in this respect she found Marjorie rather cold; felt somehow the same difficulty in talking to her that she had in talking to men. Marjorie never giggled, was never frightened, seldom embarrassed, and in fact had very few of the qualities which

Bernice considered appropriately and blessedly feminine.

As Bernice busied herself with toothbrush and paste this night she wondered for the hundredth time why she never had any attention when she was away from home. That her family were the wealthiest in Eau Claire; that her mother entertained tremendously, gave little dinners for her daughter before all dances and bought her a car of her own to drive round in, never occurred to her as factors in her hometown social success. Like most girls she had been brought up on the warm milk prepared by **Annie Fellows Johnston** and on novels in which the female was beloved because of certain mysterious womanly qualities, always mentioned but never displayed.

Bernice felt a vague pain that she was not at present engaged in being popular. She did not know that had it not been for Marjorie's campaigning she would have danced the entire evening with one man; but she knew that even in Eau Claire other girls with less position and less pulchritude were given a much bigger rush. She attributed this to something subtly unscrupulous in those girls. It had never worried her, and if it had her mother would have assured her that the other girls cheapened themselves and that men really respected girls like Bernice.

She turned out the light in her bathroom, and on an impulse decided to go in and chat for a moment with her aunt Josephine, whose light was still on. Her soft slippers bore her noiselessly down the carpeted hall, but hearing voices inside she stopped near the partly opened door. Then she caught her own name, and without any definite intention of

---

**Annie Fellows Johnston:** The author (1863-1931) of the very popular "Little Colonel" book series, which tells the adventures of a rather imperious Southern girl.

eavesdropping lingered—and the thread of the conversation going on inside pierced her consciousness sharply as if it had been drawn through with a needle.

"She's absolutely hopeless!" It was Marjorie's voice. "Oh, I know what you're going to say! So many people have told you how pretty and sweet she is, and how she can cook! What of it? She has a bum time. Men don't like her."

"What's a little cheap popularity?"

Mrs. Harvey sounded annoyed.

"It's everything when you're eighteen," said Marjorie emphatically. "I've done my best. I've been polite and I've made men dance with her, but they just won't stand being bored. When I think of that gorgeous coloring wasted on such a ninny, and think what Martha Carey could do with it—oh!"

"There's no courtesy these days."

Mrs. Harvey's voice implied that modern situations were too much for her. When she was a girl all young ladies who belonged to nice families had glorious times.

"Well," said Marjorie, "no girl can permanently bolster up a lame-duck visitor, because these days it's every girl for herself. I've even tried to drop her hints about clothes and things, and she's been furious—given me the funniest looks. She's sensitive enough to know she's not getting away with much, but I'll bet she consoles herself by thinking that she's very virtuous and that I'm too gay and fickle and will come to a bad end. All unpopular girls think that way. Sour grapes! Sarah Hopkins refers to Genevieve and Roberta and me as gardenia girls! I'll bet she'd give ten years of her life and her European education to be a gardenia girl and have three or four men in love with her and be cut in on every few feet at dances."

"It seems to me," interrupted Mrs. Harvey rather wearily, "that you ought to be able to do something for Bernice. I know she's not very vivacious."

Marjorie groaned.

"Vivacious! Good grief! I've never heard her say anything to a boy except that it's hot or the floor's crowded or that she's going to school in New York next year. Sometimes she asks them what kind of car they have and tells them the kind she has. Thrilling!"

There was a short silence, and then Mrs. Harvey took up her refrain:

"All I know is that other girls not half so sweet and attractive get partners. Martha Carey, for instance, is stout and loud, and her mother is distinctly common. Roberta Dillon is so thin this year that she looks as though Arizona were the place for her. She's dancing herself to death."

"But, mother," objected Marjorie impatiently, "Martha is cheerful and awfully witty and an awfully slick girl, and Roberta's a marvellous dancer. She's been popular for ages!"

Mrs. Harvey yawned.

"I think it's that crazy Indian blood in Bernice," continued Marjorie. "Maybe she's a reversion to type. Indian women all just sat round and never said anything."

"Go to bed, you silly child," laughed Mrs. Harvey. "I wouldn't have told you that if I'd thought you were going to remember it. And I think most of your ideas are perfectly idiotic," she finished sleepily.

There was another silence, while Marjorie considered whether or not convincing her mother was worth the trouble. People over forty can seldom be permanently convinced of anything. At eighteen our convictions are ills from which we look; at forty-five they are caves in which we hide.

Having decided this, Marjorie said good night. When she came out into the hall it was quite empty.

## III

While Marjorie was breakfasting late next day Bernice came into the room with a rather formal good morning, sat down opposite, stared intently over and slightly moistened her lips.

"What's on your mind?" inquired Marjorie, rather puzzled.

Bernice paused before she threw her hand-grenade.

"I heard what you said about me to your mother last night."

Marjorie was startled, but she showed only a faintly heightened color and her voice was quite even when she spoke.

"Where were you?"

"In the hall. I didn't mean to listen—at first."

After an involuntary look of contempt Marjorie dropped her eyes and became very interested in balancing a stray corn-flake on her finger.

"I guess I'd better go back to Eau Claire—if I'm such a nuisance." Bernice's lower lip was trembling violently and she continued on a wavering note: "I've tried to be nice, and—and I've been first neglected and then insulted. No one ever visited me and got such treatment."

Marjorie was silent.

"But I'm in the way, I see. I'm a drag on you. Your friends don't like me." She paused, and then remembered another one of her grievances. "Of course I was furious last week when you tried to hint to me that that dress was unbecoming. Don't you think I know how to dress myself?"

"No," murmured Marjorie less than half-aloud.

"What?"

"I didn't hint anything," said Marjorie succinctly. "I said, as I remember, that it was better to wear a becoming dress three times straight than to alternate it with two frights."

"Do you think that was a very nice thing to say?"

"I wasn't trying to be nice." Then after a pause: "When do you want to go?"

Bernice drew in her breath sharply.

"Oh!" It was a little half-cry.

Marjorie looked up in surprise.

"Didn't you say you were going?"

"Yes, but——"

"Oh, you were only bluffing!"

They stared at each other across the breakfast-table for a moment. Misty waves were passing before Bernice's eyes, while Marjorie's face wore that rather hard expression that she used when slightly intoxicated undergraduates were courting her.

"So you were bluffing," she repeated as if it were what she might have expected.

Bernice admitted it by bursting into tears. Marjorie's eyes showed boredom.

"You're my cousin," sobbed Bernice. "I'm v-v-visiting you. I was to stay a month, and if I go home my mother will know and she'll wah-wonder——"

Marjorie waited until the shower of broken words collapsed into little sniffles.

"I'll give you my month's allowance," she said coldly, "and you can spend this last week anywhere you want. There's a very nice hotel——"

Bernice's sobs rose to a flute note, and rising of a sudden she fled from the room.

An hour later, while Marjorie was in the library absorbed in composing one of those non-committal, marvellously elusive letters that only a young girl can write, Bernice reappeared, very red-eyed and consciously calm. She cast no glance at Marjorie but took a book at random from the shelf and sat down as if to read. Marjorie seemed absorbed in her letter and continued writing. When the clock showed noon Bernice closed her book with a snap.

"I suppose I'd better get my railroad ticket."

This was not the beginning of the speech she had rehearsed upstairs, but as Marjorie was not getting her cues—wasn't urging her to be reasonable; it's all a mistake—it was the best opening she could muster.

"Just wait till I finish this letter," said Marjorie without looking round. "I want to get it off in the next mail."

After another minute, during which her pen scratched busily, she turned round and relaxed with an air of "at your service." Again Bernice had to speak.

"Do you want me to go home?"

"Well," said Marjorie, considering, "I suppose if you're not having a good time you'd better go. No use being miserable."

"Don't you think common kindness——"

"Oh, please don't quote *Little Women*!" cried Marjorie impatiently. "That's out of style."

"You think so?"

"Heavens, yes! What modern girl could live like those inane females?"

"They were the models for our mothers."

Marjorie laughed.

"Yes, they were—not! Besides, our mothers were all very well in their way, but they know very little about their daughters' problems."

Bernice drew herself up.

"Please don't talk about my mother."

Marjorie laughed.

"I don't think I mentioned her."

Bernice felt that she was being led away from her subject.

"Do you think you've treated me very well?"

"I've done my best. You're rather hard material to work with."

The lids of Bernice's eyes reddened.

"I think you're hard and selfish, and you haven't a feminine quality in you."

"Oh, my Lord!" cried Marjorie in desperation. "You little nut! Girls like you are responsible for all the tiresome colorless marriages; all those ghastly inefficiencies that pass as feminine qualities. What a blow it must be when a man with imagination marries the beautiful bundle of clothes that he's been building ideals round, and finds that she's just a weak, whining, cowardly mass of affectations!"

Bernice's mouth had slipped half open.

"The womanly woman!" continued Marjorie. "Her whole early life is occupied in whining criticisms of girls like me who really do have a good time."

Bernice's jaw descended farther as Marjorie's voice rose.

"There's some excuse for an ugly girl whining. If I'd been irretrievably ugly I'd never have forgiven my parents for bringing me into the world. But you're starting life without any handicap—" Marjorie's little fist clinched. "If you expect me to weep with you you'll be disappointed. Go or stay, just as you like." And picking up her letters she left the room.

Bernice claimed a headache and failed to appear at luncheon. They had a matinee date for the afternoon, but the headache persisting, Marjorie made explanations to a not very downcast boy. But when she returned late in the afternoon she found Bernice with a strangely set face waiting for her in her bedroom.

"I've decided," began Bernice without preliminaries,

"that maybe you're right about things—possibly not. But if you'll tell me why your friends aren't—aren't interested in me I'll see if I can do what you want me to."

Marjorie was at the mirror shaking down her hair.

"Do you mean it?"

"Yes."

"Without reservations? Will you do exactly what I say?"

"Well, I—"

"Well nothing! Will you do exactly as I say?"

"If they're sensible things."

"They're not! You're no case for sensible things."

"Are you going to make—to recommend——"

"Yes, everything. If I tell you to take boxing lessons you'll have to do it. Write home and tell your mother you're going to stay another two weeks."

"If you'll tell me——"

"All right—I'll just give you a few examples now. First, you have no ease of manner. Why? Because you're never sure about your personal appearance. When a girl feels that she's perfectly groomed and dressed she can forget that part of her. That's charm. The more parts of yourself you can afford to forget the more charm you have."

"Don't I look all right?"

"No; for instance, you never take care of your eyebrows. They're black and lustrous, but by leaving them straggly they're a blemish. They'd be beautiful if you'd take care of them in one-tenth the time you take doing nothing. You're going to brush them so that they'll grow straight."

Bernice raised the brows in question.

"Do you mean to say that men notice eyebrows?" "Yes—subconsciously. And when you go home you ought to have your teeth straightened a little. It's almost imperceptible, still——"

"But I thought," interrupted Bernice in bewilderment, "that you despised little dainty feminine things like that."

"I hate dainty minds," answered Marjorie. "But a girl has to be dainty in person. If she looks like a million dollars she can talk about Russia, ping-pong, or the League of Nations and get away with it."

"What else?"

"Oh, I'm just beginning! There's your dancing."

"Don't I dance all right?"

"No, you don't—you lean on a man; yes, you do—ever so slightly. I noticed it when we were dancing together yesterday. And you dance standing up straight instead of bending over a little. Probably some old lady on the side-line once told you that you looked so dignified that way. But except with a very small girl it's much harder on the man, and he's the one that counts."

"Go on." Bernice's brain was reeling.

"Well, you've got to learn to be nice to men who are sad birds. You look as if you'd been insulted whenever you're thrown with any except the most popular boys. Why, Bernice, I'm cut in on every few feet—and who does most of it? Why, those very sad birds. No girl can afford to neglect them. They're the big part of any crowd. Young boys too shy to talk are the very best conversational practice. Clumsy boys are the best dancing practice. If you can follow them and yet look graceful you can follow a baby tank across a barb-wire skyscraper."

Bernice sighed profoundly, but Marjorie was not through.

"If you go to a dance and really amuse, say, three sad birds that dance with you; if you talk so well to them that they forget they're stuck with you, you've done something. They'll come back next time, and gradually so many sad birds will dance with you that the attractive boys will see there's no danger of being stuck—then they'll dance with you."

"Yes," agreed Bernice faintly. "I think I begin to see."

"And finally," concluded Marjorie, "poise and charm will just come. You'll wake up some morning knowing you've attained it, and men will know it too."

Bernice rose.

"It's been awfully kind of you—but nobody's ever talked to me like this before, and I feel sort of startled."

Marjorie made no answer but gazed pensively at her own image in the mirror.

"You're a peach to help me," continued Bernice.

Still Marjorie did not answer, and Bernice thought she had seemed too grateful.

"I know you don't like sentiment," she said timidly.

Marjorie turned to her quickly.

"Oh, I wasn't thinking about that. I was considering whether we hadn't better bob your hair."

Bernice collapsed backward upon the bed.

## IV

On the following Wednesday evening there was a dinner-dance at the country club. When the guests strolled in Bernice found her place-card with a slight feeling of irritation. Though at her right sat G. Reece Stoddard, a most desirable and distinguished young bachelor, the all-important left held only Charley Paulson. Charley lacked height, beauty, and social shrewdness, and in her new enlightenment Bernice decided that his only qualification to be her partner was that he had never been stuck with her. But this feeling of irritation left with the last of the soup-plates, and Marjorie's specific instruction came to her. Swallowing her pride she turned to Charley Paulson and plunged.

"Do you think I ought to bob my hair, Mr. Charley Paulson?"

Charley looked up in surprise.

"Why?"

"Because I'm considering it. It's such a sure and easy way of attracting attention."

Charley smiled pleasantly. He could not know this had been rehearsed. He replied that he didn't know much about bobbed hair. But Bernice was there to tell him.

"I want to be a society vampire, you see," she announced coolly, and went on to inform him that bobbed hair was the necessary prelude. She added that she wanted to ask his advice, because she had heard he was so critical about girls.

Charley, who knew as much about the psychology of women as he did of the mental states of Buddhist contemplatives, felt vaguely flattered.

"So I've decided," she continued, her voice rising slightly, "that early next week I'm going down to the Sevier Hotel barbershop, sit in the first chair, and get my hair bobbed." She faltered, noticing that the people near her had paused in their conversation and were listening; but after a confused second Marjorie's coaching told, and she finished her paragraph to the vicinity at large. "Of course I'm charging admission, but if you'll all come down and encourage me I'll issue passes for the inside seats."

There was a ripple of appreciative laughter, and under cover of it G. Reece Stoddard leaned over quickly and said close to her ear: "I'll take a box right now."

She met his eyes and smiled as if he had said something surpassingly brilliant.

"Do you believe in bobbed hair?" asked G. Reece in the

same undertone.

"I think it's unmoral," affirmed Bernice gravely. "But, of course, you've either got to amuse people or feed 'em or shock 'em." Marjorie had culled this from **Oscar Wilde.** It was greeted with a ripple of laughter from the men and a series of quick, intent looks from the girls. And then as though she had said nothing of wit or moment Bernice turned again to Charley and spoke confidentially in his ear.

"I want to ask you your opinion of several people. I imagine you're a wonderful judge of character."

Charley thrilled faintly—paid her a subtle compliment by overturning her water.

Two hours later, while Warren McIntyre was standing passively in the stag line abstractedly watching the dancers and wondering whither and with whom Marjorie had disappeared, an unrelated perception began to creep slowly upon him—a perception that Bernice, cousin to Marjorie, had been cut in on several times in the past five minutes. He closed his eyes, opened them and looked again. Several minutes back she had been dancing with a visiting boy, a matter easily accounted for; a visiting boy would know no better. But now she was dancing with some one else, and there was Charley Paulson headed for her with enthusiastic determination in his eye. Funny—Charley seldom danced with more than three girls an evening.

Warren was distinctly surprised when—the exchange having been effected—the man relieved proved to be none other than G. Reece Stoddard himself. And G. Reece seemed not at all jubilant at being relieved. Next time Bernice danced near, Warren regarded her intently. Yes, she was pretty, dis-

---

**Oscar Wilde** : Irish author (1854-1900) famous for his brilliantly clever wit. *The Importance of Being Earnest* is considered his masterpiece.

tinctly pretty; and tonight her face seemed really vivacious. She had that look that no woman, however histrionically proficient, can successfully counterfeit—she looked as if she were having a good time. He liked the way she had her hair arranged, wondered if it was brilliantine that made it glisten so. And that dress was becoming—a dark red that set off her shadowy eyes and high coloring. He remembered that he had thought her pretty when she first came to town, before he had realized that she was dull. Too bad she was dull—dull girls—unbearable—certainly pretty though.

His thoughts zigzagged back to Marjorie. This disappearance would be like other disappearances. When she reappeared he would demand where she had been—would be told emphatically that it was none of his business. What a pity she was so sure of him! She basked in the knowledge that no other girl in town interested him; she defied him to fall in love with Genevieve or Roberta.

Warren sighed. The way to Marjorie's affections was a labyrinth indeed. He looked up. Bernice was again dancing with the visiting boy. Half unconsciously he took a step out from the stag line in her direction, and hesitated. Then he said to himself that it was charity. He walked toward her—collided suddenly with G. Reece Stoddard.

"Pardon me," said Warren.

But G. Reece had not stopped to apologize. He had again cut in on Bernice.

That night at one o'clock Marjorie, with one hand on the electric-light switch in the hall, turned to take a last look at Bernice's sparkling eyes.

"So it worked?"

"Oh, Marjorie, yes!" cried Bernice.

"I saw you were having a gay time."

"I did! The only trouble was that about midnight I ran

short of talk. I had to repeat myself—with different men of course. I hope they won't compare notes."

"Men don't," said Marjorie, yawning, "and it wouldn't matter if they did—they'd think you were even trickier."

She snapped out the light, and as they started up the stairs Bernice grasped the banister thankfully. For the first time in her life she had been danced tired.

"You see," said Marjorie at the top of the stairs, "one man sees another man cut in and he thinks there must be something there. Well, we'll fix up some new stuff tomorrow. Good night."

"Good night."

As Bernice took down her hair she passed the evening before her in review. She had followed instructions exactly. Even when Charley Paulson cut in for the eighth time she had simulated delight and had apparently been both interested and flattered. She had not talked about the weather or Eau Claire or automobiles or her school, but had confined her conversation to me, you, and us.

But a few minutes before she fell asleep a rebellious thought was churning drowsily in her brain—after all, it was she who had done it. Marjorie, to be sure, had given her her conversation, but then Marjorie got much of her conversation out of things she read. Bernice had bought the red dress, though she had never valued it highly before Marjorie dug it out of her trunk—and her own voice had said the words, her own lips had smiled, her own feet had danced. Marjorie nice girl—vain, though—nice evening—nice boys—like Warren—Warren—Warren—what's-his-name—Warren.

She fell asleep.

V

To Bernice the next week was a revelation. With the feeling that people really enjoyed looking at her and listening to her came the foundation of self-confidence. Of course there were numerous mistakes at first. She did not know, for instance, that Draycott Deyo was studying for the ministry; she was unaware that he had cut in on her because he thought she was a quiet, reserved girl. Had she known these things she would not have treated him to the line which began "Hello, Shell Shock!" and continued with the bathtub story—"It takes a frightful lot of energy to fix my hair in the summer—there's so much of it—so I always fix it first and powder my face and put on my hat; then I get into the bathtub, and dress afterward. Don't you think that's the best plan?"

Though Draycott Deyo was in the throes of difficulties concerning baptism by immersion and might possibly have seen a connection, it must be admitted that he did not. He considered feminine bathing an immoral subject, and gave her some of his ideas on the depravity of modern society.

But to offset that unfortunate occurrence Bernice had several signal successes to her credit. Little Otis Ormonde pleaded off from a trip East and elected instead to follow her with a puppylike devotion, to the amusement of his crowd and to the irritation of G. Reece Stoddard, several of whose afternoon calls Otis completely ruined by the disgusting tenderness of the glances he bent on Bernice. He even told her the story of the two-by-four and the dressing-room to show her how frightfully mistaken he and every one else had been in their first judgment of her. Bernice laughed off that incident with a slight sinking sensation.

Of all Bernice's conversation perhaps the best known and most universally approved was the line about the bobbing of her hair.

"Oh, Bernice, when you goin' to get the hair bobbed?"

"Day after tomorrow maybe," she would reply, laughing. "Will you come and see me? Because I'm counting on you, you know."

"Will we? You know! But you better hurry up."

Bernice, whose tonsorial intentions were strictly dishonorable, would laugh again.

"Pretty soon now. You'd be surprised."

But perhaps the most significant symbol of her success was the gray car of the hypercritical Warren McIntyre, parked daily in front of the Harvey house. At first the parlor-maid was distinctly startled when he asked for Bernice instead of Marjorie; after a week of it she told the cook that Miss Bernice had gotta holda Miss Marjorie's best fella.

And Miss Bernice had. Perhaps it began with Warren's desire to rouse jealousy in Marjorie; perhaps it was the familiar though unrecognized strain of Marjorie in Bernice's conversation; perhaps it was both of these and something of sincere attraction besides. But somehow the collective mind of the younger set knew within a week that Marjorie's most reliable beau had made an amazing about-face and was giving an indisputable rush to Marjorie's guest. The question of the moment was how Marjorie would take it. Warren called Bernice on the phone twice a day, sent her notes, and they were frequently seen together in his roadster, obviously engrossed in one of those tense, significant conversations as to whether or not he was sincere.

Marjorie on being twitted only laughed. She said she was mighty glad that Warren had at last found some one who appreciated him. So the younger set laughed, too, and guessed that Marjorie didn't care and let it go at that.

One afternoon when there were only three days left of her visit Bernice was waiting in the hall for Warren, with whom she was going to a bridge party. She was in rather a blissful mood, and when Marjorie—also bound for the party—appeared beside her and began casually to adjust her hat in the mirror. Bernice was utterly unprepared for anything in the nature of a clash. Marjorie did her work very coldly and succinctly in three sentences.

"You may as well get Warren out of your head," she said coldly.

"What?" Bernice was utterly astounded.

"You may as well stop making a fool of yourself over Warren McIntyre. He doesn't care a snap of his fingers about you."

For a tense moment they regarded each other—Marjorie scornful, aloof; Bernice astounded, half-angry, half-afraid. Then two cars drove up in front of the house and there was a riotous honking. Both of them gasped faintly, turned, and side by side hurried out.

All through the bridge party Bernice strove in vain to master a rising uneasiness. She had offended Marjorie, the sphinx of sphinxes. With the most wholesome and innocent intentions in the world she had stolen Marjorie's property. She felt suddenly and horribly guilty. After the bridge game, when they sat in an informal circle and the conversation became general, the storm gradually broke. Little Otis Ormonde inadvertently precipitated it.

"When you going back to kindergarten, Otis?" some one had asked.

"Me? Day Bernice gets her hair bobbed."

"Then your education's over," said Marjorie quickly. "That's only a bluff of hers. I should think you'd have realized."

"That a fact?" demanded Otis, giving Bernice a reproachful glance.

Bernice's ears burned as she tried to think up an effectual comeback. In the face of this direct attack her imagination was paralyzed.

"There's a lot of bluffs in the world," continued Marjorie quite pleasantly. "I should think you'd be young enough to know that, Otis."

"Well," said Otis, "maybe so. But gee! With a line like Bernice's——"

"Really?" yawned Marjorie. "What's her latest ***bon mot***?"

No one seemed to know. In fact, Bernice, having trifled with her muse's beau, had said nothing memorable of late.

"Was that really all a line?" asked Roberta curiously.

Bernice hesitated. She felt that wit in some form was demanded of her, but under her cousin's suddenly frigid eyes she was completely incapacitated.

"I don't know," she stalled.

"Splush!" said Marjorie. "Admit it!"

Bernice saw that Warren's eyes had left a ukulele he had been tinkering with and were fixed on her questioningly.

"Oh, I don't know!" she repeated steadily. Her cheeks were glowing.

"Splush!" remarked Marjorie again.

"Come through, Bernice," urged Otis. "Tell her where to get off."

Bernice looked round again—she seemed unable to get away from Warren's eyes.

"I like bobbed hair," she said hurriedly, as if he had asked her a question, "and I intend to bob mine."

---

**Bon mot**: A clever remark or witticism; literally, "good word" in French.

"When?" demanded Marjorie.

"Any time."

"No time like the present," suggested Roberta.

Otis jumped to his feet.

"Good stuff!" he cried. "We'll have a summer bobbing party. Sevier Hotel barbershop, I think you said."

In an instant all were on their feet. Bernice's heart throbbed violently.

"What?" she gasped.

Out of the group came Marjorie's voice, very clear and contemptuous.

"Don't worry—she'll back out!"

"Come on, Bernice!" cried Otis, starting toward the door.

Four eyes—Warren's and Marjorie's—stared at her, challenged her, defied her. For another second she wavered wildly.

"All right," she said swiftly, "I don't care if I do."

An eternity of minutes later, riding downtown through the late afternoon beside Warren, the others following in Roberta's car close behind, Bernice had all the sensations of Marie Antoinette bound for the guillotine in a **tumbrel**. Vaguely she wondered why she did not cry out that it was all a mistake. It was all she could do to keep from clutching her hair with both hands to protect it from the suddenly hostile world. Yet she did neither. Even the thought of her mother was no deterrent now. This was the test supreme of her sportsmanship; her right to walk unchallenged in the starry heaven of popular girls.

Warren was moodily silent, and when they came to the hotel he drew up at the curb and nodded to Bernice to pre-

---

**Tumbrel**: A two-wheeled farm cart.

cede him out. Roberta's car emptied a laughing crowd into the shop, which presented two bold plate-glass windows to the street.

Bernice stood on the curb and looked at the sign, Sevier Barbershop. It was a guillotine indeed, and the hangman was the first barber, who, attired in a white coat and smoking a cigarette, leaned nonchalantly against the first chair. He must have heard of her; he must have been waiting all week, smoking eternal cigarettes beside that portentous, too-often-mentioned first chair. Would they blindfold her? No, but they would tie a white cloth round her neck lest any of her blood—nonsense—hair—should get on her clothes.

"All right, Bernice," said Warren quickly.

With her chin in the air she crossed the sidewalk, pushed open the swinging screen-door, and giving not a glance to the uproarious, riotous row that occupied the waiting bench, went up to the first barber.

"I want you to bob my hair."

The first barber's mouth slid somewhat open. His cigarette dropped to the floor.

"Huh?"

"My hair—bob it!"

Refusing further preliminaries, Bernice took her seat on high. A man in the chair next to her turned on his side and gave her a glance, half lather, half amazement. One barber started and spoiled little Willy Schuneman's monthly haircut. Mr. O'Reilly in the last chair grunted and swore musically in ancient Gaelic as a razor bit into his cheek. Two bootblacks became wide-eyed and rushed for her feet. No, Bernice didn't care for a shine.

Outside a passerby stopped and stared; a couple joined him; half a dozen small boys' noses sprang into life, flattened against the glass; and snatches of conversation borne on the summer breeze drifted in through the screen-door.

"Lookada long hair on a kid!"

"Where'd yuh get 'at stuff? 'At's a bearded lady he just finished shavin'."

But Bernice saw nothing, heard nothing. Her only living sense told her that this man in the white coat had removed one tortoiseshell comb and then another; that his fingers were fumbling clumsily with unfamiliar hairpins; that this hair, this wonderful hair of hers, was going—she would never again feel its long voluptuous pull as it hung in a dark-brown glory down her back. For a second she was near breaking down, and then the picture before her swam mechanically into her vision—Marjorie's mouth curling in a faint ironic smile as if to say:

"Give up and get down! You tried to buck me and I called your bluff. You see you haven't got a prayer."

And some last energy rose up in Bernice, for she clinched her hands under the white cloth, and there was a curious narrowing of her eyes that Marjorie remarked on to some one long afterward.

Twenty minutes later the barber swung her round to face the mirror, and she flinched at the full extent of the damage that had been wrought. Her hair was not curly, and now it lay in lank lifeless blocks on both sides of her suddenly pale face. It was ugly as sin—she had known it would be ugly as sin. Her face's chief charm had been a Madonna-like simplicity. Now that was gone and she was—well, frightfully mediocre—not stagy; only ridiculous, like a Greenwich Villager who had left her spectacles at home.

As she climbed down from the chair she tried to smile—failed miserably. She saw two of the girls exchange glances; noticed Marjorie's mouth curved in attenuated mockery—and that Warren's eyes were suddenly very cold.

"You see"—her words fell into an awkward pause—"I've done it."

"Yes, you've—done it," admitted Warren.

"Do you like it?"

There was a halfhearted "Sure" from two or three voices, another awkward pause, and then Marjorie turned swiftly and with serpentlike intensity to Warren.

"Would you mind running me down to the cleaners?" she asked. "I've simply got to get a dress there before supper. Roberta's driving right home and she can take the others."

Warren stared abstractedly at some infinite speck out the window. Then for an instant his eyes rested coldly on Bernice before they turned to Marjorie.

"Be glad to," he said slowly.

## VI

Bernice did not fully realize the outrageous trap that had been set for her until she met her aunt's amazed glance just before dinner.

"Why, Bernice!"

"I've bobbed it, Aunt Josephine."

"Why, child!"

"Do you like it?"

"Why, Ber-nice!"

"I suppose I've shocked you."

"No, but what'll Mrs. Deyo think tomorrow night? Bernice, you should have waited until after the Deyos' dance—you should have waited if you wanted to do that."

"It was sudden, Aunt Josephine. Anyway, why does it matter to Mrs. Deyo particularly?"

"Why, child," cried Mrs. Harvey, "in her paper on 'The

Foibles of the Younger Generation' that she read at the last meeting of the Thursday Club she devoted fifteen minutes to bobbed hair. It's her pet abomination. And the dance is for you and Marjorie!"

"I'm sorry."

"Oh, Bernice, what'll your mother say? She'll think I let you do it."

"I'm sorry."

Dinner was an agony. She had made a hasty attempt with a curling-iron, and burned her finger and much hair. She could see that her aunt was both worried and grieved, and her uncle kept saying, "Well, I'll be darned!" over and over in a hurt and faintly hostile tone. And Marjorie sat very quietly, entrenched behind a faint smile, a faintly mocking smile.

Somehow she got through the evening. Three boys called; Marjorie disappeared with one of them, and Bernice made a listless unsuccessful attempt to entertain the two others—sighed thankfully as she climbed the stairs to her room at half past ten. What a day!

When she had undressed for the night the door opened and Marjorie came in.

"Bernice," she said, "I'm awfully sorry about the Deyo dance. I'll give you my word of honor I'd forgotten all about it."

"'Sall right," said Bernice shortly. Standing before the mirror she passed her comb slowly through her short hair.

"I'll take you downtown tomorrow," continued Marjorie, "and the hairdresser'll fix it so you'll look slick. I didn't imagine you'd go through with it. I'm really mighty sorry."

"Oh, 'sall right!"

"Still it's your last night, so I suppose it won't matter much."

Then Bernice winced as Marjorie tossed her own hair

over her shoulders and began to twist it slowly into two long blond braids until in her cream-colored negligee she looked like a delicate painting of some Saxon princess. Fascinated, Bernice watched the braids grow. Heavy and luxurious they were, moving under the supple fingers like restive snakes—and to Bernice remained this relic and the curling-iron and a tomorrow full of eyes. She could see G. Reece Stoddard, who liked her, assuming his Harvard manner and telling his dinner partner that Bernice shouldn't have been allowed to go to the movies so much; she could see Draycott Deyo exchanging glances with his mother and then being conscientiously charitable to her. But then perhaps by tomorrow Mrs. Deyo would have heard the news; would send round an icy little note requesting that she fail to appear—and behind her back they would all laugh and know that Marjorie had made a fool of her; that her chance at beauty had been sacrificed to the jealous whim of a selfish girl. She sat down suddenly before the mirror, biting the inside of her cheek.

"I like it," she said with an effort. "I think it'll be becoming."

Marjorie smiled.

"It looks all right. For heaven's sake, don't let it worry you!"

"I won't."

"Good night, Bernice."

But as the door closed something snapped within Bernice. She sprang dynamically to her feet, clinching her hands, then swiftly and noiselessly crossed over to her bed and from underneath it dragged out her suitcase. Into it she tossed toilet articles and a change of clothing. Then she turned to her trunk and quickly dumped in two drawerfuls of lingerie and summer dresses. She moved quietly, but with deadly efficiency, and in three-quarters of an hour her trunk was locked and strapped and she was fully dressed in a becoming new travelling suit that Marjorie had helped her pick out.

Sitting down at her desk she wrote a short note to Mrs. Harvey, in which she briefly outlined her reasons for going. She sealed it, addressed it, and laid it on her pillow. She glanced at her watch. The train left at one, and she knew that if she walked down to the Marborough Hotel two blocks away she could easily get a taxicab.

Suddenly she drew in her breath sharply and an expression flashed into her eyes that a practiced character reader might have connected vaguely with the set look she had worn in the barber's chair—somehow a development of it. It was quite a new look for Bernice—and it carried consequences.

She went stealthily to the bureau, picked up an article that lay there, and turning out all the lights stood quietly until her eyes became accustomed to the darkness. Softly she pushed open the door to Marjorie's room. She heard the quiet, even breathing of an untroubled conscience asleep.

She was by the bedside now, very deliberate and calm. She acted swiftly. Bending over she found one of the braids of Marjorie's hair, followed it up with her hand to the point nearest the head, and then holding it a little slack so that the sleeper would feel no pull, she reached down with the shears and severed it. With the pigtail in her hand she held her breath. Marjorie had muttered something in her sleep. Bernice deftly amputated the other braid, paused for an instant, and then flitted swiftly and silently back to her own room.

Downstairs she opened the big front door, closed it carefully behind her, and feeling oddly happy and exuberant stepped off the porch into the moonlight, swinging her heavy grip like a shopping bag. After a minute's brisk walk she discovered that her left hand still held the two blond braids. She laughed unexpectedly—had to shut her mouth hard to keep from emitting an absolute peal. She was passing Warren's house now, and on the impulse she set down her baggage, and swinging the braids like pieces of rope flung them at the wooden porch, where they landed with a slight thud. She laughed again, no longer restraining herself.

"Huh!" she giggled wildly. "Scalp the selfish thing!"

Then picking up her suitcase she set off at a half-run down the moonlit street.

## James Joyce

# *Araby*

North Richmond street, being **blind**, was a quiet street except at the hour when the Christian Brothers' School set the boys free. An uninhabited house of two stories stood at the blind end, detached from its neighbors in a square ground. The other houses of the street, conscious of decent lives within them, gazed at one another with brown imperturbable faces.

The former tenant of our house, a priest, had died in the back drawing-room. Air, musty from having been long enclosed, hung in all the rooms, and the waste room behind the kitchen was littered with old useless papers. Among these I found a few paper-covered books, the pages of which were curled and damp: *The Abbot*, by Walter Scott, *The Devout Communicant* and *The Memoirs of Vidocq*. I liked the last best because its leaves were yellow. The wild garden behind the house contained a central apple tree and a few straggling bushes under one of which I found the late tenant's rusty bicycle-pump. He had been a very charitable priest; in his will

**Blind:** A dead-end street.

he had left all his money to institutions and the furniture of his house to his sister.

When the short days of winter came, dusk fell before we had well eaten our dinners. When we met in the street the houses had grown somber. The space of sky above us was the color of ever-changing violet and towards it the lamps of the street lifted their feeble lanterns. The cold air stung us and we played till our bodies glowed. Our shouts echoed in the silent street. The career of our play brought us through the dark muddy lanes behind the houses where we ran the gauntlet of the rough tribes from the cottages, to the back doors of the dark dripping gardens where odors arose from the ashpits, to the dark odorous stables where a coachman smoothed and combed the horse or shook music from the buckled harness. When we returned to the street, light from the kitchen windows had filled the areas. If my uncle was seen turning the corner we hid in the shadow until we had seen him safely housed. Or if Mangan's sister came out on the doorstep to call her brother in to his tea we watched her from our shadow peer up and down the street. We waited to see whether she would remain or go in and, if she remained, we left our shadow and walked up to Mangan's steps resignedly. She was waiting for us, her figure defined by the light from the half-opened door. Her brother always teased her before he obeyed and I stood by the railings looking at her. Her dress swung as she moved her body and the soft rope of her hair tossed from side to side.

Every morning I lay on the floor in the front parlor watching her door. The blind was pulled down to within an inch of the sash so that I could not be seen. When she came out on the doorstep my heart leaped. I ran to the hall, seized my books and followed her. I kept her brown figure always in my eye and, when we came near the point at which our ways diverged, I quickened my pace and passed her. This happened morning after morning. I had never spoken to her, except for a few casual words, and yet her name was like a summons to all my foolish blood.

Her image accompanied me even in places the most hostile to romance. On Saturday evenings when my aunt went marketing I had to go to carry some of the parcels. We walked through the flaring streets, jostled by drunken men and bargaining women, amid the curses of laborers, the shrill litanies of shop-boys who stood on guard by the barrels of pigs' cheeks, the nasal chanting of street-singers, who sang a *come-all-you* about **O'Donovan Rossa**, or a ballad about the troubles in our native land. These noises converged in a single sensation of life for me: I imagined that I bore my chalice safely through a throng of foes. Her name sprang to my lips at moments in strange prayers and praises which I myself did not understand. My eyes were often full of tears (I could not tell why) and at times a flood from my heart seemed to pour itself out into my bosom. I thought little of the future. I did not know whether I would ever speak to her or not or, if I spoke to her, how I could tell her of my confused adoration. But my body was like a harp and her words and gestures were like fingers running upon the wires.

One evening I went into the back drawing-room in which the priest had died. It was a dark rainy evening and there was no sound in the house. Through one of the broken panes I heard the rain impinge upon the earth, the fine inces-

---

**Jeremiah O'Donovan Rossa**: An Irish patriot (1831-1915) who was a leader in the Fenian movement, which called for the use of force to achieve independence from Britain. He was jailed for his role in the Fenian Rising of 1867. Four years later, the British sent him into exile in the United States to try to end the repeated attempts to free Fenian prisoners.

sant needles of water playing in the sodden beds. Some distant lamp or lighted window gleamed below me. I was thankful that I could see so little. All my senses seemed to desire to veil themselves and, feeling that I was about to slip from them, I pressed the palms of my hands together until they trembled, murmuring: *O love! O love!* many times.

At last she spoke to me. When she addressed the first words to me I was so confused that I did not know what to answer. She asked me was I going to *Araby*. I forget whether I answered yes or no. It would be a splendid bazaar, she said; she would love to go.

—And why can't you? I asked.

While she spoke she turned a silver bracelet round and round her wrist. She could not go, she said, because there would be a retreat that week in her convent. Her brother and two other boys were fighting for their caps and I was alone at the railings. She held one of the spikes, bowing her head towards me. The light from the lamp opposite our door caught the white curve of her neck, lit up her hair that rested there and, falling, lit up the hand upon the railing. It fell over one side of her dress and caught the white border of a petticoat, just visible as she stood at ease.

—It's well for you, she said.

—If I go, I said, I will bring you something.

What innumerable follies laid waste my waking and sleeping thoughts after that evening! I wished to annihilate the tedious intervening days. I chafed against the work of school. At night in my bedroom and by day in the classroom her image came between me and the page I strove to read. The syllables of the word *Araby* were called to me through the silence in which my soul luxuriated and cast an Eastern enchantment over me. I asked for leave to go to the bazaar on Saturday night. My aunt was surprised and hoped it was not some **Freemason** affair. I answered few questions in class. I watched my master's face pass from amiability to sternness; he hoped I was not beginning to idle. I could not call my wandering thoughts together. I had hardly any patience with the serious work of life which, now that it stood between me and my desire, seemed to me child's play, ugly monotonous child's play.

On Saturday morning I reminded my uncle that I wished to go to the bazaar in the evening. He was fussing at the hall-stand, looking for the hat-brush, and answered me curtly:

—Yes, boy, I know.

As he was in the hall I could not go into the front parlor and lie at the window. I left the house in bad humor and walked slowly towards the school. The air was pitilessly raw and already my heart misgave me.

When I came home to dinner my uncle had not yet been home. Still it was early. I sat staring at the clock for some time and, when its ticking began to irritate me, I left the room. I mounted the staircase and gained the upper part of the house. The high cold empty gloomy rooms liberated me and I went from room to room singing. From the front window I saw my companions playing below in the street. Their cries reached me weakened and indistinct and, leaning my forehead against the cool glass, I looked over at the dark house where she lived. I may have stood there for an hour, seeing nothing but the brown-clad figure cast by my imagination, touched discreetly by the lamplight at the curved neck, at the hand upon the railings and at the border below the dress.

When I came downstairs again I found Mrs. Mercer sit-

---

**Freemason:** An international secret society that uses the tools of stonemasons for its symbols. Its bylaws stress religious toleration and political compromise.

ting at the fire. She was an old garrulous woman, a pawnbroker's widow, who collected used stamps for some pious purpose. I had to endure the gossip of the tea-table. The meal was prolonged beyond an hour and still my uncle did not come. Mrs. Mercer stood up to go: she was sorry she couldn't wait any longer, but it was after eight o'clock and she did not like to be out late, as the night air was bad for her. When she had gone I began to walk up and down the room, clenching my fists. My aunt said:

—I'm afraid you may put off your bazaar for this night of Our Lord.

At nine o'clock I heard my uncle's latchkey in the halldoor. I heard him talking to himself and heard the hallstand rocking when it had received the weight of his overcoat. I could interpret these signs. When he was midway through his dinner I asked him to give me the money to go to the bazaar. He had forgotten.

—The people are in bed and after their first sleep, now, he said.

I did not smile. My aunt said to him energetically:

—Can't you give him the money and let him go? You've kept him late enough as it is.

My uncle said he was very sorry he had forgotten. He said he believed in the old saying: *All work and no play makes Jack a dull boy*. He asked me where I was going and, when I had told him a second time he asked me did I know *The Arab's Farewell to his Steed*. When I left the kitchen he was about to recite the opening lines of the piece to my aunt.

I held a **florin** tightly in my hand as I strode down Buckingham Street towards the station. The sight of the

---

**Florin:** In Britain, a silver coin worth two shillings that takes its name from gold coins first minted in Florence, Italy.

streets thronged with buyers and glaring with gas recalled to me the purpose of my journey. I took my seat in a third-class carriage of a deserted train. After an intolerable delay the train moved out of the station slowly. It crept onward among ruinous houses and over the twinkling river. At Westland Row Station a crowd of people pressed to the carriage doors; but the porters moved them back, saying that it was a special train for the bazaar. I remained alone in the bare carriage. In a few minutes the train drew up beside an improvised wooden platform. I passed out on to the road and saw by the lighted dial of a clock that it was ten minutes to ten. In front of me was a large building which displayed the magical name.

I could not find any sixpenny entrance and, fearing that the bazaar would be closed, I passed in quickly through a turnstile, handing a shilling to a weary-looking man. I found myself in a big hall girdled at half its height by a gallery. Nearly all the stalls were closed and the greater part of the hall was in darkness. I recognized a silence like that which pervades a church after a service. I walked into the center of the bazaar timidly. A few people were gathered about the stalls which were still open. Before a curtain, over which the words *Café Chantant* were written in colored lamps, two men were counting money on a **salver**. I listened to the fall of the coins.

Remembering with difficulty why I had come I went over to one of the stalls and examined porcelain vases and flowered tea-sets. At the door of the stall a young lady was talking and laughing with two young gentlemen. I remarked their English accents and listened vaguely to their conversation.

—O, I never said such a thing!

—O, but you did!

---

**Salver**: A serving tray.

—O, but I didn't!

—Didn't she say that?

—Yes. I heard her.

—O, there's a . . . fib!

Observing me the young lady came over and asked me did I wish to buy anything. The tone of her voice was not encouraging; she seemed to have spoken to me out of a sense of duty. I looked humbly at the great jars that stood like eastern guards at either side of the dark entrance to the stall and murmured:

—No, thank you.

The young lady changed the position of one of the vases and went back to the two young men. They began to talk of the same subject. Once or twice the young lady glanced at me over her shoulder.

I lingered before her stall, though I knew my stay was useless, to make my interest in her wares seem the more real. Then I turned away slowly and walked down the middle of the bazaar. I allowed the two pennies to fall against the sixpence in my pocket. I heard a voice call from one end of the gallery that the light was out. The upper part of the hall was now completely dark.

Gazing up into the darkness I saw myself as a creature driven and derided by vanity; and my eyes burned with anguish and anger.

## Guy De Maupassant

# *The Piece of String*

Along all the roads around Goderville the peasants and their wives were coming toward the town because it was market day. The men were proceeding with slow steps, the whole body bent forward at each movement of their long twisted legs, deformed by their hard work, by the weight on the plow which, at the same time, raised the left shoulder and swerved the figure, by the reaping of the wheat which made the knees spread to make a firm "purchase," by all the slow and painful labors of the country. Their blouses, blue, "stiff-starched," shining as if varnished, ornamented with a little design in white at the neck and wrists, puffed about their bony bodies, seemed like balloons ready to carry them off. From each of them a head, two arms, and two feet protruded.

Some led a cow or a calf by a cord, and their wives, walking behind the animal, whipped its haunches with a leafy branch to hasten its progress. On their arms they carried large baskets from which, in some cases, chickens and, in others, ducks thrust out their heads. And they walked with a quicker, livelier step than their husbands. Their spare straight figures were wrapped in scanty little shawls, pinned over their flat bosoms, and their heads were enveloped in white cloths glued to the hair and surmounted by caps.

Then a wagon passed at the jerky trot of a nag, shaking strangely, two men seated side by side and a woman in the bottom of the vehicle, the latter holding on to the sides to lessen the hard jolts.

In the public square of Goderville there was a crowd, a throng of human beings and animals mixed together. The horns of the cattle, the tall hats with the long nap of the rich peasant, and the headgear of the peasant women rose above the surface of the assembly. And the clamorous, shrill, screaming voices made a continuous and savage din which sometimes was dominated by the robust lungs of some countryman's laugh, or the long lowing of a cow tied to the wall of a house.

All that smacked of the stable, the dairy and the dirt heap, hay and sweat, giving forth that unpleasant odor, human and animal, peculiar to the people of the field.

**Maître** Hauchecome, of Breaute, had just arrived at Goderville, and he was directing his steps toward the public square, when he perceived upon the ground a little piece of string. Maître Hauchecome, economical like a true Norman, thought that everything useful ought to be picked up, and he bent painfully, for he suffered from rheumatism. He took the bit of thin cord from the ground and began to roll it carefully when he noticed Maître Malandain, the harness-maker, on the threshold of his door, looking at him. They had heretofore had business together on the subject of a halter, and they were on bad terms, being both good haters. Maître Hauchecome was seized with a sort of shame to be seen thus by his enemy, picking a bit of string out of the dirt. He con-

**Maître:** A French term of polite address meaning mister or, literally, master.

cealed his "find" quickly under his blouse, then in his trousers' pocket; then he pretended to be still looking on the ground for something which he did not find, and he went toward the market, his head forward, bent double by his pains.

He was soon lost in the noisy and slowly moving crowd, which was busy with interminable bargainings. The peasants milked, went and came, perplexed, always in fear of being cheated, not daring to decide, watching the vendor's eye, ever trying to find the trick in the man and the flaw in the beast.

The women, having placed their great baskets at their feet, had taken out the poultry which lay upon the ground, tied together by the feet, with terrified eyes and scarlet crests.

They heard offers, stated their prices with a dry air and impassive face, or perhaps, suddenly deciding on some proposed reduction, shouted to the customer who was slowly going away: "All right, Maître Authirne, I'll give it to you for that."

Then little by little the square was deserted, and when the **Angelus** rang at noon, those who had stayed too long scattered to their shops.

At Jourdain's the great room was full of people eating, as the big court was full of vehicles of all kinds, carts, gigs, wagons, dump carts, yellow with dirt, mended and patched, raising their shafts to the sky like two arms, or perhaps with their shafts in the ground and their backs in the air.

Just opposite the diners seated at the table, the immense fireplace, filled with bright flames, cast a lively heat on the backs of the row on the right. Three spits were turning on

---

**Angelus:** A Roman Catholic devotion that is said three times daily at six in the morning, noon, and six in the evening, and announced each time by ringing a bell.

which were chickens, pigeons, and legs of mutton; and an appetizing odor of roast beef and gravy dripping over the nicely browned skin rose from the hearth, increased the jovialness, and made everybody's mouth water.

All the aristocracy of the plow ate there, at Maître Jourdain's, tavern keeper and horse dealer, a rascal who had money.

The dishes were passed and emptied, as were the jugs of yellow cider. Everyone told his affairs, his purchases, and sales. They discussed the crops. The weather was favorable for the green things but not for the wheat.

Suddenly the drum beat in the court, before the house. Everybody rose except a few indifferent persons, and ran to the door, or to the windows, their mouths still full and napkins in their hands.

After the public crier had ceased his drum-beating, he called out in a jerky voice, speaking his phrases irregularly:

"It is hereby made known to the inhabitants of Goderville, and in general to all persons present at the market, that there was lost this morning, on the road to Benzeville, between nine and ten o'clock, a black leather pocketbook containing five hundred francs and some business papers. The finder is requested to return same with all haste to the mayor's office or to Maître Fortune Houlbreque of Manneville. There will be twenty francs reward."

Then the man went away. The heavy roll of the drum and the crier's voice were again heard at a distance.

Then they began to talk of this event, discussing the chances that Maître Houlbreque had of finding or not finding his pocketbook.

And the meal concluded. They were finishing their coffee when a chief of the gendarmes appeared upon the threshold.

He inquired: "Is Maître Hauchecome, of Breaute, here?"

Maître Hauchecome, seated at the other end of the table, replied: "Here I am."

And the officer resumed: "Maître Hauchecome, will you have the goodness to accompany me to the mayor's office? The mayor would like to talk to you."

The peasant, surprised and disturbed, swallowed at a draught his tiny glass of brandy, rose, and, even more bent than in the morning, for the first steps after each rest were specially difficult, set out, repeating: "Here I am, here I am."

The mayor was awaiting him, seated on an armchair. He was the notary of the vicinity, a stout, serious man, with pompous phrases.

"Maître Hauchecome," said he, "you were seen this morning to pick up, on the road to Benzeville, the pocketbook lost by Maître Houlbreque, of Manneville."

The countryman, astounded, looked at the mayor, already terrified by this suspicion resting on him without his knowing why.

"Me? Me? Me pick up the pocketbook?"

"Yes, you, yourself."

"Word of honor, I never heard of it."

"But you were seen."

"I was seen, me? Who says he saw me?"

"Monsieur Malandain, the harness-maker."

The old man remembered, understood, and flushed with anger.

"Ah, he saw me, the clodhopper, he saw me pick up this string, here, M'sieu' the Mayor." And rummaging in his pocket, he drew out the little piece of string.

But the mayor, incredulous, shook his head.

"You will not make me believe, Maître Hauchecome, that Monsieur Malandain, who is a man worthy of credence, mistook this cord for a pocketbook."

The peasant, furious, lifted his hand, spat at one side to attest his honor, repeating: "It is nevertheless the truth of the good God, the sacred truth, M'sieu' the Mayor. I repeat it on my soul and my salvation."

The mayor resumed: "After picking up the object, you stood like a stilt, looking a long while in the mud to see if any piece of money had fallen out."

The good, old man choked with indignation and fear.

"How anyone can tell—how anyone can tell—such lies to take away an honest man's reputation! How can anyone—"

There was no use in his protesting; nobody believed him. He was confronted with Monsieur Malandain, who repeated and maintained his affirmation. They abused each other for an hour. At his own request, Maître Hauchecome was searched; nothing was found on him.

Finally the mayor, very much perplexed, discharged him with the warning that he would consult the public prosecutor and ask for further orders.

The news had spread. As he left the mayor's office, the old man was surrounded and questioned with a serious or bantering curiosity, in which there was no indignation. He began to tell the story of the string. No one believed him. They laughed at him.

He went along, stopping his friends, beginning endlessly his statement and his protestations, showing his pockets turned inside out, to prove that he had nothing.

They said: "Old rascal, get out!"

And he grew angry, becoming exasperated, hot, and distressed at not being believed, not knowing what to do and always repeating himself.

Night came. He must depart. He started on his way with three neighbors to whom he pointed out the place where he had picked up the bit of string; and all along the road he spoke of his adventure.

In the evening he took a turn in the village of Breaute, in order to tell it to everybody. He only met with incredulity.

It made him ill at night.

The next day about one o'clock in the afternoon, Marius Paumelle, a hired man in the employ of Maître Breton, husbandman at Ymanville, returned the pocketbook and its contents to Maître Houlbreque of Manneville.

This man claimed to have found the object in the road; but not knowing how to read, he had carried it to the house and given it to his employer.

The news spread through the neighborhood. Maître Hauchecome was informed of it. He immediately went the circuit and began to recount his story completed by the happy climax. He was in triumph.

"What grieved me so much was not the thing itself, as the lying. There is nothing so shameful as to be placed under a cloud on account of a lie."

He talked of his adventure all day long; he told it on the highway to people who were passing by, in the wineshop to people who were drinking there, and to persons coming out of church the following Sunday. He stopped strangers to tell them about it. He was calm now, and yet something disturbed him without his knowing exactly what it was. People had the air of joking while they listened. They did not seem convinced. He seemed to feel that remarks were being made behind his back.

On Tuesday of the next week he went to the market at Goderville, urged solely by the necessity he felt of discussing the case.

Malandain, standing at his door, began to laugh on seeing him pass. Why?

He approached a farmer from Crequetot, who did not let

him finish, and giving him a thump in the stomach said to his face: "You big rascal."

Then he turned his back on him.

Maître Hauchecome was confused. Why was he called a big rascal?

When he was seated at the table in Jourdain's tavern, he commenced to explain "the affair."

A horse dealer from Monvilliers called to him: "Come, come, old sharper, that's an old trick; I know all about your piece of string!"

Hauchecome stammered: "But since the pocketbook was found."

But the other man replied: "Shut up, papa, there is one that finds, and there is one that reports. At any rate you are mixed up with it."

The peasant stood choking. He understood. They accused him of having had the pocketbook returned by a confederate, by an accomplice.

He tried to protest. All the table began to laugh.

He could not finish his dinner and went away, in the midst of jeers.

He went home ashamed and indignant, choking with anger and confusion, the more dejected because he was capable with his Norman cunning of doing what they had accused him of, and even boasting of it as of a good turn. His innocence to him, in a confused way, was impossible to prove, as his sharpness was known. And he was stricken to the heart by the injustice of the suspicion.

Then he began to recount the adventures again, prolonging his history every day, adding each time new reasons, more energetic protestations, more solemn oaths which he imagined and prepared in his hours of solitude, his whole mind given up to the story of the string. He was believed so much the less as his defense was more complicated and his arguing more subtle.

"Those are lying excuses," they said behind his back.

He felt it, consumed his heart over it, and wore himself out with useless efforts. He wasted away before their very eyes.

The wags now made him tell about the string to amuse them, as they make a soldier who has been on a campaign tell about his battles. His mind, touched to the depth, began to weaken.

Toward the end of December he took to his bed.

He died in the first days of January, and in the delirium of his death struggles he kept claiming his innocence, reiterating:

"A piece of string, a piece of string—look—here it is, M'sieu' the Mayor."

## Frank O'Connor

# *My Oedipus Complex*

FATHER WAS IN THE ARMY ALL THROUGH THE WAR—the first war, I mean—so, up to the age of five, I never saw much of him, and what I saw did not worry me. Sometimes I woke and there was a big figure in khaki peering down at me in the candlelight. Sometimes in the early morning I heard the slamming of the front door and the clatter of nailed boots down the cobbles of the lane. These were Father's entrances and exits. Like Santa Claus he came and went mysteriously.

In fact, I rather liked his visits, though it was an uncomfortable squeeze between Mother and him when I got into the big bed in the early morning. He smoked, which gave him a pleasant musty smell, and shaved, an operation of astounding interest. Each time he left a trail of souvenirs—model tanks and **Gurkha** knives with handles made of bullet cases, and German helmets and cap badges and button-sticks, and all sorts of military equipment—carefully stowed away in a long box on top of the wardrobe, in case they ever came in

---

**Gurkha:** Gurkhas were soldiers from Nepal serving in the British army. They are known for carrying a short curved sword called a kukri.

handy. There was a bit of the magpie about Father; he expected everything to come in handy. When his back was turned, Mother let me get a chair and rummage through his treasures. She didn't seem to think so highly of them as he did.

The war was the most peaceful period of my life. The window of my attic faced southeast. My mother had curtained it, but that had small effect. I always woke with the first light and, with all the responsibilities of the previous day melted, feeling myself rather like the sun, ready to illumine and rejoice. Life never seemed so simple and clear and full of possibilities as then. I put my feet out from under the clothes—I called them Mrs. Left and Mrs. Right—and invented dramatic situations for them in which they discussed the problems of the day. At least Mrs. Right did; she was very demonstrative, but I hadn't the same control of Mrs. Left, so she mostly contented herself with nodding agreement.

They discussed what Mother and I should do during the day, what Santa Claus should give a fellow for Christmas, and what steps should be taken to brighten the home. There was that little matter of the baby, for instance. Mother and I could never agree about that. Ours was the only house in the terrace without a new baby, and Mother said we couldn't afford one till Father came back from the war because they cost seventeen and six. That showed how simple she was. The Geneys up the road had a baby, and everyone knew they couldn't afford seventeen and six. It was probably a cheap baby, and Mother wanted something really good, but I felt she was too exclusive. The Geneys' baby would have done us fine.

Having settled my plans for the day, I got up, put a chair under the attic window, and lifted the frame high enough to stick out my head. The window overlooked the front gardens of the terrace behind ours, and beyond these it looked over a deep valley to the tall, red-brick houses terraced up the opposite hillside, which were all still in shadow, while those at our side of the valley were all lit up, though with long strange shadows that made them seem unfamiliar, rigid and painted. After that I went into Mother's room and climbed into the big bed. She woke and I began to tell her of my schemes. By this time, though I never seem to have noticed it, I was petrified in my nightshirt, and I thawed as I talked until, the last frost melted, I fell asleep beside her and woke again only when I heard her below in the kitchen, making the breakfast.

After breakfast we went into town; heard Mass at St. Augustine's and said a prayer for Father, and did the shopping. If the afternoon was fine we either went for a walk in the country or a visit to Mother's great friend in the convent, Mother St. Dominic. Mother had them all praying for Father, and every night, going to bed, I asked God to send him back safe from the war to us. Little, indeed, did I know what I was praying for!

One morning, I got into the big bed, and there, sure enough, was Father in his usual Santa Claus manner, but later, instead of uniform, he put on his best blue suit, and Mother was as pleased as anything. I saw nothing to be pleased about, because, out of uniform, Father was altogether less interesting, but she only beamed, and explained that our prayers had been answered, and off we went to Mass to thank God for having brought Father safely home.

The irony of it! That very day when he came in to dinner he took off his boots and put on his slippers, donned the dirty old cap he wore about the house to save him from colds, crossed his legs, and began to talk gravely to Mother, who looked anxious. Naturally, I disliked her looking anxious, because it destroyed her good looks, so I interrupted him.

"Just a moment, Larry!" she said gently.

This was only what she said when we had boring visitors, so I attached no importance to it and went on talking.

"Do be quiet, Larry!" she said impatiently. "Don't you hear me talking to Daddy?"

This was the first time I had heard those ominous words, "talking to Daddy," and I couldn't help feeling that if this was how God answered prayers, he couldn't listen to them very attentively.

"Why are you talking to Daddy?" I asked with as great a show of indifference as I could muster.

"Because Daddy and I have business to discuss. Now, don't interrupt again!"

In the afternoon, at Mother's request, Father took me for a walk. This time we went into town instead of out to the country, and I thought at first, in my usual optimistic way, that it might be an improvement. It was nothing of the sort. Father and I had quite different notions of a walk in town. He had no proper interest in trams, ships, and horses, and the only thing that seemed to divert him was talking to fellows as old as himself. When I wanted to stop he simply went on, dragging me behind him by the hand; when he wanted to stop I had no alternative but to do the same. I noticed that it seemed to be a sign that he wanted to stop for a long time whenever he leaned against a wall. The second time I saw him do it I got wild. He seemed to be settling himself forever. I pulled him by the coat and trousers, but, unlike Mother who, if you were too persistent, got into a **wax** and said: "Larry, if you don't behave yourself, I'll give you a good slap," Father had an extraordinary capacity for amiable inattention. I sized him up and wondered would I cry, but he seemed to be too remote to be annoyed even by that. Really, it was like

---

**Wax:** A rage.

going for a walk with a mountain! He either ignored the wrenching and pummelling entirely, or else glanced down with a grin of amusement from his peak. I had never met anyone so absorbed in himself as he seemed.

At teatime, "talking to Daddy" began again, complicated this time by the fact that he had an evening paper, and every few minutes he put it down and told Mother something new out of it. I felt this was foul play. Man for man, I was prepared to compete with him any time for Mother's attention, but when he had it all made up for him by other people it left me no chance. Several times I tried to change the subject without success.

"You must be quiet while Daddy is reading, Larry," Mother said impatiently.

It was clear that she either genuinely liked talking to Father better than talking to me, or else that he had some terrible hold on her which made her afraid to admit the truth.

"Mummy," I said that night when she was tucking me up, "do you think if I prayed hard God would send Daddy back to the war?"

She seemed to think about that for a moment.

"No, dear," she said with a smile. "I don't think he would."

"Why wouldn't he, Mummy?"

"Because there isn't a war any longer, dear."

"But, Mummy, couldn't God make another war, if He liked?"

"He wouldn't like to, dear. It's not God who makes wars, but bad people."

"Oh!" I said.

I was disappointed about that. I began to think that God wasn't quite what he was cracked up to be.

Next morning I woke at my usual hour, feeling like a bottle of champagne. I put out my feet and invented a long conversation in which Mrs. Right talked of the trouble she had with her own father till she put him in the Home. I didn't quite know what the Home was but it sounded the right place for Father. Then I got my chair and stuck my head out of the attic window. Dawn was just breaking, with a guilty air that made me feel I had caught it in the act. My head bursting with stories and schemes, I stumbled in next door, and in the half-darkness scrambled into the big bed. There was no room at Mother's side so I had to get between her and Father. For the time being I had forgotten about him, and for several minutes I sat bolt upright, racking my brains to know what I could do with him. He was taking up more than his fair share of the bed, and I couldn't get comfortable, so I gave him several kicks that made him grunt and stretch. He made room all right, though. Mother waked and felt for me. I settled back comfortably in the warmth of the bed with my thumb in my mouth.

"Mummy!" I hummed, loudly and contentedly.

"Sssh! dear," she whispered. "Don't wake Daddy!"

This was a new development, which threatened to be even more serious than "talking to Daddy." Life without my early-morning conferences was unthinkable.

"Why?" I asked severely.

"Because poor Daddy is tired."

This seemed to me a quite inadequate reason, and I was sickened by the sentimentality of her "poor Daddy." I never liked that sort of gush; it always struck me as insincere.

"Oh!" I said lightly. Then in my most winning tone: "Do you know where I want to go with you today, Mummy?"

"No, dear," she sighed.

"I want to go down the Glen and fish for thornybacks with my new net, and then I want to go out to the Fox and

Hounds, and—"

"Don't-wake-Daddy!" she hissed angrily, clapping her hand across my mouth.

But it was too late. He was awake, or nearly so. He grunted and reached for the matches. Then he stared incredulously at his watch.

"Like a cup of tea, dear?" asked Mother in a meek, hushed voice I had never heard her use before. It sounded almost as though she were afraid.

"Tea?" he exclaimed indignantly. "Do you know what the time is?"

"And after that I want to go up the Rathcooney Road," I said loudly, afraid I'd forget something in all those interruptions.

"Go to sleep at once, Larry!" she said sharply.

I began to snivel. I couldn't concentrate, the way that pair went on, smothering my early-morning schemes.

Father said nothing, but lit his pipe and sucked it, looking out into the shadows without minding Mother or me. I knew he was mad. Every time I made a remark Mother hushed me irritably. I was mortified. I felt it wasn't fair; there was even something sinister in it. Every time I had pointed out to her the waste of making two beds when we could both sleep in one, she had told me it was healthier like that, and now here was this man, this stranger, sleeping with her without the least regard for her health!

He got up early and made tea, but though he brought Mother a cup he brought none for me.

"Mummy," I shouted, "I want a cup of tea, too."

"Yes, dear," she said patiently. "You can drink from Mummy's saucer."

That settled it. Either Father or I would have to leave the house. I didn't want to drink from Mother's saucer; I wanted to be treated as an equal in my own home, so, just to spite her, I drank it all and left none for her. She took that quietly, too.

But that night when she was putting me to bed she said gently:

"Larry, I want you to promise me something."

"What is it?" I asked.

"Not to come in and disturb poor Daddy in the morning. Promise?"

"Poor Daddy" again! I was becoming suspicious of everything involving that quite impossible man.

"Why?" I asked.

"Because poor Daddy is worried and tired and he doesn't sleep well."

"Why doesn't he, Mummy?"

"Well, you know, don't you, that while he was at the war Mummy got the pennies from the Post Office?"

"From Miss MacCarthy?"

"That's right. But now, you see, Miss MacCarthy hasn't any more pennies, so Daddy must go out and find us some. You know what would happen if he couldn't?"

"No," I said, "tell us."

"Well, I think we might have to go out and beg for them like the poor old woman on Fridays. We wouldn't like that, would we?"

"No," I agreed. "We wouldn't."

"So you'll promise not to come in and wake him?"

"Promise."

Mind you, I meant that. I knew pennies were a serious matter, and I was all against having to go out and beg like the old woman on Fridays. Mother laid out all my toys in a complete ring round the bed so that, whatever way I got out, I was bound to fall over one of them.

When I woke I remembered my promise all right. I got up and sat on the floor and played—for hours, it seemed to me. Then I got my chair and looked out the attic window for more hours. I wished it was time for Father to wake; I wished someone would make me a cup of tea. I didn't feel in the least like the sun; instead, I was bored and so very, very cold! I simply longed for the warmth and depth of the big featherbed.

At last I could stand it no longer. I went into the next room. As there was still no room at Mother's side I climbed over her and she woke with a start.

"Larry," she whispered, gripping my arm very tightly, "what did you promise?"

"But I did, Mummy," I wailed, caught in the very act. "I was quiet for ever so long."

"Oh, dear, and you're perished!" she said sadly, feeling me all over. "Now, if I let you stay will you promise not to talk?"

"But I want to talk, Mummy," I wailed.

"That has nothing to do with it," she said with a firmness that was new to me. "Daddy wants to sleep. Now, do you understand that?"

I understood it only too well. I wanted to talk, he wanted to sleep—whose house was it, anyway?

"Mummy," I said with equal firmness, "I think it would be healthier for Daddy to sleep in his own bed."

That seemed to stagger her, because she said nothing for a while.

"Now, once for all," she went on, "you're to be perfectly quiet or go back to your own bed. Which is it to be?"

The injustice of it got me down. I had convicted her out of her own mouth of inconsistency and unreasonableness, and she hadn't even attempted to reply. Full of spite, I gave Father a kick, which she didn't notice but which made him grunt and open his eyes in alarm.

"What time is it?" he asked in a panic-stricken voice, not looking at Mother but at the door, as if he saw someone there.

"It's early yet," she replied soothingly. "It's only the child. Go to sleep again. . . . Now, Larry," she added, getting out of bed, "you've wakened Daddy and you must go back."

This time, for all her quiet air, I knew she meant it, and knew that my principal rights and privileges were as good as lost unless I asserted them at once. As she lifted me, I gave a screech, enough to wake the dead, not to mind Father. He groaned.

"That damn child! Doesn't he ever sleep?"

"It's only a habit, dear," she said quietly, though I could see she was vexed.

"Well, it's time he got out of it," shouted Father, beginning to heave in the bed. He suddenly gathered all the bedclothes about him, turned to the wall, and then looked back over his shoulder with nothing showing only two small, spiteful, dark eyes. The man looked very wicked.

To open the bedroom door, Mother had to let me down, and I broke free and dashed for the farthest corner, screeching. Father sat bolt upright in bed.

"Shut up, you little puppy!" he said in a choking voice.

I was so astonished that I stopped screeching. Never, never had anyone spoken to me in that tone before. I looked at him incredulously and saw his face convulsed with rage. It was only then that I fully realized how God had **codded** me, listening to my prayers for the safe return of this monster.

"Shut up, you!" I bawled, beside myself.

"What's that you said?" shouted Father, making a wild

---

**Codded:** Teased or kidded.

leap out of the bed.

"Mick, Mick!" cried Mother. "Don't you see the child isn't used to you?"

"I see he's better fed than taught," snarled Father, waving his arms wildly. "He wants his bottom smacked."

All his previous shouting was as nothing to these obscene words referring to my person. They really made my blood boil.

"Smack your own!" I screamed hysterically. "Smack your own! Shut up! Shut up!"

At this he lost his patience and let fly at me. He did it with the lack of conviction you'd expect of a man under Mother's horrified eyes, and it ended up as a mere tap, but the sheer indignity of being struck at all by a stranger, a total stranger who had cajoled his way back from the war into our big bed as a result of my innocent intercession, made me completely dotty. I shrieked and shrieked, and danced in my bare feet, and Father, looking awkward and hairy in nothing but a short gray army shirt, glared down at me like a mountain out for murder. I think it must have been then that I realized he was jealous too. And there stood Mother in her nightdress, looking as if her heart was broken between us. I hoped she felt as she looked. It seemed to me that she deserved it all.

From that morning out my life was a hell. Father and I were enemies, open and avowed. We conducted a series of skirmishes against one another, he trying to steal my time with Mother and I his. When she was sitting on my bed, telling me a story, he took to looking for some pair of old boots which he alleged he had left behind him at the beginning of the war. While he talked to Mother I played loudly with my toys to show my total lack of concern. He created a terrible scene one evening when he came in from work and found me at his box, playing with his regimental badges,

Gurkha knives and button-sticks. Mother got up and took the box from me.

"You mustn't play with Daddy's toys unless he lets you, Larry," she said severely. "Daddy doesn't play with yours."

For some reason Father looked at her as if she had struck him and then turned away with a scowl.

"Those are not toys," he growled, taking down the box again to see had I lifted anything. "Some of those curios are very rare and valuable."

But as time went on I saw more and more how he managed to alienate Mother and me. What made it worse was that I couldn't grasp his method or see what attraction he had for Mother. In every possible way he was less winning than I. He had a common accent and made noises at his tea. I thought for a while that it might be the newspapers she was interested in, so I made up bits of news of my own to read to her. Then I thought it might be the smoking, which I personally thought attractive, and took his pipes and went round the house dribbling into them till he caught me. I even made noises at my tea, but Mother only told me I was disgusting. It all seemed to hinge round that unhealthy habit of sleeping together, so I made a point of dropping into their bedroom and nosing round, talking to myself, so that they wouldn't know I was watching them, but they were never up to anything that I could see. In the end it beat me. It seemed to depend on being grownup and giving people rings, and I realized I'd have to wait.

But at the same time I wanted him to see that I was only waiting, not giving up the fight. One evening when he was being particularly obnoxious, chattering away well above my head, I let him have it.

"Mummy," I said, "do you know what I'm going to do when I grow up?"

"No, dear," she replied. "What?"

"I'm going to marry you," I said quietly.

Father gave a great guffaw out of him, but he didn't take me in. I knew it must only be pretense. And Mother, in spite of everything, was pleased. I felt she was probably relieved to know that one day Father's hold on her would be broken.

"Won't that be nice?" she said with a smile.

"It'll be very nice," I said confidently. "Because we're going to have lots and lots of babies."

"That's right, dear," she said placidly. "I think we'll have one soon, and then you'll have plenty of company."

I was no end pleased about that because it showed that in spite of the way she gave in to Father she still considered my wishes. Besides, it would put the Geneys in their place.

It didn't turn out like that, though. To begin with, she was very preoccupied—I supposed about where she would get the seventeen and six—and though Father took to staying out late in the evenings it did me no particular good. She stopped taking me for walks, became as touchy as blazes, and smacked me for nothing at all. Sometimes I wished I'd never mentioned the confounded baby—I seemed to have a genius for bringing calamity on myself.

And calamity it was! Sonny arrived in the most appalling hullabaloo—even that much he couldn't do without a fuss—and from the first moment I disliked him. He was a difficult child—so far as I was concerned he was always difficult—and demanded far too much attention. Mother was simply silly about him, and couldn't see when he was only showing off. As company he was worse than useless. He slept all day, and I had to go round the house on tiptoe to avoid waking him. It wasn't any longer a question of not waking Father. The slogan now was "Don't-wake-Sonny!" I couldn't understand why the child wouldn't sleep at the proper time, so whenever Mother's back was turned I woke him. Sometimes to keep him awake I pinched him as well. Mother caught me at it one day and gave me a most unmerciful flaking.

One evening, when Father was coming in from work, I was playing trains in the front garden. I let on not to notice him; instead, I pretended to be talking to myself, and said in a loud voice: "If another **bloody** baby comes into this house, I'm going out."

Father stopped dead and looked at me over his shoulder.

"What's that you said?" he asked sternly.

"I was only talking to myself," I replied, trying to conceal my panic. "It's private."

He turned and went in without a word. Mind you, I intended it as a solemn warning, but its effect was quite different. Father started being quite nice to me. I could understand that, of course. Mother was quite sickening about Sonny. Even at mealtimes she'd get up and gawk at him in the cradle with an idiotic smile, and tell Father to do the same. He was always polite about it, but he looked so puzzled you could see he didn't know what she was talking about. He complained of the way Sonny cried at night, but she only got cross and said that Sonny never cried except when there was something up with him—which was a flaming lie, because Sonny never had anything up with him, and only cried for attention. It was really painful to see how simpleminded she was. Father wasn't attractive, but he had a fine intelligence. He saw through Sonny, and now he knew that I saw through him as well.

One night I woke with a start. There was someone beside me in the bed. For one wild moment I felt sure it must be

---

**Bloody:** Used in British English to convey strong feeling, usually of disgust; often considered vulgar.

Mother, having come to her senses and left Father for good, but then I heard Sonny in convulsions in the next room, and Mother saying: "There! There! There!" and I knew it wasn't she. It was Father. He was lying beside me, wide awake, breathing hard and apparently as mad as hell.

After a while it came to me what he was mad about. It was his turn now. After turning me out of the big bed, he had been turned out himself. Mother had no consideration now for anyone but that poisonous pup, Sonny. I couldn't help feeling sorry for Father. I had been through it all myself, and even at that age I was magnanimous. I began to stroke him down and say: "There! There!" He wasn't exactly responsive.

"Aren't you asleep either?" he snarled.

"Ah, come on and put your arm around us, can't you?" I said, and he did, in a sort of way. Gingerly, I suppose, is how you'd describe it. He was very bony but better than nothing.

At Christmas he went out of his way to buy me a really nice model railway.

Katherine Anne Porter

# *The Jilting of Granny Weatherall*

She flicked her wrist neatly out of Doctor Harry's pudgy careful fingers and pulled the sheet up to her chin. The brat ought to be in knee breeches. Doctoring around the country with spectacles on his nose! "Get along now, take your schoolbooks and go. There's nothing wrong with me."

Doctor Harry spread a warm paw like a cushion on her forehead where the forked green vein danced and made her eyelids twitch. "Now, now, be a good girl, and we'll have you up in no time."

"That's no way to speak to a woman nearly eighty years old just because she's down. I'd have you respect your elders, young man."

"Well, Missy, excuse me." Doctor Harry patted her cheek. "But I've got to warn you, haven't I? You're a marvel, but you must be careful or you're going to be good and sorry."

"Don't tell me what I'm going to be. I'm on my feet now, morally speaking. It's Cornelia. I had to go to bed to get rid of her."

Her bones felt loose, and floated around in her skin, and Doctor Harry floated like a balloon around the foot of the bed. He floated and pulled down his waistcoat and swung his glasses on a cord. "Well, stay where you are, it certainly can't hurt you."

"Get along and doctor your sick," said Granny Weatherall. "Leave a well woman alone. I'll call for you when I want you. . . . Where were you forty years ago when I pulled through **milk-leg** and double pneumonia? You weren't even born. Don't let Cornelia lead you on," she shouted, because Doctor Harry appeared to float up to the ceiling and out. "I pay my own bills, and I don't throw my money away on nonsense!"

She meant to wave goodbye, but it was too much trouble. Her eyes closed of themselves, it was like a dark curtain drawn around the bed. The pillow rose and floated under her, pleasant as a hammock in a light wind. She listened to the leaves rustling outside the window. No, somebody was swishing newspapers: no, Cornelia and Doctor Harry were whispering together. She leaped broad awake, thinking they whispered in her ear.

"She was never like this, *never* like this!" "Well, what can we expect?" "Yes, eighty years old. . . ."

Well, and what if she was? She still had ears. It was like Cornelia to whisper around doors. She always kept things secret in such a public way. She was always being tactful and kind. Cornelia was dutiful; that was the trouble with her. Dutiful and good: "So good and dutiful," said Granny, "that I'd like to spank her." She saw herself spanking Cornelia and making a fine job of it.

---

**Milk-leg:** A painful swelling of the legs during childbirth caused by blood clotting in the veins.

"What'd you say, Mother?"

Granny felt her face tying up in hard knots.

"Can't a body think, I'd like to know?"

"I thought you might want something."

"I do. I want a lot of things. First off, go away and don't whisper."

She lay and drowsed, hoping in her sleep that the children would keep out and let her rest a minute. It had been a long day. Not that she was tired. It was always pleasant to snatch a minute now and then. There was always so much to be done, let me see: tomorrow.

Tomorrow was far away and there was nothing to trouble about. Things were finished somehow when the time came; thank God there was always a little margin over for peace: then a person could spread out the plan of life and tuck in the edges orderly. It was good to have everything clean and folded away, with the hair brushes and tonic bottles sitting straight on the white embroidered linen: the day started without fuss and the pantry shelves laid out with rows of jelly glasses and brown jugs and white stone-china jars with blue whirligigs and words painted on them: coffee, tea, sugar, ginger, cinnamon, allspice: and the bronze clock with the lion on top nicely dusted off. The dust that lion could collect in twenty-four hours! The box in the attic with all those letters tied up, well, she'd have to go through that tomorrow. All those letters—George's letters and John's letters and her letters to them both—lying around for the children to find afterwards made her uneasy. Yes, that would be tomorrow's business. No use to let them know how silly she had been once.

While she was rummaging around she found death in her mind and it felt clammy and unfamiliar. She had spent so much time preparing for death there was no need for bringing it up again. Let it take care of itself now. When she was sixty she had felt very old, finished, and went around making farewell trips to see her children and grandchildren, with a secret in her mind: This is the very last of your mother, children! Then she made her will and came down with a long fever. That was all just a notion like a lot of other things, but it was lucky too, for she had once for all got over the idea of dying for a long time. Now she couldn't be worried. She hoped she had better sense now. Her father had lived to be one hundred and two years old and had drunk a noggin of strong hot toddy on his last birthday. He told the reporters it was his daily habit, and he owed his long life to that. He had made quite a scandal and was very pleased about it. She believed she'd just plague Cornelia a little.

"Cornelia! Cornelia!" No footsteps, but a sudden hand on her cheek. "Bless you, where have you been?"

"Here, mother."

"Well, Cornelia, I want a noggin of hot toddy."

"Are you cold, darling?"

"I'm chilly, Cornelia. Lying in bed stops the circulation. I must have told you that a thousand times."

Well, she could just hear Cornelia telling her husband that Mother was getting a little childish and they'd have to humor her. The thing that most annoyed her was that Cornelia thought she was deaf, dumb, and blind. Little hasty glances and tiny gestures tossed around her and over her head saying, "Don't cross her, let her have her way, she's eighty years old," and she sitting there as if she lived in a thin glass cage. Sometimes Granny almost made up her mind to pack up and move back to her own house where nobody could remind her every minute that she was old. Wait, wait, Cornelia, till your own children whisper behind your back!

In her day she had kept a better house and had got more work done. She wasn't too old yet for Lydia to be driving eighty miles for advice when one of the children jumped the track, and Jimmy still dropped in and talked things over: "Now, Mammy, you've a good business head, I want to know what you think of this? ..." Old. Cornelia couldn't change the furniture around without asking. Little things, little things! They had been so sweet when they were little. Granny wished the old days were back again with the children young and everything to be done over. It had been a hard pull, but not too much for her. When she thought of all the food she had cooked, and all the clothes she had cut and sewed, and all the gardens she had made—well, the children showed it. There they were, made out of her, and they couldn't get away from that. Sometimes she wanted to see John again and point to them and say, Well, I didn't do so badly, did I? But that would have to wait. That was for tomorrow. She used to think of him as a man, but now all the children were older than their father, and he would be a child beside her if she saw him now. It seemed strange and there was something wrong in the idea. Why, he couldn't possibly recognize her. She had fenced in a hundred acres once, digging the post holes herself and clamping the wires with just a Negro boy to help. That changed a woman. John would be looking for a young woman with the peaked Spanish comb in her hair and the painted fan. Digging post holes changed a woman. Riding country roads in the winter when women had their babies was another thing: sitting up nights with sick horses and sick negroes and sick children and hardly ever losing one. John, I hardly ever lost one of them! John would see that in a minute, that would be something he could understand, she wouldn't have to explain anything!

It made her feel like rolling up her sleeves and putting the whole place to rights again. No matter if Cornelia was determined to be everywhere at once, there were a great many things left undone on this place. She would start tomorrow and do them. It was good to be strong enough for everything, even if all you made melted and changed and slipped under your hands, so that by the time you finished you almost forgot what you were working for. What was it I set out to do? she asked herself intently, but she could not remember. A fog rose over the valley, she saw it marching across the creek swallowing the trees and moving up the hill like an army of ghosts. Soon it would be at the near edge of the orchard, and then it was time to go in and light the lamps. Come in, children, don't stay out in the night air.

Lighting the lamps had been beautiful. The children huddled up to her and breathed like little calves waiting at the bars in the twilight. Their eyes followed the match and watched the flame rise and settle in a blue curve, then they moved away from her. The lamp was lit, they didn't have to be scared and hang on to mother any more. Never, never, never more. God, for all my life I thank Thee. Without Thee, my God, I could never have done it. Hail, Mary, full of grace.

I want you to pick all the fruit this year and see that nothing is wasted. There's always someone who can use it. Don't let good things rot for want of using. You waste life when you waste good food. Don't let things get lost. It's bitter to lose things. Now, don't let me get to thinking, not when I am tired and taking a little nap before supper. . . .

The pillow rose about her shoulders and pressed against her heart and the memory was being squeezed out of it: oh, push down the pillow, somebody: it would smother her if she tried to hold it. Such a fresh breeze blowing and such a green day with no threats in it. But he had not come, just the same. What does a woman do when she has put on the white veil and set out the white cake for a man and he doesn't come? She tried to remember. No, I swear he never harmed me but in that. He never harmed me but in that . . . and what if he did? There was the day, the day, but a whirl of dark smoke rose and covered it, crept up and over into the bright field where everything was planted so carefully in orderly rows. That was hell, she knew hell when she saw it. For sixty years she had prayed against remembering him and against losing her soul in the deep pit of hell, and now the two things were mingled in one and the thought of him was a smoky cloud from hell that moved and crept in her head when she had just got rid of Doctor Harry and was trying to rest a minute. Wounded vanity, Ellen, said a sharp voice in the top of her mind. Don't let your wounded vanity get the upper hand of you. Plenty of girls get jilted. You were jilted, weren't you? Then stand up to it. Her eyelids wavered and let in streamers of blue-gray light like tissue paper over her eyes. She must get up and pull the shades down or she'd never sleep. She was in bed again and the shades were not down. How could that happen? Better turn over, hide from the light, sleeping in the light gave you nightmares. "Mother, how do you feel now?" and a stinging wetness on her forehead. But I don't like having my face washed in cold water!

Hapsy? George? Lydia? Jimmy? No, Cornelia, and her features were swollen and full of little puddles. "They're coming, darling, they'll all be here soon." Go wash your face, child, you look funny.

Instead of obeying, Cornelia knelt down and put her head on the pillow. She seemed to be talking but there was no sound. "Well, are you tongue-tied? Whose birthday is it? Are you going to give a party?"

Cornelia's mouth moved urgently in strange shapes. "Don't do that, you bother me, daughter."

"Oh, no, Mother. Oh, no. . . ."

Nonsense. It was strange about children. They disputed

your every word. "No what, Cornelia?"

"Here's Doctor Harry."

"I won't see that boy again. He just left five minutes ago."

"That was this morning, Mother. It's night now. Here's the nurse."

"This is Doctor Harry, Mrs. Weatherall. I never saw you look so young and happy!"

"Ah, I'll never be young again—but I'd be happy if they'd let me lie in peace and get rested."

She thought she spoke up loudly, but no one answered. A warm weight on her forehead, a warm bracelet on her wrist, and a breeze went on whispering, trying to tell her something. A shuffle of leaves in the everlasting hand of God, He blew on them and they danced and rattled. "Mother, don't mind, we're going to give you a little hypodermic." "Look here, daughter, how do ants get in this bed? I saw sugar ants yesterday." Did you send for Hapsy too?

It was Hapsy she really wanted. She had to go a long way back through a great many rooms to find Hapsy standing with a baby on her arm. She seemed to herself to be Hapsy also, and the baby on Hapsy's arm was Hapsy and himself and herself, all at once, and there was no surprise in the meeting. Then Hapsy melted from within and turned flimsy as gray gauze and the baby was a gauzy shadow, and Hapsy came up close and said, "I thought you'd never come," and looked at her very searchingly and said, "You haven't changed a bit!" They leaned forward to kiss, when Cornelia began whispering from a long way off, "Oh, is there anything you want to tell me? Is there anything I can do for you?"

Yes, she had changed her mind after sixty years and she would like to see George. I want you to find George. Find him and be sure to tell him I forgot him. I want him to know I had my husband just the same and my children and my house like any other woman. A good house too and a good husband that I loved and fine children out of him. Better than I hoped for even. Tell him I was given back everything he took away and more. Oh, no, oh, God, no, there was something else besides the house and the man and the children. Oh, surely they were not all? What was it? Something not given back.... Her breath crowded down under her ribs and grew into a monstrous frightening shape with cutting edges; it bored up into her head, and the agony was unbelievable: Yes, John, get the Doctor now, no more talk, my time has come.

When this one was born it should be the last. The last. It should have been born first, for it was the one she had truly wanted. Everything came in good time. Nothing left out, left over. She was strong, in three days she would be as well as ever. Better. A woman needed milk in her to have her full health.

"Mother, do you hear me?"

"I've been telling you—"

"Mother, Father Connolly's here."

"I went to Holy Communion only last week. Tell him I'm not so sinful as all that."

"Father just wants to speak to you."

He could speak as much as he pleased. It was like him to drop in and inquire about her soul as if it were a teething baby, and then stay on for a cup of tea and a round of cards and gossip. He always had a funny story of some sort, usually about an Irishman who made his little mistakes and confessed them, and the point lay in some absurd thing he would blurt out in the confessional showing his struggles between native piety and original sin. Granny felt easy about her soul. Cornelia, where are your manners? Give Father Connolly a chair. She had her secret comfortable understanding with a few favorite saints who cleared a straight road to God for her. All as surely signed and sealed as the papers for the new Forty Acres. Forever . . . heirs and assigns, forever. Since the day the wedding cake was not cut, but thrown out and wasted. The whole bottom dropped out of the world, and there she was blind and sweating with nothing under her feet and the walls falling away. His hand had caught her under the breast, she had not fallen, there was the freshly polished floor with the green rug on it, just as before. He had cursed like a sailor's parrot and said, "I'll kill him for you." Don't lay a hand on him, for my sake leave something to God. "Now, Ellen, you must believe what I tell you. . . ."

So there was nothing, nothing to worry about any more, except sometimes in the night one of the children screamed in a nightmare, and they both hustled out shaking and hunting for the matches and calling, "There, wait a minute, here we are!" John, get the doctor now, Hapsy's time has come. But there was Hapsy standing by the bed in a white cap. "Cornelia, tell Hapsy to take off her cap. I can't see her plain."

Her eyes opened very wide and the room stood out like a picture she had seen somewhere. Dark colors with the shadows rising towards the ceiling in long angles. The tall black dresser gleamed with nothing on it but John's picture, enlarged from a little one, with John's eyes very black when they should have been blue. You never saw him, so how do you know how he looked? But the man insisted the copy was perfect, it was very rich and handsome. For a picture, yes, but it's not my husband. The table by the bed had a linen cover and a candle and a crucifix. The light was blue from Cornelia's silk lampshades. No sort of light at all, just frippery. You had to live forty years with kerosene lamps to appreciate honest electricity. She felt very strong and she saw Doctor Harry with a rosy nimbus around him.

"You look like a saint, Doctor Harry, and I vow that's as

near as you'll ever come to it."

"She's saying something."

"I heard you, Cornelia. What's all this carrying-on?"

"Father Connolly's saying—"

Cornelia's voice staggered and bumped like a cart in a bad road. It rounded corners and turned back again and arrived nowhere. Granny stepped up in the cart very lightly and reached for the reins, but a man sat beside her and she knew him by his hands, driving the cart. She did not look in his face, for she knew without seeing, but looked instead down the road where the trees leaned over and bowed to each other and a thousand birds were singing a Mass. She felt like singing too, but she put her hand in the bosom of her dress and pulled out a rosary, and Father Connolly murmured Latin in a very solemn voice and tickled her feet. My God, will you stop that nonsense? I'm a married woman. What if he did run away and leave me to face the priest by myself? I found another a whole world better. I wouldn't have exchanged my husband for anybody except St. Michael himself, and you may tell him that for me with a thank you in the bargain.

Light flashed on her closed eyelids, and a deep roaring shook her. Cornelia, is that lightning? I hear thunder. There's going to be a storm. Close all the windows. Call the children in. . . . "Mother, here we are, all of us." "Is that you, Hapsy?" "Oh, no, I'm Lydia. We drove as fast as we could." Their faces drifted above her, drifted away. The **rosary** fell out of her hands and Lydia put it back. Jimmy tried to help, their hands fumbled together, and Granny closed two fingers around Jimmy's thumb. Beads wouldn't do, it must be something

---

**Rosary:** A Roman Catholic prayer that meditates on 15 events in the lives of Jesus and Mary and uses a chain of beads as counters.

alive. She was so amazed her thoughts ran round and round. So, my dear Lord, this is my death and I wasn't even thinking about it. My children have come to see me die. But I can't, it's not time. Oh, I always hated surprises. I wanted to give Cornelia the amethyst set—Cornelia, you're to have the amethyst set, but Hapsy's to wear it when she wants, and, Doctor Harry, do shut up. Nobody sent for you. Oh, my dear Lord, do wait a minute. I meant to do something about the Forty Acres, Jimmy doesn't need it and Lydia will later on, with that worthless husband of hers. I meant to finish the altar cloth and send six bottles of wine to Sister Borgia for her dyspepsia. I want to send six bottles of wine to Sister Borgia, Father Connolly, now don't let me forget.

Cornelia's voice made short turns and tilted over and crashed. "Oh, Mother, oh, Mother, oh, Mother. . . ."

"I'm not going, Cornelia. I'm taken by surprise. I can't go."

You'll see Hapsy again. What about her? "I thought you'd never come." Granny made a long journey outward, looking for Hapsy. What if I don't find her? What then? Her heart sank down and down, there was no bottom to death, she couldn't come to the end of it. The blue light from Cornelia's lampshade drew into a tiny point in the center of her brain, it flickered and winked like an eye, quietly it fluttered and dwindled. Granny lay curled down within herself, amazed and watchful, staring at the point of light that was herself; her body was now only a deeper mass of shadow in an endless darkness and this darkness would curl around the light and swallow it up. God, give a sign!

For the second time there was no sign. Again no bridegroom and the priest in the house. She could not remember any other sorrow because this grief wiped them all away. Oh, no, there's nothing more cruel than this—I'll never forgive it. She stretched herself with a deep breath and blew out the light.

# ESSAYS

## George Orwell

# *Shooting an Elephant*

In Moulmein, in **Lower Burma** I was hated by large numbers of people—the only time in my life that I have been important enough for this to happen to me. I was sub-divisional police officer of the town, and in an aimless, petty kind of way anti-European feeling was very bitter. No one had the guts to raise a riot, but if a European woman went through the bazaars alone somebody would probably spit betel juice over her dress. As a police officer I was an obvious target and was baited whenever it seemed safe to do so. When a nimble Burman tripped me up on the **football** field and the referee (another Burman) looked the other way, the crowd yelled with hideous laughter. This happened more than once. In the end the sneering yellow faces of young men that met me everywhere, the insults hooted after me when I was at a safe distance, got badly on my nerves. The young Buddhist priests were the worst of all. There were several thousands of them in the town and none of them seemed to

**Lower Burma:** Now known as Myanmar. At the time this essay was written in 1940 it was a colonially administered territory of the British Empire.

**Football:** Known as soccer in the United States.

have anything to do except stand on street corners and jeer at Europeans.

All this was perplexing and upsetting. For at that time I had already made up my mind that imperialism was an evil thing and the sooner I chucked up my job and got out of it the better. Theoretically—and secretly, of course—I was all for the Burmese and all against their oppressors, the British. As for the job I was doing, I hated it more bitterly than I can perhaps make clear. In a job like that you see the dirty work of Empire at close quarters. The wretched prisoners huddling in the stinking cages of the lock-ups, the grey, cowed faces of the long-term convicts, the scarred buttocks of the men who had been flogged with bamboos—all these oppressed me with an intolerable sense of guilt. But I could get nothing into perspective. I was young and ill-educated and I had had to think out my problems in the utter silence that is imposed on every Englishman in the East. I did not even know that the British Empire is dying, still less did I know that it is a great deal better than the younger empires that are going to supplant it. All I knew was that I was stuck between my hatred of the empire I served and my rage against the evil-spirited little beasts who tried to make my job impossible. With one part of my mind I thought of the **British Raj** as an unbreakable tyranny, as something clamped down, ***in saecula saeculorum,*** upon the will of prostrate peoples; with another part I thought that the greatest joy in the world would be to drive a bayonet into a Buddhist priest's guts. Feelings like these are the normal byproducts of imperialism; ask any

---

**British Raj:** The term given to the period from 1757 to 1949 when the British ruled what are now the nations of India, Pakistan, Bangladesh and Myanmar.

**In saecula saeculorum:** For ages and ages, forever.

Anglo-Indian official, if you can catch him off duty.

One day something happened which in a roundabout way was enlightening. It was a tiny incident in itself, but it gave me a better glimpse than I had had before of the real nature of imperialism—the real motives for which despotic governments act. Early one morning the sub-inspector at a police station at the other end of the town rang me up on the phone and said that an elephant was ravaging the bazaar. Would I please come and do something about it? I did not know what I could do, but I wanted to see what was happening and I got on to a pony and started out. I took my rifle, an old .44 Winchester and much too small to kill an elephant, but I thought the noise might be useful ***in terrorem.*** Various Burmans stopped me on the way and told me about the elephant's doings. It was not, of course, a wild elephant, but a tame one which had gone "**must**." It had been chained up as tame elephants always are when their attack of "must" is due, but on the previous night it had broken its chain and escaped. Its **mahout**, the only person who could manage it when it was in that state, had set out in pursuit, but he had taken the wrong direction and was now twelve hours' journey away, and in the morning the elephant had suddenly reappeared in the town. The Burmese population had no weapons and were quite helpless against it. It had already destroyed somebody's bamboo hut, killed a cow and raided some fruit-stalls and devoured the stock; also it had met the municipal rubbish van, and, when the driver jumped out and took to his heels, had turned the van over and inflicted vio-

---

**In terrorem:** As a way of threatening or intimidating; Latin, literally "for terror."

**Mahout:** The keeper and driver of an elephant.

**Must:** In season for breeding.

lence upon it.

The Burmese sub-inspector and some Indian constables were waiting for me in the quarter where the elephant had been seen. It was a very poor quarter, a labyrinth of squalid bamboo huts, thatched with palm-leaf, winding all over a steep hillside. I remember that it was a cloudy stuffy morning at the beginning of the rains. We began questioning the people as to where the elephant had gone, and, as usual, failed to get any definite information. That is invariably the case in the East; a story always sounds clear enough at a distance, but the nearer you get to the scene of events the vaguer it becomes. Some of the people said that the elephant had gone in one direction, some said that he had gone in another, some professed not even to have heard of any elephant. I had almost made up my mind that the whole story was a pack of lies, when we heard yells a little distance away. There was a loud, scandalized cry of "Go away, child! Go away this instant!" and an old woman with a switch in her hand came round the corner of a hut, violently shooing away a crowd of naked children. Some more women followed, clicking their tongues and exclaiming; evidently there was something there that the children ought not to have seen. I rounded the hut and saw a man's dead body sprawling in the mud. He was an Indian, a black **Dravidian** coolie, almost naked, and he could not have been dead many minutes. The people said that the elephant had come suddenly upon him round the corner of the hut, caught him with its trunk, put its foot on his back and ground him into the earth. This was the rainy season

**Dravidian:** People of southern India and Sri Lanka who speak any of the family of 23 Dravidian languages, believed to have been spoken since at least 3,500 years ago. They have their own alphabets and are unrelated to any other existing languages.

and the ground was soft, and his face had scored a trench a foot deep and a couple of yards long. He was lying on his belly with arms crucified and head sharply twisted to one side. His face was coated with mud, the eyes wide open, the teeth bared and grinning with an expression of unendurable agony. (Never tell me, by the way, that the dead look peaceful. Most of the corpses I have seen looked devilish.) The friction of the great beast's foot had stripped the skin from his back as neatly as one skins a rabbit. As soon as I saw the dead man I sent an orderly to a friend's house nearby to borrow an elephant rifle. I had already sent back the pony, not wanting it to go mad with fright and throw me if it smelled the elephant.

The orderly came back in a few minutes with a rifle and five cartridges, and meanwhile some Burmans had arrived and told us that the elephant was in the paddy fields below, only a few hundred yards away. As I started forward practically the whole population of the quarter flocked out of their houses and followed me. They had seen the rifle and were all shouting excitedly that I was going to shoot the elephant. They had not shown much interest in the elephant when he was merely ravaging their homes, but it was different now that he was going to be shot. It was a bit of fun to them, as it would be to an English crowd; besides, they wanted the meat. It made me vaguely uneasy. I had no intention of shooting the elephant—I had merely sent for the rifle to defend myself if necessary—and it is always unnerving to have a crowd following you. I marched down the hill, looking and feeling a fool, with the rifle over my shoulder and an ever-growing army of people jostling at my heels. At the bottom, when you got away from the huts, there was a metalled road and beyond that a miry waste of paddy fields a thousand yards across, not yet ploughed but soggy from the first rains and dotted with coarse grass. The elephant was standing eighty yards from the road, his left side towards us. He took not the slightest notice of the crowd's approach. He was tearing up bunches of grass, beating them against his knees to clean them and stuffing them into his mouth.

I had halted on the road. As soon as I saw the elephant I knew with perfect certainty that I ought not to shoot him. It is a serious matter to shoot a working elephant—it is comparable to destroying a huge and costly piece of machinery—and obviously one ought not to do it if it can possibly be avoided. And at that distance, peacefully eating, the elephant looked no more dangerous than a cow. I thought then and I think now that his attack of "must" was already passing off; in which case he would merely wander harmlessly about until the mahout came back and caught him. Moreover, I did not in the least want to shoot him. I decided that I would watch him for a little while to make sure that he did not turn savage again and then go home.

But at that moment I glanced round at the crowd that had followed me. It was an immense crowd, two thousand at the least and growing every minute. It blocked the road for a long distance on either side. I looked at the sea of yellow faces above the garish clothes —faces all happy and excited over this bit of fun, all certain that the elephant was going to be shot. They were watching me as they would watch a conjuror about to perform a trick. They did not like me, but with the magical rifle in my hands I was momentarily worth watching. And suddenly I realized that I should have to shoot the elephant after all. The people expected it of me and I had got to do it; I could feel their two thousand wills pressing me forward, irresistibly. And it was at this moment, as I stood there with the rifle in my hands, that I first grasped the hollowness, the futility of the white man's dominion in the

East. Here was I, the white man with his gun, standing in front of the unarmed native crowd—seemingly the leading actor of the piece; but in reality I was only an absurd puppet pushed to and fro by the will of those yellow faces behind. I perceived in this moment that when the white man turns tyrant it is his own freedom that he destroys. He becomes a sort of hollow, posing dummy, the conventionalized figure of a **sahib**. For it is the condition of his rule that he shall spend his life in trying to impress the "natives" and so in every crisis he has got to do what the "natives" expect of him. He wears a mask, and his face grows to fit it. I had got to shoot the elephant. I had committed myself to doing it when I sent for the rifle. A sahib has got to act like a sahib; he has got to appear resolute, to know his own mind and do definite things. To come all that way, rifle in hand, with two thousand people marching at my heels, and then to trail feebly away, having done nothing—no, that was impossible. The crowd would laugh at me. And my whole life, every white man's life in the East, was one long struggle not to be laughed at.

But I did not want to shoot the elephant. I watched him beating his bunch of grass against his knees, with that preoccupied grandmotherly air that elephants have. It seemed to me that it would be murder to shoot him. At that age I was not squeamish about killing animals, but I had never shot an elephant and never wanted to. (Somehow it always seems worse to kill a *large* animal.) Besides, there was the beast's owner to be considered. Alive, the elephant was worth at least a hundred pounds; dead, he would only be worth the value of his tusks—five pounds, possibly. But I had got to act quickly. I turned to some experienced-looking Burmans who had

---

**Sahib:** A Hindi term meaning sir or master used during the Raj by Muslims and Hindus to address Europeans who had official rank.

been there when we arrived and asked them how the elephant had been behaving. They all said the same thing: he took no notice of you if you left him alone, but he might charge if you went too close to him.

It was perfectly clear to me what I ought to do. I ought to walk up to within, say, twenty-five yards of the elephant and test his behavior. If he charged I could shoot, if he took no notice of me it would be safe to leave him until the mahout came back. But also I knew that I was going to do no such thing. I was a poor shot with a rifle and the ground was soft mud into which one would sink at every step. If the elephant charged and I missed him, I should have about as much chance as a toad under a steamroller. But even then I was not thinking particularly of my own skin, only the watchful yellow faces behind. For at that moment, with the crowd watching me, I was not afraid in the ordinary sense, as I would have been if I had been alone. A white man mustn't be frightened in front of "natives"; and so, in general, he isn't frightened. The sole thought in my mind was that if anything went wrong those two thousand Burmans would see me pursued, caught, trampled on and reduced to a grinning corpse like that Indian up the hill. And if that happened it was quite probable that some of them would laugh. That would never do. There was only one alternative. I shoved the cartridges into the magazine and lay down on the road to get a better aim.

The crowd grew very still, and a deep, low, happy sigh, as of people who see the theater curtain go up at last, breathed from innumerable throats. They were going to have their bit of fun after all. The rifle was a beautiful German thing with cross-hair sights. I did not then know that in shooting an elephant one should shoot to cut an imaginary bar running from ear-hole to ear-hole. I ought therefore, as the elephant was sideways on, to have aimed straight at his ear-hole; actually I aimed several inches in front of this, thinking the brain would be further forward.

When I pulled the trigger I did not hear the bang or feel the kick—one never does when a shot goes home—but I heard the devilish roar of glee that went up from the crowd. In that instant, in too short a time, one would have thought, even for the bullet to get there, a mysterious, terrible change had come over the elephant. He neither stirred nor fell, but every line of his body had altered. He looked suddenly stricken, shrunken, immensely old, as though the frightful impact of the bullet had paralysed him without knocking him down. At last, after what seemed a long time—it might have been five seconds, I dare say—he sagged flabbily to his knees. His mouth slobbered. An enormous senility seemed to have settled upon him. One could have imagined him thousands of years old. I fired again into the same spot. At the second shot he did not collapse but climbed with desperate slowness to his feet and stood weakly upright, with legs sagging and head drooping. I fired a third time. That was the shot that did for him. You could see the agony of it jolt his whole body and knock the last remnant of strength from his legs. But in falling he seemed for a moment to rise, for as his hind legs collapsed beneath him he seemed to tower upwards like a huge rock toppling, his trunk reaching skyward like a tree. He trumpeted, for the first and only time. And then down he came, his belly towards me, with a crash that seemed to shake the ground even where I lay.

I got up. The Burmans were already racing past me across the mud. It was obvious that the elephant would never rise again, but he was not dead. He was breathing very rhythmically with long rattling gasps, his great mound of a side painfully rising and falling. His mouth was wide open—I could see far down into caverns of pale pink throat. I waited a long time for him to die, but his breathing did not weaken. Finally I fired my two remaining shots into the spot where I thought his heart must be. The thick blood welled out of him like red velvet, but still he did not die. His body did not even jerk when the shots hit him, the tortured breathing continued without a pause. He was dying, very slowly and in great agony, but in some world remote from me where not even a bullet could damage him further. I felt that I had got to put an end to that dreadful noise. It seemed dreadful to see the great beast lying there, powerless to move and yet powerless to die, and not even to be able to finish him. I sent back for my small rifle and poured shot after shot into his heart and down his throat. They seemed to make no impression. The tortured gasps continued as steadily as the ticking of a clock.

In the end I could not stand it any longer and went away. I heard later that it took him half an hour to die. Burmans were arriving with dahs and baskets even before I left, and I was told they had stripped his body almost to the bones by the afternoon.

Afterwards, of course, there were endless discussions about the shooting of the elephant. The owner was furious, but he was only an Indian and could do nothing. Besides, legally I had done the right thing, for a mad elephant has to be killed, like a mad dog, if its owner fails to control it. Among the Europeans opinion was divided. The older men said I was right, the younger men said it was a damn shame to shoot an elephant for killing a coolie, because an elephant was worth more than any damn Coringhee coolie. And afterwards I was very glad that the coolie had been killed; it put me legally in the right and it gave me a sufficient pretext for shooting the elephant. I often wondered whether any of the others grasped that I had done it solely to avoid looking a fool.

## James Thurber

# *The Night the Bed Fell*

I SUPPOSE THAT THE HIGH-WATER MARK OF MY YOUTH in Columbus, Ohio, was the night the bed fell on my father. It makes a better recitation (unless, as some friends of mine have said, one has heard it five or six times) than it does a piece of writing, for it is almost necessary to throw furniture around, shake doors, and bark like a dog, to lend the proper atmosphere and verisimilitude to what is admittedly a somewhat incredible tale. Still, it did take place.

It happened, then, that my father had decided to sleep in the attic one night, to be away where he could think. My mother opposed the notion strongly because, she said, the old wooden bed up there was unsafe: it was wobbly and the heavy headboard would crash down on father's head in case the bed fell, and kill him. There was no dissuading him, however, and at a quarter past ten he closed the attic door behind him and went up the narrow twisting stairs. We later heard ominous creakings as he crawled into bed. Grandfather, who usually slept in the attic bed when he was with us, had disappeared some days before. (On these occasions he was usually gone six or eight days and returned growling and out of temper, with the news that the federal Union was run by a passel of blockheads and that the Army of the Potomac didn't have any more chance than a fiddler's bitch.)

We had visiting us at this time a nervous first cousin of mine named Briggs Beall, who believed that he was likely to cease breathing when he was asleep. It was his feeling that if he were not awakened every hour during the night, he might die of suffocation. He had been accustomed to setting an alarm clock to ring at intervals until morning, but I persuaded him to abandon this. He slept in my room and I told him that I was such a light sleeper that if anybody quit breathing in the same room with me, I would wake instantly. He tested me the first night—which I had suspected he would—by holding his breath after my regular breathing had convinced him I was asleep. I was not asleep, however, and called to him. This seemed to allay his fears a little, but he took the precaution of putting a glass of spirits of camphor on a little table at the head of his bed. In case I didn't arouse him until he was almost gone, he said, he would sniff the camphor, a powerful reviver. Briggs was not the only member of his family who had his crotchets. Old Aunt Melissa Beall (who could whistle like a man, with two fingers in her mouth) suffered under the premonition that she was destined to die on South High Street, because she had been born on South High Street and married on South High Street. Then there was Aunt Sarah Shoaf, who never went to bed at night without the fear that a burglar was going to get in and blow chloroform under her door through a tube. To avert this calamity—for she was in greater dread of anesthetics than of losing her household goods—she always piled her money, silverware, and other valuables in a neat stack just outside her bedroom, with a note reading: "This is all I have. Please take it and do not use your chloroform, as this is all I have." Aunt Gracie

Shoaf also had a burglar phobia, but she met it with more fortitude. She was confident that burglars had been getting into her house every night for forty years. The fact that she never missed anything was to her no proof to the contrary. She always claimed that she scared them off before they could take anything by throwing shoes down the hallway. When she went to bed she piled, where she could get at them handily, all the shoes there were about her house. Five minutes after she had turned off the light, she would sit up in bed and say "Hark!" Her husband, who had learned to ignore the whole situation as long ago as 1903, would either be sound asleep or pretend to be sound asleep. In either case he would not respond to her tugging and pulling, so that presently she would arise, tiptoe to the door, open it slightly and heave a shoe down the hall in one direction, and its mate down the hall in the other direction. Some nights she threw them all, some nights only a couple of pair.

But I am straying from the remarkable incidents that took place during the night that the bed fell on father. By midnight we were all in bed. The layout of the rooms and the disposition of their occupants is important to an understanding of what later occurred. In the front room upstairs (just under father's attic bedroom) were my mother and my brother Herman, who sometimes sang in his sleep, usually "Marching Through Georgia" or "Onward, Christian Soldiers." Briggs Beall and myself were in a room adjoining this one. My brother Roy was in a room across the hall from ours. Our bull terrier, Rex, slept in the hall.

My bed was an army cot, one of those affairs which are made wide enough to sleep on comfortably only by putting up, flat with the middle section, the two sides which ordinarily hang down like the sideboards of a drop-leaf table. When these sides are up, it is perilous to roll too far toward the edge, for then the cot is likely to tip completely over, bringing the whole bed down on top of one, with a tremendous banging crash. This, in fact, is precisely what happened, about two o'clock in the morning. (It was my mother who, in recalling the scene later, first referred to it as "the night the bed fell on your father.")

Always a deep sleeper, slow to arouse (I had lied to Briggs), I was at first unconscious of what had happened when the iron cot rolled me onto the floor and toppled over on me. It left me still warmly bundled up and unhurt, for the bed rested above me like a canopy. Hence I did not wake up, only reached the edge of consciousness and went back. The racket, however, instantly awakened my mother in the next room, who came to the immediate conclusion that her worst dread was realized: the big wooden bed upstairs had fallen on father. She therefore screamed, "Let's go to your poor father!" It was this shout, rather than the noise of my cot falling, that awakened Herman, in the same room with her. He thought that mother had become, for no apparent reason, hysterical. "You're all right, Mamma!" he shouted, trying to calm her. They exchanged shout for shout for perhaps ten seconds: "Let's go to your poor father!" and "You're all right!" That woke up Briggs. By this time I was conscious of what was going on, in a vague way, but did not yet realize that I was under my bed instead of on it. Briggs, awakening in the midst of loud shouts of fear and apprehension, came to the quick conclusion that he was suffocating and that we were all trying to "bring him out." With a low moan, he grasped the glass of camphor at the head of his bed and instead of sniffing it poured it over himself. The room reeked of camphor. "Ugf, ahfg," choked Briggs, like a drowning man, for he had almost succeeded in stopping his breath under the deluge of pungent spirits. He leaped out of bed and groped toward the open window, but he came up against one that was closed. With his hand, he beat out the glass, and I could hear it crash and tinkle on the alleyway below. It was at this juncture that I, in trying to get up, had the uncanny sensation of feeling my bed above me! Foggy with sleep, I now suspected, in my turn, that the whole uproar was being made in a frantic endeavor to extricate me from what must be an unheard-of and perilous situation. "Get me out of this!" I bawled. "Get me out!" I think I had the nightmarish belief that I was entombed in a mine. "Gugh," gasped Briggs, floundering in his camphor.

By this time my mother, still shouting, pursued by Herman, still shouting, was trying to open the door to the attic, in order to go up and get my father's body out of the wreckage. The door was stuck, however, and wouldn't yield. Her frantic pulls on it only added to the general banging and confusion. Roy and the dog were now up, the one shouting questions, the other barking.

Father, farthest away and soundest sleeper of all, had by this time been awakened by the battering on the attic door. He decided that the house was on fire. "I'm coming, I'm coming!" he wailed in a slow, sleepy voice—it took him many minutes to regain full consciousness. My mother, still believing he was caught under the bed, detected in his "I'm coming!" the mournful, resigned note of one who is preparing to meet his Maker. "He's dying!" she shouted.

"I'm all right!" Briggs yelled to reassure her. "I'm all right!" He still believed that it was his own closeness to death that was worrying mother. I found at last the light switch in my room, unlocked the door, and Briggs and I joined the others at the attic door. The dog, who never did like Briggs, jumped for him—assuming that he was the culprit in whatever was going on—and Roy had to throw Rex and hold him. We could hear father crawling out of bed upstairs. Roy pulled the attic door open, with a mighty jerk, and father came down the stairs, sleepy and irritable but safe and sound. My mother began to weep when she saw him. Rex began to howl. "What in the name of God is going on here?" asked father.

The situation was finally put together like a gigantic jigsaw puzzle. Father caught a cold from prowling around in his bare feet but there were no other bad results. "I'm glad," said mother, who always looked on the bright side of things, "that your grandfather wasn't here."

# SPEECHES

## Franklin Delano Roosevelt

# *Declaration of War Against Japan*

MR. VICE PRESIDENT, MR. SPEAKER, MEMBERS OF THE SENATE AND THE HOUSE OF REPRESENTATIVES:

YESTERDAY, DEC. 7, 1941—A DATE WHICH WILL LIVE in infamy—the United States of America was suddenly and deliberately attacked by naval and air forces of the empire of Japan.

The United States was at peace with that nation, and, at the solicitation of Japan, was still in conversation with its government and its Emperor looking toward the maintenance of peace in the Pacific.

Indeed, one hour after Japanese air squadrons had commenced bombing in the American island of Oahu, the Japanese Ambassador to the United States and his colleague delivered to our Secretary of State a formal reply to a recent American message. And, while this reply stated that it seemed useless to continue the existing diplomatic negotiations, it contained no threat or hint of war or of armed attack.

It will be recorded that the distance of Hawaii from

Japan makes it obvious that the attack was deliberately planned many days or even weeks ago. During the intervening time the Japanese Government has deliberately sought to deceive the United States by false statements and expressions of hope for continued peace.

The attack yesterday on the Hawaiian Islands has caused severe damage to American naval and military forces. I regret to tell you that very many American lives have been lost. In addition, American ships have been reported torpedoed on the high seas between San Francisco and Honolulu.

Yesterday the Japanese Government also launched an attack against Malaya.

Last night Japanese forces attacked Hong Kong.

Last night Japanese forces attacked Guam.

Last night Japanese forces attacked the Philippine Islands.

Last night the Japanese attacked Wake Island.

And this morning the Japanese attacked Midway Island.

Japan has therefore undertaken a surprise offensive extending throughout the Pacific area. The facts of yesterday and today speak for themselves. The people of the United States have already formed their opinions and well understand the implications to the very life and safety of our nation.

As Commander in Chief of the Army and Navy I have directed that all measures be taken for our defense, that always will our whole nation remember the character of the onslaught against us.

No matter how long it may take us to overcome this premeditated invasion, the American people, in their righteous might, will win through to absolute victory.

I believe that I interpret the will of the Congress and of the people when I assert that we will not only defend ourselves to the uttermost but will make it very certain that this form of treachery shall never again endanger us.

Hostilities exist. There is no blinking at the fact that our people, our territory and our interests are in grave danger.

With confidence in our armed forces, with the unbounding determination of our people, we will gain the inevitable triumph. So help us God.

I ask that the Congress declare that since the unprovoked and dastardly attack by Japan on Sunday, Dec. 7, 1941, a state of war has existed between the United States and the Japanese Empire.

# Winston Churchill

## *"Blood, Sweat and Tears"*

*Churchill's first speech before Parliament after his appointment as Prime Minister of Great Britain, delivered on May 13, 1940.*

On Friday evening last I received from His Majesty the mission to form a new administration.

It was the evident will of Parliament and the nation that this should be conceived on the broadest possible basis and that it should include all parties.

I have already completed the most important part of this task. A war cabinet has been formed of five members, representing, with the Labor, Opposition and Liberals, the unity of the nation.

It was necessary that this should be done in one single day on account of the extreme urgency and rigor of events. Other key positions were filled yesterday. I am submitting a further list to the King tonight. I hope to complete the appointment of principal Ministers during tomorrow.

The appointment of other Ministers usually takes a little longer. I trust when Parliament meets again this part of my task will be completed and that the administration will be complete in all respects.

I considered it in the public interest to suggest to the Speaker that the House should be summoned today. At the end of today's proceedings, the adjournment of the House will be proposed until May 21 with provision for earlier meeting if need be. Business for that will be notified to **M. P.'s** at the earliest opportunity.

I now invite the House by a resolution to record its approval of the steps taken and declare its confidence in the new government. The resolution:

"That this House welcomes the formation of a government representing the united and inflexible resolve of the nation to prosecute the war with Germany to a victorious conclusion."

To form an administration of this scale and complexity is a serious undertaking in itself. But we are in the preliminary phase of one of the greatest battles in history. We are in action at many other points—in Norway and in Holland—and we have to be prepared in the Mediterranean. The air battle is continuing, and many preparations have to be made here at home.

In this crisis I think I may be pardoned if I do not address the House at any length today, and I hope that any of my friends and colleagues or former colleagues who are affected by the political reconstruction will make all allowances for any lack of ceremony with which it has been necessary to act.

I say to the House, as I said to Ministers who have joined this government, I have nothing to offer but blood, toil, tears and sweat. We have before us an ordeal of the most grievous kind. We have before us many, many months of struggle and suffering.

You ask, what is our policy? I say it is to wage war by land, sea and air. War with all our might and with all the strength

---

**M. P.'s**: Members of Parliament

God has given us, and to wage war against a monstrous tyranny never surpassed in the dark and lamentable catalogue of human crime. That is our policy.

You ask, what is our aim? I can answer in one word. It is victory. Victory at all costs—victory in spite of all terrors—victory, however long and hard the road may be, for without victory there is no survival.

Let that be realized. No survival for the British Empire, no survival for all that the British Empire has stood for, no survival for the urge, the impulse of the ages, that mankind shall move forward toward his goal.

I take up my task in buoyancy and hope. I feel sure that our cause will not be suffered to fail among men.

I feel entitled at this juncture, at this time, to claim the aid of all and to say, "Come then, let us go forward together with our united strength."

# Winston Churchill

## *"Their Finest Hour"*

*Delivered June 18, 1940, in the British House of Commons*

I SPOKE THE OTHER DAY OF THE COLOSSAL MILITARY disaster which occurred when the French High Command failed to withdraw the northern armies from Belgium at a moment when they knew that the French front was decisively broken at **Sedan and on the Meuse.**

This delay entailed the loss of fifteen or sixteen French divisions and threw out of action the whole of the British Expeditionary Force.

Our army were indeed rescued by the British Navy from Dunkirk, but only with the loss of all their cannon, vehicles and modern equipment. This loss inevitably took some weeks to repair, and in the first two of these weeks the Battle of France had been lost.

When we consider the heroic resistance made by the

---

**Sedan and on the Meuse:** Sedan, a strategically situated town in northeastern France, was the scene of France's defeat by the Prussians in 1870, of bloody fighting in World War I, and of the German breakthrough that resulted in the conquest of France in 1940. The Meuse river flows through Sedan and eventually forms part of the boundary between Belgium and Holland.

French Army against heavy odds in this battle, and the enormous loss inflicted upon the enemy and the evident exhaustion of the enemy, it might well be thought that these twenty-five divisions of the best troops—best trained and equipped—might have turned the scales. However, General Weygand had to fight without them.

Only three British divisions or their equivalent were able to stand in the line with their French comrades. They have suffered severely, but they have fought well. We sent every man we could to France, as fast as we could re-equip and transport their formations.

I am not reciting these facts for the purpose of recrimination. That I judge to be utterly futile and even harmful. We cannot afford it. I recite them in order to explain why it was we did not have, as we could have had, between twelve and fourteen British divisions fighting in the line in this battle instead of only three.

Now I put all this aside. I put it on the shelf from which the historians may select their documents in order to tell their story. We have to think of the future and not of the past. This also applies in a small way to our own affairs at home.

There are many who wish to hold an inquest upon the conduct of the government and of Parliament during the years which led up to this catastrophe. They wish to indict those who were responsible for the guidance of our affairs.

This also would be a foolish and pernicious process. There are too many in it. Let each man search his conscience and search his speeches, as I frequently search mine. Of this I am quite sure, that if we open a quarrel between the past and the present we shall find that we have lost the future.

Therefore I cannot accept the drawing of any distinctions between members of the present government which was formed in a moment of crisis in order to unite members of all parties and all sections of opinion. It has received the almost unanimous support of both Houses of Parliament and its members are going to stand together and, subject to the authority of the House of Commons, we are going to govern the country and fight the war.

It is absolutely necessary at a time like this that every Minister who tries each day to do his duty shall be respected and their subordinates must know that their chiefs are not threatened men who are here today and gone tomorrow.

Their directions must be punctually and effectively given. Without this concentrated power we cannot do what lies before us. I do not think it would be very advantageous for the House to prolong this debate this afternoon under the conditions of a public sitting. We are to have a secret session on Thursday that would be a better opportunity for many earnest expressions of opinion which may be desired for the House to discuss our vital matters without having everything read the next morning by our dangerous foe.

The military events which have happened in France during the last fortnight have not come to me with any sense of surprise; indeed, I indicated a fortnight ago as clearly as I could to the House, that the worst possibilities were open and I made it perfectly clear that whatever happened in France, it would make no difference to the resolve of Britain and the British Empire to fight on, if necessary for years, and if necessary alone....

The invasion of Great Britain at this time would require the transport across the seas of hostile armies on a very large scale, and after they had been so transported, they would have to be continually maintained with all the immense mass of munitions and supplies which are required for continuous battle, as continuous battle it would be....

It seems to me that as far as seaborne invasion on a great

scale is concerned, we are far more capable of meeting it than we were at many periods in the last war and during the early months of this war before our troops were trained and while the British Expeditionary Force was abroad.

The navy was never intended to prevent the raids of bodies of five or ten thousand men flung across and thrown suddenly ashore at several points on the coast some dark night or foggy morning. The efficacy of sea power, especially under modern conditions, depends upon the invading force being of a large size and, if it is of a large size, the navy has something they can find and, as it were, bite on.

Now we must remember that even five divisions, even lightly equipped, would require 200 to 250 ships, and with modern air reconnaissance and photography it would not be easy to collect such an armada and marshal it across the seas with any powerful naval force to escort it with any possibility that it would not be intercepted long before it reached the coast and the men all drowned in the sea, or, at the worst, blown to pieces with their equipment when they were trying to land . . .

These are the well-tested and well-proved arguments on which we have relied for many years, but the question is whether there are any new methods by which they can be circumvented. Odd as it may seem, some attention has been given to this by the Admiralty, whose prime duty and responsibility it is to destroy any large seaborne expedition before it reaches or at the moment when it reaches these shores. It would not be useful to go into details and it might even suggest ideas to other people that they have not got and who would not be likely to give us any of their ideas in exchange.

All I would say is that untiring vigilance and mind-searching must be devoted to the subject, because the enemy is crafty, cunning and full of novel treacheries and strategies. . . .

This brings me naturally to the great question of invasion from the air and the impending struggle between the British and German Air Forces.

It seems quite clear that no invasion on a scale beyond the capacity of our ground forces to crush speedily is likely to take place from the air until our air force has been definitely overpowered. In the meantime, there may be raids by parachute troops and attempted descents by airborne soldiers. We ought to be able to give those gentry a warm reception, both in the air and if they reach the ground in any condition to continue their dispute. The great question is, can we break Hitler's air weapon?

Now, of course, it is a very great pity that we have not got an air force at least equal to that of the most powerful enemy within reach of our shores, but we have a very powerful air force, which has proved itself far superior in quality both in men and in many types of machines to what we have met so far in the numerous fierce air battles which have been fought.

In France, where we were at a considerable disadvantage and lost many machines on the ground in the airdromes, we were accustomed to inflict upon the enemy a loss of two to two-and-a-half to one. In the fighting over Dunkirk, which was a sort of No Man's Land, we undoubtedly gained a local mastery of the air and inflicted on the German Air Force losses on the scale of three or four to one.

Any one looking at the photographs of the re-embarkation showing the masses of troops assembled on the beaches, affording an ideal target for hours at a time, must realize that this embarkation would not have been possible unless the enemy had resigned all hope of recovery of air superiority at that point.

In these islands the advantage to the defenders will be very great. We ought to improve upon that rate of three or four to one, which was realized at Dunkirk.

In addition, there are, of course, a great many injured machines and men who get down safely after an air fight. But all those who fall in an attack upon this island would land on friendly soil and live to fight another day, whereas all the injured enemy machines and their complements will be total losses, as far as the Germans are concerned.

During the great battle in France we gave very great and continuous aid to the French, both by fighters and bombers, but in spite of all pressure, we never allowed the entire metropolitan strength of our air force in fighters to be consumed. This decision was painful, but it was also right.

The battle was, however, lost by the unfortunate strategic opening and by the extraordinary unforeseen power of the armored columns and by the very great preponderance of the German Army in numbers.

Our fighter air force might easily have been exhausted as a mere incident in that struggle and we should have found ourselves at the present time in a very unhappy plight. I am happy to inform the House that our fighter air strength is stronger at the present time relatively to the German, which has suffered terrible losses, than it has ever been. Consequently we believe ourselves to possess the capacity to continue the war in the air under better conditions than we have ever experienced before.

I look forward confidently to the exploits of our fighter pilots, who will have the glory of saving their native land and our island home from the most deadly of all attacks.

There remains the danger of the bombing attacks, which will certainly be made very soon upon us by the bomber forces of the enemy. It is quite true that these forces are superior in number to ours, but we have a very large bombing force also which we shall use to strike at the military targets in Germany without intermission.

I do not at all underrate the severity of the ordeal which lies before us, but I believe that our countrymen will show themselves capable of standing up to it and carrying on in spite of it at least as well as any other people in the world.

It will depend upon themselves, and every man and woman will have the chance of showing the finest qualities of their race and of rendering the highest service to their cause.

For all of us, whatever our sphere or station, it will be a help to remember the famous lines:

**He nothing common did, or mean**
**Upon that memorable scene.**

I have thought it right on this occasion to give the House and the country some indication of the solid, practical grounds upon which we are basing our invincible resolve to continue the war, and I can assure them that our professional advisers of the three services unitedly advise that we should do it, and that there are good and reasonable hopes of final victory.

We have fully informed all the self-governing dominions and we have received from all Prime Ministers messages couched in the most moving terms, in which they endorse our decision and declare themselves ready to share our fortunes and persevere to the end.

We may now ask ourselves in what way has our position worsened since the beginning of the war. It is worsened by the fact that the Germans have conquered a large part of the coast of the Allies in Western Europe, and many small coun-

---

**He . . . scene:** Lines from "An Horation Ode upon Cromwell's Return from Ireland" by the English poet Andrew Marvell (1621-1678).

tries have been overrun by them. This aggravates the possibility of air attack and adds to our naval preoccupation, but it in no way diminishes, but on the contrary definitely increases, the power of our long-distance blockade.

Should military resistance come to an end in France—which is not yet, though it will in any case be greatly diminished—the Germans can concentrate their forces both military and industrial upon us. But for the reason given to the House, this will not be easy to apply.

If invasion becomes more imminent, we have been relieved from the task of maintaining a large army in France and we have a far larger and more efficient force here to meet it.

If Hitler can bring under despotic control the industries of the countries he has conquered, this will add greatly to his already vast armament output. On the other hand, this will not happen immediately and we are now assured of immense continued and increasing support in munitions of all kinds from the United States, and especially of airplanes and pilots from across the ocean. They will come from regions beyond the reach of enemy bombers.

I do not see how any of these factors can operate to our detriment, on balance, before the winter comes, and the winter will impose a strain upon the Nazi regime, with half Europe writhing and starving under its heel, which, for all their ruthlessness, will run them very hard.

We must not forget that from the moment we declared war on Sept. 3, it was always possible for Germany to turn all her air force on this country. There would also be other devices of invasion, and France could do little or nothing to prevent her. We have therefore lived under this danger during all these months.

In the meanwhile, however, we have enormously

improved our methods of defense and we have learned what we had no right to assume at the beginning, of the individual superiority of our aircraft and pilots.

Therefore in casting up this dread balance sheet and contemplating our dangers with a disillusioned eye, I see great reasons for intense exertion and vigilance, but none whatever for panic or despair. During the first four months of the last war the Allies experienced nothing but disaster and disappointment, and yet at the end their morale was higher than that of the Germans, who had moved from one aggressive triumph to another.

During that war we repeatedly asked ourselves the question, "How are we going to win?" and no one was ever able to answer it with much precision, until at the end, quite suddenly and unexpectedly, our terrible foe collapsed before us and we were so glutted with victory that in our folly we cast it away.

We do not yet know what will happen in France or whether the French resistance will be prolonged both in France and in the French Empire overseas. The French Government will be throwing away great opportunities and casting away their future if they do not continue the war in accordance with their treaty obligations, from which we have not felt able to release them.

The House will have read the historic declaration in which, at the desire of many Frenchmen and of our own hearts, we have proclaimed our willingness to conclude at the darkest hour in French history a union of common citizenship in their struggle.

However matters may go in France or with the French Government, or another French Government, we in this island and in the British Empire will never lose our sense of comradeship with the French people.

If we are now called upon to endure what they have suffered, we shall emulate their courage, and if final victory rewards our toils they shall share the gain—aye, freedom shall be restored to all. We abate nothing of our just demands. Czechs, Poles, Norwegians, Dutch and Belgians, who have joined their causes with our own, all shall be restored.

What General Weygand called the Battle of France is over. The Battle of Britain is about to begin. On this battle depends the survival of Christian civilization.

Upon it depends our own British life and the long continuity of our institutions and our empire. The whole fury and might of the enemy must very soon be turned upon us. Hitler knows he will have to break us in this island or lose the war.

If we can stand up to him, all Europe may be freed and the life of the world may move forward into broad sunlit uplands; but if we fail, the whole world, including the United States and all that we have known and cared for, will sink into the abyss of a new dark age made more sinister and perhaps more prolonged by the lights of a perverted science.

Let us therefore brace ourselves to our duty and so bear ourselves that if the British Commonwealth and Empire last for a thousand years, men will still say "This was their finest hour."

# Huey P. Long

## *Every Man a King*

*Exerpted from a radio address delivered in January of 1935 while Long was serving as a U.S. Senator from Louisiana.*

I CONTEND, MY FRIENDS, THAT WE HAVE NO DIFFICULT problem to solve in America, and that is the view of nearly everyone with whom I have discussed the matter here in Washington and elsewhere throughout the United States—that we have no very difficult problem to solve.

It is not the difficulty of the problem which we have; it is the fact that the rich people of this country—and by rich people I mean the super-rich—will not allow us to solve the problems, or rather the one little problem that is afflicting this country, because in order to cure all of our woes it is necessary to scale down the big fortunes, that we may scatter the wealth to be shared by all of the people. . . .

I believe that was the judgment and the view and the law of the Lord, that we would have to distribute wealth every so often, in order that there could not be people starving to death in a land of plenty, as there is in America today.

We have in America today more wealth, more goods, more food, more clothing, more houses than we have ever had. We have everything in abundance here.

We have the farm problem, my friends, because we have too much cotton, because we have too much wheat, and have too much corn, and too much potatoes.

We have a home-loan problem, because we have too many houses, and yet nobody can buy them and live in them.

We have trouble, my friends, in the country, because we have too much money owing, the greatest indebtedness that has ever been given to civilization, where it has been shown that we are incapable of distributing the actual things that are here, because the people have not money enough to supply themselves with them, and because the greed of a few men is such that they think it is necessary that they own everything, and their pleasure consists in the starvation of the masses, and in their possessing things they cannot use, and their children cannot use, but who bask in the splendor of sunlight and wealth, casting darkness and despair and impressing it on everyone else.

"So, therefore," said the Lord in effect, "if you see these things that now have occurred and exist in this and other countries, there must be a constant scattering of wealth in any country if this country is to survive."...

Now, my friends, if you were off on an island where there were a hundred lunches, you could not let one man eat up the hundred lunches, or take the hundred lunches and not let anybody else eat any of them. If you did, there would not be anything else for the balance of the people to consume.

So, we have in America today, my friends, a condition by which about ten men dominate the means of activity in at least 85 percent of the activities that you own. They either own directly everything or they have got some kind of mortgage on it, with a very small percentage to be excepted. They own the banks, they own the steel mills, they own the railroads, they own the bonds, they own the mortgages, they own the stores, and they have chained the country from one end to the other until there is not any kind of business that a small, independent man could go into today and make a living, and there is not any kind of business that an independent man can go into and make any money to buy an automobile with; and they have finally and gradually and steadily eliminated everybody from the fields in which there is a living to be made, and still they have got little enough sense to think they ought to be able to get more business out of it anyway.

If you reduce a man to the point where he is starving to death and bleeding and dying, how do you expect that man to get hold of any money to spend with you? It is not possible.

Then, ladies and gentlemen, how do you expect people to live, when the wherewith cannot be had by the people?...

Now, we have organized a society, and we call it Share Our Wealth Society, a society with the motto "Every Man a King."

Every man a king, so there would be no such thing as a man or woman who did not have the necessities of life, who would not be dependent upon the whims and caprices and ***ipse dixit*** of the financial barons for a living. What do we propose by this society? We propose to limit the wealth of big men in the country. There is an average of $15,000 in wealth to every family in America. That is right here today.

We do not propose to divide it up equally. We do not propose a division of wealth, but we propose to limit poverty that we will allow to be inflicted upon any man's family. We will not say we are going to try to guarantee any equality, or

---

**Ipse dixit:** Something asserted but not proven; Latin, literally "he himself said it."

$15,000 to a family. No; but we do say that one-third of the average is low enough for any one family to hold, that there should be a guarantee of a family wealth of around $5,000; enough for a home, an automobile, a radio, and the ordinary conveniences, and the opportunity to educate their children; a fair share of the income of this land thereafter to that family, so there will be no such thing as merely the select to have those things, and so there will be no such thing as a family living in poverty and distress.

We have to limit fortunes. Our present plan is that we will allow no one man to own more than $50 million. We think that with that limit we will be able to carry out the balance of the program. It may be necessary that we limit it to less than $50 million. It may be necessary, in working out of the plans, that no man's fortune would be more than $10 million or $15 million. But be that as it may, it will still be more than any one man, or any one man and his children and their children, will be able to spend in their lifetimes; and it is not necessary or reasonable to have wealth piled up beyond that point where we cannot prevent poverty among the masses.

Another thing we propose is old-age pension of $30 a month for everyone that is sixty years old. Now, we do not give this pension to a man making $1,000 a year, and we do not give it to him if he has $10,000 in property, but outside of that we do.

We will limit hours of work. There is not any necessity of having over-production. I think all you have got to do, ladies and gentlemen, is just limit the hours of work to such an extent as people will work only so long as it is necessary to produce enough for all of the people to have what they need. Why, ladies and gentlemen, let us say that all of these labor-saving devices reduce hours down to where you do not have to work but four hours a day; that is enough for these people, and then praise be the name of the Lord, if it gets that good. Let it be good and not a curse, and then we will have five hours a day and five days a week, or even less than that, and we might give a man a whole month off during a year, or give him two months; and we might do what other countries have seen fit to do, and what I did in Louisiana, by having schools by which adults could go back and learn the things that have been discovered since they went to school.

We will not have any trouble taking care of the agricultural situation. All you have to do is balance your production with your consumption. You simply have to abandon a particular crop that you have too much of, and all you have to do is store the surplus for the next year, and the government will take it over...

Those are the things we propose to do. "Every Man a King." Every man to eat when there is something to eat; all to wear something when there is something to wear. That makes us all a sovereign....

And we ought to take care of the veterans of the wars in this program. That is a small matter. Suppose it does cost a billion dollars a year—that means that the money will be scattered throughout this country. We ought to pay them a bonus. We can do it....

Now, my friends, we have got to hit the root with the ax. Centralized power in the hands of a few, with centralized credit in the hands of a few, is the trouble.

# George C. Marshall

## *European Unity*

*Delivered when General Marshall was U. S. Secretary of State, June 5, 1947, at Harvard University*

I NEED NOT TELL YOU GENTLEMEN THAT THE WORLD situation is very serious. That must be apparent to all intelligent people. I think one difficulty is that the problem is one of such enormous complexity that the very mass of facts presented to the public by press and radio make it exceedingly difficult for the man in the street to reach a clear appraisement of the situation. Furthermore, the people of this country are distant from the troubled areas of the earth and it is hard for them to comprehend the plight and consequent reactions of the long-suffering peoples, and the effect of those reactions on their governments in connection with our efforts to promote peace in the world.

In considering the requirements for the rehabilitation of Europe, the physical loss of life, the visible destruction of cities, factories, mines and railroads was correctly estimated, but it has become obvious during recent months that this visible destruction was probably less serious that the dislocation of the entire fabric of European economy. For the past ten years conditions have been highly abnormal. The feverish preparation for war and the more feverish maintenance of the war effort engulfed all aspects of national economics. Machinery has fallen into disrepair or is entirely obsolete. Under the arbitrary and destructive Nazi rule, virtually every possible enterprise was geared into the German war machine. Long-standing commercial ties, private institutions, banks, insurance companies and shipping companies disappeared, through loss of capital, absorption through nationalization or by simple destruction. In many countries, confidence in the local currency has been severely shaken. The breakdown of the business structure of Europe during the war was complete. Recovery has been seriously retarded by the fact that two years after the close of hostilities a peace settlement with Germany and Austria has not been agreed upon. But even given a more prompt solution of these difficult problems, the rehabilitation of the economic structure of Europe quite evidently will require a much longer time and greater effort that had been foreseen.

There is a phase of this matter which is both interesting and serious. The farmer has always produced the foodstuffs to exchange with the city dweller for the other necessities of life. This division of labor is the basis of modern civilization. At the present time it is threatened with breakdown. The town and city industries are not producing adequate goods to exchange with the food-producing farmer. Raw materials and fuel are in short supply. Machinery is lacking or worn out. The farmer or the peasant cannot find the goods for sale which he desires to purchase. So the sale of his farm produce for money which he cannot use seems to him an unprofitable transaction. He, therefore, has withdrawn many fields from crop cultivation and is using them for grazing. He feeds more grain to stock and finds for himself and his family an ample supply of food, however short he may be on clothing and the other ordinary gadgets of civilization. Meanwhile people in the cities are short of food and fuel. So the governments are forced to use their foreign money and credits to procure these necessities abroad. This process exhausts funds which are urgently needed for reconstruction. Thus a very serious situation is rapidly developing which bodes no good for the world. The modern system of the division of labor upon which the exchange of products is based is in danger of breaking down.

The truth of the matter is that Europe's requirements for the next three or four years of foreign food and other essential products — principally from America — are so much greater than her present ability to pay that she must have substantial additional help, or face economic, social and political deterioration of a very grave character.

The remedy lies in breaking the vicious circle and restoring the confidence of the European people in the economic future of their own countries and of Europe as a whole. The manufacturer and the farmer throughout wide areas must be able and willing to exchange their products for currencies the continuing value of which is not open to question.

Aside from the demoralizing effect on the world at large and the possibilities of disturbances arising as a result of the desperation of the people concerned, the consequences to the economy of the United States should be apparent to all. It is logical that the United States should do whatever it is able to do to assist in the return of normal economic health in the world, without which there can be no political stability and no assured peace. Our policy is directed not against any country or doctrine but against hunger, poverty, desperation and chaos. Its purpose should be the revival of a working economy in the world so as to permit the emergence of political and social conditions in which free institutions can exist. Such assistance, I am convinced, must not be on a piece-meal basis as various crises develop. Any assistance that this government may render in the future should provide a cure rather than a mere palliative. Any government that is willing to assist in the task of recovery will find full cooperation, I am sure, on the part of the United States Government. Any government which maneuvers to block the recovery of other countries cannot expect help from us. Furthermore, governments, political parties or groups which seek to perpetuate human misery in order to profit therefrom politically or otherwise will encounter the opposition of the United States.

It is already evident that, before the United Sates Government can proceed much further in its efforts to alleviate the situation and help start the European world on its way to recovery, there must be some agreement among the countries of Europe as to the requirements of the situation and the part those countries themselves will take in order to give proper effect to whatever action might be undertaken by this government. It would be neither fitting nor efficacious for this government to undertake to draw up unilaterally a program designed to place Europe on its feet economically. This is the business of the Europeans. The initiative, I think, must come from Europe. The role of this country should consist of friendly aid in the drafting of a European program and of later support of such a program so far as it may be practical for us to do so. The program should be a joint one, agreed to by a number, if not all, European nations.

An essential part of any successful action on the part of the United States is an understanding on the part of the people of America of the character of the problem and the remedies to be applied. Political passion and prejudice should have no part. With foresight, and a willingness on the part of our people to face up to the vast responsibility which history has clearly placed upon our country, the difficulties I have outlined can and will be overcome.

## Franklin Delano Roosevelt

# *The Four Freedoms*

*Delivered to Congress, January 6, 1941*

MR. SPEAKER, MEMBERS OF THE 77TH CONGRESS:

I ADDRESS YOU, THE MEMBERS OF THIS NEW CONGRESS, at a moment unprecedented in the history of the union. I use the word "unprecedented" because at no previous time has American security been as seriously threatened from without as it is today.

Since the permanent formation of our government under the Constitution in 1789, most of the periods of crisis in our history have related to our domestic affairs. And, fortunately, only one of these—the four-year war between the States—ever threatened our national unity. Today, thank God, 130,000,000 Americans in forty-eight States have forgotten points of the compass in our national unity.

It is true that prior to 1914 the United States often has been disturbed by events in other continents. We have even engaged in two wars with European nations and in a number of undeclared wars in the West Indies, in the Mediterranean and in the Pacific, for the maintenance of American rights and for the principles of peaceful commerce. But in no case had a serious threat been raised against our national safety or our continued independence.

What I seek to convey is the historic truth that the United States as a nation has at all times maintained opposition—clear, definite opposition—to any attempt to lock us in behind an ancient Chinese wall while the procession of civilization went past. Today, thinking of our children and of their children, we oppose enforced isolation for ourselves or for any other part of the Americas.

That determination of ours, extending over all these years, was proved, for example, in the early days during the quarter-century of wars following the French Revolution.

While the Napoleonic struggle did threaten interests of the United States because of the French foothold in the West Indies and in Louisiana, and while we engaged in the War of 1812 to vindicate our right to peaceful trade, it is nevertheless clear that neither France nor Great Britain nor any other nation was aiming at domination of the whole world.

And in like fashion, from 1815 to 1914—ninety-nine years—no single war in Europe or in Asia constituted a real threat against our future or against the future of any other American nation.

Except in the Maximilian interlude in Mexico, no foreign power sought to establish itself in this hemisphere. And the strength of the British fleet in the Atlantic has been a friendly strength; it is still a friendly strength.

Even when the World War broke out in 1914 it seemed to contain only small threat of danger to our own American future. But as time went on, as we remember, the American people began to visualize what the downfall of democratic nations might mean to our own democracy.

We need not overemphasize imperfections in the peace of Versailles. We need not harp on failure of the democracies to deal with problems of world reconstruction. We should remember that the peace of 1919 was far less unjust than the kind of pacification which began even before Munich, and which is being carried on under the new order of tyranny that seeks to spread over every continent today.

The American people have unalterably set their faces against that tyranny.

I suppose that every realist knows that the democratic way of life is at this moment being directly assailed in every part of the world—assailed either by arms or by secret spreading of poisonous propaganda by those who seek to destroy unity and promote discord in nations that are still at peace.

During sixteen long months this assault has blotted out the whole pattern of democratic life in an appalling number of independent nations, great and small. And the assailants are still on the march, threatening other nations, great and small.

Therefore, as your President, performing my constitutional duty to "give to the Congress information of the state of the union," I find it unhappily necessary to report that the future and the safety of our country and of our democracy are overwhelmingly involved in events far beyond our borders.

Armed defense of democratic existence is now being gallantly waged in four continents. If that defense fails, all the population and all the resources of Europe and Asia, Africa and Australia will be dominated by conquerors. And let us remember that the total of those populations in those four continents, the total of those populations and their resources greatly exceeds the sum total of the population and the resources of the whole of the Western Hemisphere—yes, many times over.

In times like these it is immature—and, incidentally,

untrue—for anybody to brag that an unprepared America, single-handed and with one hand tied behind its back, can hold off the whole world.

No realistic American can expect from a dictator's peace international generosity, or return of true independence, or world disarmament, or freedom of expression, or freedom of religion—or even good business. Such a peace would bring no security for us or for our neighbors. Those who would give up essential liberty to purchase a little temporary safety deserve neither liberty nor safety.

As a nation we may take pride in the fact that we are soft-hearted, but we cannot afford to be soft-headed. We must always be wary of those who with sounding brass and a tinkling cymbal preach the *ism* of appeasement. We must especially beware of that small group of selfish men who would clip the wings of the American eagle in order to feather their own nests.

I have recently pointed out how quickly the tempo of modern warfare could bring into our very midst the physical attack which we must eventually expect if the dictator nations win this war.

There is much loose talk of our immunity from immediate and direct invasion from across the seas. Obviously, as long as the British Navy retains its power, no such danger exists. Even if there were no British Navy, it is not probable that any enemy would be stupid enough to attack us by landing troops in the United States from across thousands of miles of ocean, until it had acquired strategic bases from which to operate.

But we learn much from the lessons of the past years in Europe—particularly the lesson of Norway, whose essential seaports were captured by treachery and surprise built up over a series of years.

The first phase of the invasion of this hemisphere would not be the landing of regular troops. The necessary strategic points would be occupied by secret agents and by their dupes—and great numbers of them are already here and in Latin America.

As long as the aggressor nations maintain the offensive, they, not we, will choose the time and the place and the method of their attack.

And that is why the future of all the American Republics is today in serious danger. That is why this annual message to the Congress is unique in our history. That is why every member of the executive branch of the government and every member of the Congress face great responsibility—great accountability.

The need of the moment is that our actions and our policy should be devoted primarily—almost exclusively—to meeting this foreign peril. For all our domestic problems are now a part of the great emergency.

Just as our national policy in internal affairs has been based upon a decent respect for the rights and the dignity of all of our fellow men within our gates, so our national policy in foreign affairs has been based on a decent respect for the rights and the dignity of all nations, large and small. And the justice of morality must and will win in the end.

Our national policy is this:

First, by an impressive expression of the public will and without regard to partisanship, we are committed to all-inclusive national defense.

Second, by an impressive expression of the public will and without regard to partisanship, we are committed to full support of all those resolute people everywhere who are resisting aggression and are thereby keeping war away from our hemisphere. By this support we express our determination that the democratic cause shall prevail, and we strengthen the defense and the security of our own nation.

Third, by an impressive expression of the public will and without regard to partisanship, we are committed to the proposition that principles of morality and considerations for our own security will never permit us to acquiesce in a peace dictated by aggressors and sponsored by appeasers. We know that enduring peace cannot be bought at the cost of other people's freedom.

In the recent national election there was no substantial difference between the two great parties in respect to that national policy. No issue was fought out on the line before the American electorate. And today it is abundantly evident that American citizens everywhere are demanding and supporting speedy and complete action in recognition of obvious danger.

Therefore, the immediate need is a swift and driving increase in our armament production. Leaders of industry and labor have responded to our summons. Goals of speed have been set. In some cases these goals are being reached ahead of time. In some cases we are on schedule; in other cases there are slight but not serious delays. And in some cases—and, I am sorry to say, very important cases—we are all concerned by the slowness of the accomplishment of our plans.

The Army and Navy, however, have made substantial progress during the past year. Actual experience is improving and speeding up our methods of production with every passing day. And today's best is not good enough for tomorrow.

I am not satisfied with the progress thus far made. The men in charge of the program represent the best in training, in ability and in patriotism. They are not satisfied with the progress thus far made. None of us will be satisfied until the job is done.

No matter whether the original goal was set too high or too low, our objective is quicker and better results.

To give you two illustrations:

We are behind schedule in turning out finished airplanes. We are working day and night to solve the innumerable problems and to catch up.

We are ahead of schedule in building warships, but we are working to get even further ahead of that schedule.

To change a whole nation from a basis of peacetime production of implements of peace to a basis of wartime production of implements of war is no small task. The greatest difficulty comes at the beginning of the program, when new tools, new plant facilities, new assembly lines, new shipways must first be constructed before the actual material begins to flow steadily and speedily from them.

The Congress, of course, must rightly keep itself informed at all times of the progress of the program. However, there is certain information, as the Congress itself will readily recognize, which, in the interests of our own security and those of the nations that we are supporting, must of needs be kept in confidence.

New circumstances are constantly begetting new needs for our safety. I shall ask this Congress for greatly increased new appropriations and authorizations to carry on what we have begun.

I also ask this Congress for authority and for funds sufficient to manufacture additional munitions and war supplies of many kinds, to be turned over to those nations which are now in actual war with aggressor nations. Our most useful and immediate role is to act as an arsenal for them as well as for ourselves. They do not need manpower, but they do need billions of dollars' worth of the weapons of defense.

The time is near when they will not be able to pay for them all in ready cash. We cannot, and we will not, tell them that they must surrender merely because of present inability to pay for the weapons which we know they must have.

I do not recommend that we make them a loan of dollars with which to pay for these weapons—a loan to be repaid in dollars. I recommend that we make it possible for those nations to continue to obtain war materials in the United States, fitting their orders into our own program. And nearly all of their material would, if the time ever came, be useful in our own defense.

Taking counsel of expert military and naval authorities, considering what is best for our own security, we are free to decide how much should be kept here and how much should be sent abroad to our friends who, by their determined and heroic resistance, are giving us time in which to make ready our own defense.

For what we send abroad we shall be repaid, repaid within a reasonable time following the close of hostilities, repaid in similar materials, or at our option in other goods of many kinds which they can produce and which we need.

Let us say to the democracies: "We Americans are vitally concerned in your defense of freedom. We are putting forth our energies, our resources and our organizing powers to give you the strength to regain and maintain a free world. We shall send you, in ever-increasing numbers, ships, planes, tanks, guns. That is our purpose and our pledge."

In fulfillment of this purpose we will not be intimidated by the threats of dictators that they will regard as a breach of international law or as an act of war our aid to the democracies which dare to resist their aggression. Such aid is not an act of war, even if a dictator should unilaterally proclaim it so to be.

And when the dictators—if the dictators—are ready to make war upon us, they will not wait for an act of war on our part.

They did not wait for Norway or Belgium or the Netherlands to commit an act of war. Their only interest is in a new one-way international law which lacks mutuality in its observance and therefore becomes an instrument of oppression. The happiness of future generations of Americans may well depend on how effective and how immediate we can make our aid felt. No one can tell the exact character of the emergency situations that we may be called upon to meet. The nation's hands must not be tied when the nation's life is in danger.

Yes, and we must prepare, all of us prepare, to make the sacrifices that the emergency—almost as serious as war itself—demands. Whatever stands in the way of speed and efficiency in defense, in defense preparations at any time, must give way to the national need.

A free nation has the right to expect full cooperation from all groups. A free nation has the right to look to the leaders of business, of labor and of agriculture to take the lead in stimulating effort, not among other groups but within their own groups.

The best way of dealing with the few slackers or troublemakers in our midst is, first, to shame them by patriotic example, and if that fails, to use the sovereignty of government to save government.

As men do not live by bread alone, they do not fight by armaments alone. Those who man our defenses and those behind them who build our defenses must have the stamina and the courage which come from unshakable belief in the manner of life which they are defending. The mighty action that we are calling for cannot be based on a disregard of all the things worth fighting for.

The nation takes great satisfaction and much strength from the things which have been done to make its people conscious of their individual stake in the preservation of democratic life in America. Those things have toughened the fiber of our people, have renewed their faith and strengthened their devotion to the institutions we make ready to protect.

Certainly this is no time for any of us to stop thinking about the social and economic problems which are the root cause of the social revolution which is today a supreme factor in the world. For there is nothing mysterious about the foundations of a healthy and strong democracy.

The basic things expected by our people of their political and economic systems are simple. They are:

Equality of opportunity for youth and for others. Jobs for those who can work. Security for those who need it.

The ending of special privilege for the few.

The preservation of civil liberties for all.

The enjoyment of the fruits of scientific progress in a wider and constantly rising standard of living.

These are the simple, the basic things that must never be lost sight of in the turmoil and unbelievable complexity of our modern world. The inner and abiding strength of our economic and political systems is dependent upon the degree to which they fulfill these expectations.

Many subjects connected with our social economy call for immediate improvement. As examples:

We should bring more citizens under the coverage of old-age pensions and unemployment insurance.

We should widen the opportunities for adequate medical care.

We should plan a better system by which persons deserving or needing gainful employment may obtain it.

I have called for personal sacrifice, and I am assured of the willingness of almost all Americans to respond to that call. A part of the sacrifice means the payment of more money in taxes. In my budget message I will recommend that a greater portion of this great defense program be paid for from taxation than we are paying for today. No person should try, or be allowed, to get rich out of the program, and the principle of tax payments in accordance with ability to pay should be constantly before our eyes to guide our legislation.

If the Congress maintains these principles, the voters, putting patriotism ahead of pocketbooks, will give you their applause.

In the future days which we seek to make secure, we look forward to a world founded upon four essential human freedoms.

The first is freedom of speech and expression—everywhere in the world.

The second is freedom of every person to worship God in his own way—everywhere in the world.

The third is freedom from want, which, translated into world terms, means economic understandings which will secure to every nation a healthy peacetime life for its inhabitants—everywhere in the world.

The fourth is freedom from fear, which, translated into world terms, means a worldwide reduction of armaments to such a point and in such a thorough fashion that no nation will be in a position to commit an act of physical aggression against any neighbor—anywhere in the world.

That is no vision of a distant millennium. It is a definite basis for a kind of world attainable in our own time and generation. That kind of world is the very antithesis of the so-called "new order" of tyranny which the dictators seek to create with the crash of a bomb.

To that new order we oppose the greater conception—the moral order. A good society is able to face schemes of world domination and foreign revolutions alike without fear.

Since the beginning of our American history we have been engaged in change, in a perpetual, peaceful revolution, a revolution which goes on steadily, quietly, adjusting itself to changing conditions without the concentration camp or the quicklime in the ditch. The world order which we seek is the cooperation of free countries, working together in a friendly, civilized society.

This nation has placed its destiny in the hands, heads and hearts of its millions of free men and women, and its faith in freedom under the guidance of God. Freedom means the supremacy of human rights everywhere. Our support goes to those who struggle to gain those rights and keep them. Our strength is our unity of purpose.

To that high concept there can be no end save victory.

## Woodrow Wilson

# *The Fourteen Points*

*Delivered before a joint session of Congress on January 8, 1918.*

GENTLEMEN OF THE CONGRESS:

ONCE MORE, AS REPEATEDLY BEFORE, THE spokesmen of the Central Empires have indicated their desire to discuss the objects of the war and the possible basis of a general peace. Parleys have been in progress at Brest-Litovsk between Russian representatives and representatives of the Central Powers to which the attention of all the belligerents has been invited for the purpose of ascertaining whether it may be possible to extend these parleys into a general conference with regard to terms of peace and settlement.

The Russian representatives presented not only a perfectly definite statement of the principles upon which they would be willing to conclude peace, but also an equally definite program of the concrete application of those principles. The representatives of the Central Powers, on their part, presented an outline of settlement which, if much less definite, seemed susceptible of liberal interpretation until their specific program of practical terms was added.

That program proposed no concessions at all, either to

the sovereignty of Russia or to the preferences of the population with whose fortunes it dealt, but meant, in a word, that the Central Empires were to keep every foot of territory their armed forces had occupied—every province, every city, every point of vantage—as a permanent addition to their territories and their power. It is a reasonable conjecture that the general principles of settlement which they at first suggested originated with the more liberal statesmen of Germany and Austria, the men who have begun to feel the force of their own peoples, thought and purpose, while the concrete terms of actual settlement came from the military leaders who have no thought but to keep what they have got. The negotiations have been broken off. The Russian representatives were sincere and in earnest. They cannot entertain such proposals of conquest and domination.

The whole incident is full of significance. It is also full of perplexity. With whom are the Russian representatives dealing? For whom are the representatives of the Central Empires speaking? Are they speaking for the majorities of their respective Parliaments or for the minority parties, that military and imperialistic minority which has so far dominated their whole policy and controlled the affairs of Turkey and of the Balkan States, which have felt obliged to become their associates in this war? The Russian representatives have insisted, very justly, very wisely, and in the true spirit of modern democracy, that the conferences they have been holding with the Teutonic and Turkish statesmen should be held within open, not closed, doors, and all the world has been audience, as was desired.

To whom have we been listening, then? To those who speak the spirit and intention of the resolutions of the German Reichstag of the 9th of July last, the spirit and intention of the liberal leaders and parties of Germany, or to those who resist and defy that spirit and intention and insist upon conquest and subjugation? Or are we listening in fact, to both, unreconciled and in open and hopeless contradiction? These are very serious and pregnant questions. Upon the answer to them depends the peace of the world.

But whatever the results of the parleys at Brest-Litovsk, whatever the confusions of counsel and of purpose in the utterances of the spokesmen of the Central Empires, they have again attempted to acquaint the world with their objects in the war and have again challenged their adversaries to say what their objects are and what sort of settlement they would deem just and satisfactory. There is no good reason why that challenge should not be responded to, and responded to with the utmost candor. We did not wait for it. Not once, but again and again we have laid our whole thought and purpose before the world, not in general terms only, but each time with sufficient definition to make it clear what sort of definite terms of settlement must necessarily spring out of them.

Within the last week Mr. Lloyd George has spoken with admirable candor and in admirable spirit for the people and Government of Great Britain. There is no confusion of counsel among the adversaries of the Central Powers, no uncertainty of principle, no vagueness of detail. The only secrecy of counsel, the only lack of fearless frankness, the only failure to make definite statement of the objects of the war, lies with Germany and her allies.

The issues of life and death hang upon these definitions. No statesman who has the least conception of his responsibility ought for a moment to permit himself to continue this tragical and appalling outpouring of blood and treasure unless he is sure beyond a peradventure that the objects of the vital sacrifice are part and parcel of the very life of society and that the people for whom he speaks think them right and imperative as he does.

There is, moreover, a voice calling for these definitions of principle and of purpose which is, it seems to me, more thrilling and more compelling than any of the many moving voices with which the troubled air of the world is filled. It is the voice of the Russian people. They are prostrate and all but helpless, it would seem, before the grim power of Germany, which has hitherto known no relenting and no pity. Their power apparently is shattered. And yet their soul is not subservient. They will not yield either in principle or in action. Their conception of what is right, of what is humane and honorable for them to accept, has been stated with a frankness, a largeness of view, a generosity of spirit, and a universal human sympathy which must challenge the admiration of every friend of mankind; and they have refused to compound their ideals or desert others that they themselves may be safe.

They call to us to say what it is that we desire, in what, if in anything, our purpose and our spirit differ from theirs; and I believe that the people of the United States would wish me to respond with utter simplicity and frankness. Whether their present leaders believe it or not, it is our heartfelt desire and hope that some way may be opened whereby we may be privileged to assist the people of Russia to attain their utmost hope of liberty and ordered peace.

It will be our wish and purpose that the processes of peace, when they are begun, shall be absolutely open, and that they shall involve and permit henceforth no secret understandings of any kind. The day of conquest and aggrandizement is gone by; so is also the day of secret covenants entered into in the interest of particular governments and likely at some unlooked-for moment to upset the peace of the world. It is this happy fact, now clear to the view of every public man whose thoughts do not still linger in an age that is dead and gone, which makes it possible for every nation whose purposes are consistent with justice and the peace of the world to avow now or at any other time the objects it has in view.

We entered this war because violations of right had occurred which touched us to the quick and made the life of our own people impossible unless they were corrected and the world secured once for all against their recurrence. What we demand in this war, therefore, is nothing peculiar to ourselves. It is that the world be made fit and safe to live in; and particularly that it be made safe for every peace-loving nation which, like our own, wishes to live its own life, determine its own institutions, be assured of justice and fair dealings by the other peoples of the world, as against force and selfish aggression. All of the peoples of the world are in effect partners in this interest, and for our own part we see very clearly that unless justice be done to others it will not be done to us.

The program of the world's peace, therefore, is our program, and that program, the only possible program, as we see it, is this:

*I.* Open covenants of peace must be arrived at, after which there will surely be no private international action or rulings of any kind, but diplomacy shall proceed always frankly and in the public view.

*II.* Absolute freedom of navigation upon the seas, outside territorial waters, alike in peace and in war, except as the seas may be closed in whole or in part by international action for the enforcement of international covenants.

*III.* The removal, so far as possible, of all economic barriers and the establishment of an equality of trade conditions among all the nations consenting to the peace and associating themselves for its maintenance.

*IV.* Adequate guaranties given and taken that national

armaments will reduce to the lowest point consistent with domestic safety.

*V.* Free, open-minded, and absolutely impartial adjustment of all colonial claims, based upon a strict observance of the principle that in determining all such questions of sovereignty, the interests of the population concerned must have equal weight with the equitable claims of the government whose title is to be determined.

*VI.* The evacuation of all Russian territory and such a settlement of all questions affecting Russia as will secure the best and freest cooperation of the other nations of the world in obtaining for her an unhampered and unembarrassed opportunity for the independent determination of her own political development and national policy, and assure her of a sincere welcome into the society of free nations under institutions of her own choosing; and, more than a welcome, assistance also of every kind that she may need and may herself desire. The treatment accorded Russia by her sister nations in the months to come will be the acid test of their good-will, of their comprehension of her needs as distinguished from their own interests, and of their intelligent and unselfish sympathy.

*VII.* Belgium, the whole world will agree, must be evacuated and restored, without any attempt to limit the sovereignty which she enjoys in common with all other free nations. No other single act will serve as this will serve to restore confidence among the nations in the laws which they have themselves set and determined for the government of their relations with one another. Without this healing act the whole structure and validity of international law is forever impaired.

*VIII.* All French territory should be freed and the invaded portions restored, and the wrong done to France by Prussia in 1871 in the matter of Alsace-Lorraine, which has unsettled the peace of the world for nearly fifty years, should be righted, in order that peace may once more be made secure in the interest of all.

*IX.* A readjustment of the frontiers of Italy should be effected along clearly recognizable lines of nationality.

*X.* The peoples of Austria-Hungary, whose place among the nations we wish to see safeguarded and assured, should be accorded the freest opportunity of autonomous development.

*XI.* Romania, Serbia, and Montenegro should be evacuated; occupied territories restored; Serbia accorded free and secure access to the sea; and the relations of the several Balkan States to one another determined by friendly counsel along historically established lines of allegiance and nationality; and international guaranties of the political and economic independence and territorial integrity of the several Balkan States should be entered into.

*XII.* The Turkish portions of the present Ottoman Empire should be assured a secure sovereignty, but the other nationalities which are now under Turkish rule should be assured an undoubted security of life and an absolutely unmolested opportunity of autonomous development, and the Dardanelles should be permanently opened as a free passage to the ships and commerce of all nations under international guaranties.

*XIII.* An independent Polish state should be erected which should include the territories inhabited by indisputably Polish populations, which should be assured a free and secure access to the sea, and whose political and economic independence and territorial integrity should be guaranteed by international covenant.

*XIV.* A general association of nations must be formed

under specific covenants for the purpose of affording mutual guaranties of political independence and territorial integrity to great and small states alike.

In regard to these essential rectifications of wrong and assertions of right, we feel ourselves to be intimate partners of all the governments and peoples associated together against the imperialists. We cannot be separated in interest or divided in purpose. We stand together until the end.

For such arrangements and covenants we are willing to fight and to continue to fight until they are achieved; but only because we wish the right to prevail and desire a just and stable peace, such as can be secured only by removing the chief provocations to war, which this program does remove. We have no jealousy of German greatness, and there is nothing in this program that impairs it. We grudge her no achievement or distinction of learning or of pacific enterprise such as have made her record very bright and very enviable. We do not wish to injure her or to block in any way her legitimate influence or power. We do not wish to fight her either with arms or with hostile arrangements of trade, if she is willing to associate herself with us and the other peace-loving nations of the world in covenants of justice and law and fair dealing. We wish her only to accept a place of equality among the peoples of the world—the new world in which we now live—instead of a place of mastery.

Neither do we presume to suggest to her any alteration or modification of her institutions. But it is necessary, we must frankly say, and necessary as a preliminary to any intelligent dealings with her on our part, that we should know whom her spokesmen speak for when they speak to us, whether for the Reichstag majority or for the military party and the men whose creed is imperial domination.

We have spoken now, surely, in terms too concrete to

admit of any further doubt or question. An evident principle runs through the whole program I have outlined. It is the principle of justice to all peoples and nationalities, and their right to live on equal terms of liberty and safety with one another, whether they be strong or weak. Unless this principle be made its foundation, no part of the structure of international justice can stand. The people of the United States could act upon no other principle, and to the vindication of this principle they are ready to devote their lives, their honor, and everything that they possess. The moral climax of this, the culminating and final war for human liberty, has come, and they are ready to put their own strength, their own highest purpose, their own integrity and devotion to the test.

# AUTOBIOGRAPHY

## Benjamin Franklin

FROM
# *The Autobiography*

MY ELDER BROTHERS WERE ALL PUT APPRENTICES to different trades. I was put to the grammar school at eight years of age, my Father intending to devote me as the tithe of his sons to the service of the church. My early readiness in learning to read (which must have been very early, as I do not remember when I could not read) and the opinion of all his friends that I should certainly make a good scholar, encouraged him in this purpose of his. My Uncle Benjamin too approved of it, and proposed to give me all his shorthand volumes of sermons, I suppose as a stock to set up with, if I would learn his **character.** I continued however at the grammar school not quite one year, though in that time I had risen gradually from the middle of the class of that year to be the head of it, and further was removed into the next class above it, in order to go with that into the third at the end of the year. But my Father in the meantime, from a view of the expense of a college education which, having so large a family, he could not well afford, and

---

**Character:** His system of shorthand writing.

the mean living many so educated were afterwards able to obtain—reasons that he gave to his friends in my hearing—altered his first intention, took me from the grammar school, and sent me to a school for writing and arithmetic kept by a then famous man, Mr George Brownell, very successful in his profession generally, and that by mild encouraging methods. Under him I acquired fair writing pretty soon, but I failed in the arithmetic, and made no progress in it.

At ten years old, I was taken home to assist my Father in his business, which was that of a tallow chandler and soap-boiler, a business he was not bred to, but had assumed on his arrival in New England and on finding his dying trade would not maintain his family, being in little request. Accordingly, I was employed in cutting wick for the candles, filling the dipping mold, and the molds for cast candles, attending the shop, going of errands, etc. I disliked the trade and had a strong inclination for the sea, but my Father declared against it; however, living near the water, I was much in and about it, learnt early to swim well and to manage boats, and when in a boat or canoe with other boys I was commonly allowed to govern, especially in any case of difficulty; and upon other occasions I was generally a leader among the boys, and sometimes led them into scrapes, of which I will mention one instance, as it shows an early projecting public spirit, though not then justly conducted. There was a salt marsh that bounded part of the mill pond, on the edge of which at high-water, we used to stand to fish for minnows. By much trampling, we had made it a mere quagmire. My proposal was to build a wharf there fit for us to stand upon, and I showed my comrades a large heap of stones which were intended for a new house near the marsh, and which would very well suit our purpose. Accordingly, in the evening when the workmen were gone, I assembled a number of my playfellows, and working with them diligently like so many **emmets**, sometimes two or three to a stone, we brought them all away and built our little wharf. The next morning the workmen were surprised at missing the stones, which were found in our wharf; enquiry was made after the removers; we were discovered and complained of; several of us were corrected by our Fathers, and though I pleaded the usefulness of the work, mine convinced me that nothing was useful which was not honest.

I think you may like to know something of his person and character. He had an excellent constitution of body, was of middle stature, but well set and very strong. He was ingenious, could draw prettily, was skilled a little in music and had a clear pleasing voice, so that when he played psalm tunes on his violin and sung **withal** as he sometimes did in an evening after the business of the day was over, it was extremely agreeable to hear. He had a mechanical genius too, and on occasion was very handy in the use of other tradesmen's tools. But his great excellence lay in a sound understanding and solid judgment in prudential matters, both in private and public affairs. In the latter indeed he was never employed, the numerous family he had to educate and the straitness of his circumstances keeping him close to his trade, but I remember well his being frequently visited by leading people, who consulted him for his opinion on affairs of the town or of the church he belonged to and showed a good deal of respect for his judgment and advice. He was also much consulted by private persons about their affairs when any difficulty occurred, and frequently chosen an arbitrator between contending parties.

---

**Emmets:** Ants.

**Withal:** Besides.

At his table he liked to have as often as he could, some sensible friend or neighbor to converse with, and always took care to start some ingenious or useful topic for discourse, which might tend to improve the minds of his children. By this means he turned our attention to what was good, just, and prudent in the conduct of life; and little or no notice was ever taken of what related to the victuals on the table, whether it was well or ill dressed, in or out of season, of good or bad flavor, preferable or inferior to this or that other thing of the kind; so that I was brought up in such a perfect inattention to those matters as to be quite indifferent what kind of food was set before me; and so unobservant of it, that to this day, if I am asked I can scarce tell, a few hours after dinner, what I dined upon. This has been a convenience to me in travelling, where my companions have been sometimes very unhappy for want of a suitable gratification of their more delicate because better instructed tastes and appetites.

My Mother had likewise an excellent constitution. She suckled all her 10 children. I never knew either my Father or Mother to have any sickness but that of which they died, he at 89 and she at 85 years of age. They lie buried together at Boston, where I some years since placed a marble stone over their grave with this inscription:

Josiah Franklin<br>
And Abiah his wife<br>
Lie here interred.<br>
They lived lovingly together in wedlock<br>
Fifty-five Years.<br>
Without an estate or any gainful employment,<br>
By constant labor and industry,<br>
With God's blessing,<br>
They maintained a large family

Comfortably;
And brought up thirteen children,
And seven grandchildren
Reputably.
From this instance, reader,
Be encouraged to diligence in thy calling,
And distrust not Providence.
He was a pious and prudent man,
She a discreet and virtuous woman.
Their youngest son,
In filial regard to their memory,
Places this stone.
J. F. born 1655—died 1744—**ætas** 89
A. F. born 1667—died 1752—85

By my rambling digressions I perceive my self to be grown old. I used to write more methodically. But one does not dress for private company as for a public ball. 'Tis perhaps only negligence.

To return. I continued thus employed in my Father's business for two years, that is till I was 12 years old. My brother John, who was bred to that business, having left my Father, married and set up for himself at Rhode Island; there was all appearance that I was destined to supply his place and be a tallow chandler. But my dislike to the trade continuing, my Father was under apprehensions that if he did not find one for me more agreeable, I should break away and get to sea, as his son Josiah had done to his great vexation. He therefore sometimes took me to walk with him, and see joiners, bricklayers, turners, braziers, etc., at their work, that he might observe my inclination, and endeavor to fix it on some

---

**Aetas:** From Latin, meaning for the period of time.

trade or other on land. It has ever since been a pleasure to me to see good workmen handle their tools; and it has been useful to me, having learnt so much by it, as to be able to do little jobs myself in my house, when a workman could not readily be got; and to construct little machines for my experiments while the intention of making the experiment was fresh and warm in my mind. My Father at last fixed upon the cutler's trade, and my Uncle Benjamin's son Samuel who was bred to that business in London being about that time established in Boston, I was sent to be with him some time on liking. But his expectations of a fee with me displeasing my Father, I was taken home again.

From a child I was fond of reading, and all the little money that came into my hands was ever laid out in books. Pleased with the ***Pilgrim's Progress***, my first collection was of John Bunyan's works, in separate little volumes. I afterwards sold them to enable me to buy Richard Burton's historical collections. They were small chapmen's books and cheap, 40 or 50 in all. My Father's little library consisted chiefly of books in polemic divinity, most of which I read, and have since often regretted, that at a time when I had such a thirst for knowledge, more proper books had not fallen in my way, since it was now resolved I should not be a clergyman. **Plutarch's *Lives*** there was, in which I read abundantly, and I still think that time spent to great advantage. There was

---

***Pilgrim's Progress***: A popular allegory—a story, like a fable, that uses symbolic figures to represent deeper moral meanings—of Christian life by John Bunyan (1628-88), in which the main character seeks truth and salvation in a hostile world.

**Plutarch's *Lives:*** The Greek biographer Plutarch (c. 50-125) recounted the lives of the great heroes and kings of the classical age, careful to include events that revealed each's moral character.

also a book of Defoe's called an essay on projects and another of **Dr. Mather's** called *Essays To Do Good*, which perhaps gave me a turn of thinking that had an influence on some of the principal future events of my life.

This bookish inclination at length determined my Father to make me a printer, though he had already one son (James) of that profession. In 1717 my brother James returned from England with a press and letters to set up his business in Boston. I liked it much better than that of my Father, but still had a hankering for the sea. To prevent the apprehended effect of such an inclination, my Father was impatient to have me bound to my brother. I stood out some time, but at last was persuaded and signed the **indentures**, when I was yet but 12 years old. I was to serve as an apprentice till I was 21 years of age, only I was to be allowed journeyman's wages during the last year. In a little time I made great proficiency in the business and became a useful hand to my brother.

I now had access to better books. An acquaintance with the apprentices of booksellers enabled me sometimes to borrow a small one, which I was careful to return soon and clean. Often I sat up in my room reading the greatest part of the night, when the book was borrowed in the evening and to be returned early in the morning lest it should be missed

---

**Dr. Mather:** Cotton Mather (1663-1728) was a New England Puritan minis ter famous for his stern sermons and his part in the Salem witchcraft trials of 1692.

**Indentures:** A contract in which an apprentice agreed to learn a trade, usually over a period of seven years, in exchange for room and board with his master. At the end of his apprenticeship he was considered a journeyman and would receive wages. Journeymen could ply their skills independently, become masters of their trade and eventually accept apprentices themselves.

or wanted. And after some time an ingenious tradesman, Mr. Matthew Adams, who had a pretty collection of books, and who frequented our printing house, took notice of me, invited me to his library, and very kindly lent me such books as I chose to read. I now took a fancy to poetry, and made some little pieces. My brother, thinking it might turn to account, encouraged me, and put me on composing two occasional ballads. One was called the *Light House Tragedy*, and contained an account of the drowning of Capt. Worthilake with his two daughters. The other was a sailor song on the taking of **Teach.** They were wretched stuff, in the **Grub Street** ballad style, and when they were printed he sent me about the town to sell them. The first sold wonderfully, the event being recent, having made a great noise. This flattered my vanity. But my Father discouraged me, by ridiculing my performances and telling me verse-makers were generally beggars; so I escaped being a poet, most probably a very bad one. But as prose writing has been of great use to me in the course of my life, and was a principal means of my advancement, I shall tell you how in such a situation I acquired what little ability I have in that way.

There was another bookish lad in the town, John Collins by name, with whom I was intimately acquainted. We sometimes disputed, and very fond we were of argument, and very desirous of confuting one another. Which disputatious turn, by the way, is apt to become a very bad habit, making people

---

**Teach:** Edward Teach, known as Blackbeard the Pirate, looted shipping and settlements along the American coast from hideouts in the Bahamas and the Carolinas, becoming notorious for his cruelty, until he was killed in 1718 by the British navy.

**Grub Street:** In 18th century London, an address associated with poor hack writers and journalists of minor talent.

often extremely disagreeable in company, by the contradiction that is necessary to bring it into practice, and thence, besides souring and spoiling the conversation, is productive of disgusts and perhaps enmities where you may have occasion for friendship. I had caught it by reading my Father's books of dispute about religion. Persons of good sense, I have since observed, seldom fall into it, except lawyers, university men, and men of all sorts that have been bred at **Edinborough**. A question was once somehow or other started between Collins and me, of the propriety of educating the female sex in learning, and their abilities for study. He was of the opinion that it was improper; and that they were naturally unequal to it. I took the contrary side, perhaps a little for dispute sake. He was naturally more eloquent, had a ready plenty of words, and sometimes as I thought bore me down more by his fluency than by the strength of his reasons. As we parted without settling the point, and were not to see one another again for some time, I sat down to put my arguments in writing, which I copied fair and sent to him. He answered and I replied. Three or four letters of a side had passed, when my Father happened to find my papers and read them. Without entering into the discussion, he took occasion to talk to me about the manner of my writing, observed that though I had the advantage of my antagonist in correct spelling and pointing (which I owed to the printing house), I fell far short in elegance of expression, in method and in perspicuity, of which he convinced me by several instances. I saw the justice of his remarks, and thence grew more attentive to the manner in writing, and determined to endeavor at improvement.

---

**Edinborough:** The capital of Scotland, famous for its university, which was one of the foremost of Franklin's day.

About this time I met with an odd volume of the ***Spectator***. I had never before seen any of them. I bought it, read it over and over, and was much delighted with it. I thought the writing excellent and wished if possible to imitate it. With that view, I took some of the papers, and making short hints of the sentiment in each sentence, laid them by a few days, and then without looking at the book, tried to complete the papers again, by expressing each hinted sentiment at length and as fully as it had been expressed before, in any suitable words that should come to hand.

Then I compared my *Spectator* with the original, discovered some of my faults and corrected them. But I found I wanted a stock of words, or a readiness in recollecting and using them, which I thought I should have acquired before that time, if I had gone on making verses, since the continual occasion for words of the same import but of different length, to suit the measure, or of different sound for the rhyme, would have laid me under a constant necessity of searching for variety, and also have tended to fix that variety in my mind, and make me a master of it. Therefore I took some of the tales and turned them into verse, and after a time, when I had pretty well forgotten the prose, turned them back again. I also sometimes jumbled my collections of hints into confusion, and after some weeks, endeavored to reduce them into the best order, before I began to form the full sentences, and complete the paper. This was to teach me method in the arrangement of thoughts. By comparing my work afterwards with the original, I discovered many faults and amended them; but I sometimes had the pleasure of fancying that in certain particulars of small import, I had been lucky

---

***Spectator:*** An English periodical appearing from 1711 to 1714 that included character sketches and comments on current cultural affairs.

enough to improve the method or the language and this encouraged me to think I might possibly in time come to be a tolerable English writer, of which I was extremely ambitious.

My time for these exercises and for reading was at night after work, or before work began in the morning; or on Sundays, when I contrived to be in the printing house alone, evading as much as I could the common attendance on public worship, which my Father used to exact of me when I was under his care, and which indeed I still thought a duty; though I could not, as it seemed to me, afford the time to practice it.

When about 16 years of age, I happened to meet with a book written by one Tryon, recommending a vegetable diet. I determined to go into it. My brother being yet unmarried, did not keep house, but boarded himself and his apprentices in another family. My refusing to eat flesh occasioned an inconveniency, and I was frequently chided for my singularity. I made myself acquainted with Tryon's manner of preparing some of his dishes, such as boiling potatoes, or rice, making hasty pudding, and a few others, and then proposed to my brother, that if he would give me weekly half the money he paid for my board, I would board myself. He instantly agreed to it, and I presently found that I could save half what he paid me. This was an additional fund for buying books: but I had another advantage in it. My brother and the rest going from the printing house to their meals, I remained there alone, and dispatching presently my light repast, (which often was no more than a biscuit or a slice of bread, a handful of raisins or a tart from the pastry cook's, and a glass of water) had the rest of the time till their return for study, in which I made the greater progress from that greater clearness of head and quicker apprehension which usually attend temperance in eating and drinking. And now it was that being on some occasion made ashamed of my ignorance in figures, which I had twice failed in learning when at school, I took Cocker's book of arithmetic, and went through the whole by myself with great ease. I also read Seller's and Sturmy's books of navigation, and became acquainted with the little geometry they contain, but never proceeded far in that science. And I read about this time **Locke's** *On Human Understanding*, and the *Art of Thinking* by Mr. Du Port Royal.

While I was intent on improving my language, I met with an English grammar (I think it was Greenwood's) at the end of which there were two little sketches of the arts of rhetoric and logic, the latter finishing with a specimen of a dispute in the **Socratic method**. And soon after I procured **Xenophon's** memorable things of Socrates, wherein there are many instances of the same method. I was charmed with it, adopted it, dropped my abrupt contradiction and positive argumentation, and put on the humble enquirer and doubter. And being then, from reading **Shaftsbury** and Collins, become a real doubter in many points of our religious doctrine, I found this method safest for myself and very embar-

---

**Locke:** The great English philosopher John Locke (1632-1704) believed that human nature is essentially happy and that humans have natural rights upon which government legitimacy rests.

**Socratic method:** A method of teaching named for the Greek philosopher Socrates that proceeds by question and answer.

**Xenophon:** Xenophon (430 B.C. - 355 B.C.) was a young disciple of Socrates who later wrote accounts of him that show him in a practical light.

**Shaftsbury:** Anthony Ashley Cooper (1671-1713), third Earl of Shaftsbury, English moral philosopher tutored by John Locke. Shaftsbury argued that mankind has an altruistic instinct that counteracts selfishness and promotes a balance between social and individual needs.

rassing to those against whom I used it. Therefore I took a delight in it, practiced it continually and grew very artful and expert in drawing people even of superior knowledge into concessions the consequences of which they did not foresee, entangling them in difficulties out of which they could not extricate themselves, and so obtaining victories that neither myself nor my cause always deserved. I continued this method some few years, but gradually left it, retaining only the habit of expressing myself in terms of modest diffidence, never using, when I advance any thing that may possibly be disputed, the words 'certainly,' 'undoubtedly,' or any others that give the air of positiveness to an opinion; but rather say, I conceive, or I apprehend a thing to be so or so, it appears to me, or I think it so or so for such and such reasons, or I imagine it to be so, or it is so if I am not mistaken. This habit I believe has been of great advantage to me, when I have had occasion to inculcate my opinions and persuade men into measures that I have been from time to time engaged in promoting. And as the chief ends of conversation are to inform, or to be informed, to please or to persuade, I wish well-meaning sensible men would not lessen their power of doing good by a positive assuming manner that seldom fails to disgust, tends to create opposition, and to defeat every one of those purposes for which speech was given us, to wit, giving or receiving information, or pleasure: for if you would inform, a positive dogmatical manner in advancing your sentiments may provoke contradiction and prevent a candid attention. If you wish information and improvement from the knowledge of others and yet at the same time express yourself as firmly fixed in your present opinions, modest sensible men, who do not love disputation, will probably leave you undisturbed in the possession of your error; and by such a manner you can seldom hope to recommend yourself in pleasing your hearers, or to persuade those whose concurrence you desire.— **Pope** says, judiciously,

> Men should be taught as if you taught them not,
> And things unknown proposed as things forgot,—

further recommending, it to us,

> To speak though sure, with seeming diffidence.

And he might have coupled with this line that which he has coupled with another, I think less properly,

> For want of modesty is want of sense.

If you ask why less properly, I must repeat the lines;

> Immodest words admit of no defense;
> For want of modesty is want of sense.

Now is not want of sense (where a man is so unfortunate as to want it) some apology for his want of modesty? And would not the lines stand more justly thus?

> Immodest words admit but this defense,
> That want of modesty is want of sense.

This however I should submit to better judgments.

My brother had, in 1720 or '21, begun to print a newspaper. It was the second that appeared in America, and was called the *New England Courant*. The only one before it, was

---

**Pope:** Alexander Pope (1688-1744). English poet famous for rhyming couplets.

the *Boston News Letter*. I remember his being dissuaded by some of his friends from the undertaking, as not likely to succeed, one newspaper being in their judgment enough for America. At this time, 1771, there are not less than five and twenty. He went on, however, with the undertaking, and after having worked in composing the types and printing off the sheets, I was employed to carry the papers through the streets to the customers. He had some ingenious men among his friends who amused themselves by writing little pieces for this paper, which gained it credit, and made it more in demand; and these gentlemen often visited us.

Hearing their conversations, and their accounts of the approbation their papers were received with, I was excited to try my hand among them. But being still a boy, and suspecting that my brother would object to printing any thing of mine in his paper if he knew it to be mine, I contrived to disguise my hand, and writing an anonymous paper I put it in at night under the door of the printing house. It was found in the morning and communicated to his writing friends when they called in as usual. They read it, commented on it in my hearing, and I had the exquisite pleasure of finding it met with their approbation, and that in their different guesses at the author none were named but men of some character among us for learning and ingenuity. I suppose now that I was rather lucky in my judges, and that perhaps they were not really so very good ones as I then esteemed them. Encouraged however by this, I wrote and conveyed in the same way to the press several more papers, which were equally approved, and I kept my secret till my small fund of sense for such performances was pretty well exhausted, and then I discovered it; when I began to be considered a little more by my brother's acquaintances, and in a manner that did not quite please him, as he thought, probably with reason, that it tended to make me too vain. And perhaps this might be one occasion of the differences that we began to have about this time. Though a brother, he considered himself as my master, and me as his apprentice; and accordingly expected the same services from me as he would from another; while I thought he demeaned me too much in some he required of me, who from a brother expected more indulgence. Our disputes were often brought before our Father, and I fancy I was either generally in the right, or else a better pleader, because the judgment was generally in my favor. But my brother was passionate and had often beaten me, which I took extremely amiss; and thinking my apprenticeship very tedious, I was continually wishing for some opportunity of shortening it, which at length offered in a manner unexpected. Note: I fancy his harsh and tyrannical treatment of me might be a means of impressing me with that aversion to arbitrary power that has stuck to me through my whole life.

One of the pieces in our newspaper, on some political point which I have now forgotten, gave offence to the Assembly. He was taken up, censured and imprisoned for a month by the speaker's warrant, I suppose because he would not reveal his author. I too was taken up and examined before the council; but though I did not give them any satisfaction, they contented themselves with admonishing me, and dismissed me; considering me perhaps as an apprentice who was bound to keep his master's secrets. During my brother's confinement, which I resented a good deal, notwithstanding our private differences, I had the management of the paper, and I made bold to give our rulers some rubs in it, which my brother took very kindly, while others began to consider me in an unfavorable light, as a young genius that had a turn for libelling and satire. My brother's discharge was accompanied with an order of the house (a very odd one) that James

Franklin should no longer print the paper called the *New England Courant*. There was a consultation held in our printing house among his friends what he should do in this case. Some proposed to evade the order by changing the name of the paper; but my brother seeing inconveniences in that, it was finally concluded on as a better way, to let it be printed for the future under the name of Benjamin Franklin. And to avoid the censure of the Assembly that might fall on him, as still printing it by his apprentice, the contrivance was that my old indenture should be returned to me with a full discharge on the back of it, to be shown on occasion; but to secure to him the benefit of my service I was to sign new indentures for the remainder of the term, which were to be kept private. A very flimsy scheme it was, but however it was immediately executed, and the paper went on accordingly under my name for several months. At length a fresh difference arising between my brother and me, I took upon me to assert my freedom, presuming that he would not venture to produce the new indentures. It was not fair in me to take this advantage, and this I therefore reckon one of the first errata of my life: but the unfairness of it weighed little with me, when under the impressions of resentment for the blows his passion too often urged him to bestow upon me. Though he was otherwise not an ill-natured man: perhaps I was too saucy and provoking.

When he found I would leave him, he took care to prevent my getting employment in any other printing house of the town, by going round and speaking to every master, who accordingly refused to give me work. I then thought of going to New York as the nearest place where there was a printer and I was the rather inclined to leave Boston, when I reflected that I had already made myself a little obnoxious to the governing party; and from the arbitrary proceedings of the

Assembly in my brother's case it was likely I might if I stayed soon bring myself into scrapes; and farther that my indiscrete disputations about religion began to make me pointed at with horror by good people, as an infidel or atheist. I determined on the point: but my Father now siding with my brother, I was sensible that if I attempted to go openly, means would be used to prevent me. My friend Collins therefore undertook to manage a little for me. He agreed with the captain of a New York sloop for my passage, under the notion of my being a young acquaintance of his that had got a naughty girl with child, whose friends would compel me to marry her, and therefore I could not appear or come away publicly. So I sold some of my books to raise a little money, was taken on board privately, and as we had a fair wind, in three days I found my self in New York near 300 miles from home, a boy of but 17, without the least recommendation to or knowledge of any person in the place, and with very little money in my pocket.

# Helen Keller

## FROM *The Story of My Life*

### CHAPTER ONE

IT IS WITH A KIND OF FEAR THAT I BEGIN TO WRITE THE history of my life. I have, as it were, a superstitious hesitation in lifting the veil that clings about my childhood like a golden mist. The task of writing an autobiography is a difficult one. When I try to classify my earliest impressions, I find that fact and fancy look alike across the years that link the past with the present. The woman paints the child's experiences in her own fantasy. A few impressions stand out vividly from the first years of my life; but "the shadows of the prison-house are on the rest." Besides, many of the joys and sorrows of childhood have lost their poignancy; and many incidents of vital importance in my early education have been forgotten in the excitement of great discoveries. In order, therefore, not to be tedious I shall try to present in a series of sketches only the episodes that seem to me to be the most interesting and important.

I was born on June 27, 1880, in Tuscumbia, a little town of northern Alabama.

The family on my father's side is descended from Caspar

Keller, a native of Switzerland, who settled in Maryland. One of my Swiss ancestors was the first teacher of the deaf in Zurich and wrote a book on the subject of their education—rather a singular coincidence; though it is true that there is no king who has not had a slave among his ancestors, and no slave who has not had a king among his.

My grandfather, Caspar Keller's son, "entered" large tracts of land in Alabama and finally settled there. I have been told that once a year he went from Tuscumbia to Philadelphia on horseback to purchase supplies for the plantation, and my aunt has in her possession many of the letters to his family, which give charming and vivid accounts of these trips.

My Grandmother Keller was a daughter of one of Lafayette's aides, Alexander Moore, and granddaughter of Alexander Spotswood, an early Colonial Governor of Virginia. She was also second cousin to Robert E. Lee.

My father, Arthur H. Keller, was a captain in the Confederate Army, and my mother, Kate Adams, was his second wife and many years younger. Her grandfather, Benjamin Adams, married Susanna E. Goodhue, and lived in Newbury, Massachusetts, for many years. Their son, Charles Adams, was born in Newburyport, Massachusetts, and moved to Helena, Arkansas. When the Civil War broke out, he fought on the side of the South and became a brigadier-general. He married Lucy Helen Everett, who belonged to the same family of Everetts as Edward Everett and Dr. Edward Everett Hale. After the war was over the family moved to Memphis, Tennessee.

I lived, up to the time of the illness that deprived me of my sight and hearing, in a tiny house consisting of a large square room and a small one, in which the servant slept. It is a custom in the South to build a small house near the homestead as an annex to be used on occasion. Such a house my father built after the Civil War, and when he married my mother they went to live in it. It was completely covered with vines, climbing roses and honeysuckles. From the garden it looked like an arbor. The little porch was hidden from view by a screen of yellow roses and Southern smilax. It was the favorite haunt of hummingbirds and bees.

The Keller homestead, where the family lived, was a few steps from our little rose-bower. It was called "Ivy Green" because the house and the surrounding trees and fences were covered with beautiful English ivy. Its old-fashioned garden was the paradise of my childhood.

Even in the days before my teacher came, I used to feel along the square stiff boxwood hedges, and, guided by the sense of smell, would find the first violets and lilies. There, too, after a fit of temper, I went to find comfort and to hide my hot face in the cool leaves and grass. What joy it was to lose myself in that garden of flowers, to wander happily from spot to spot, until, coming suddenly upon a beautiful vine, I recognized it by its leaves and blossoms, and knew it was the vine which covered the tumbledown summerhouse at the farther end of the garden! Here, also, were trailing clematis, drooping jessamine, and some rare sweet flowers called butterfly lilies, because their fragile petals resemble butterflies' wings. But the roses—they were loveliest of all. Never have I found in the greenhouses of the North such heart-satisfying roses as the climbing roses of my southern home. They used to hang in long festoons from our porch, filling the whole air with their fragrance, untainted by any earthy smell; and in the early morning, washed in the dew, they felt so soft, so pure, I could not help wondering if they did not resemble the asphodels of God's garden.

The beginning of my life was simple and much like every

other little life. I came, I saw, I conquered, as the first baby in the family always does. There was the usual amount of discussion as to a name for me. The first baby in the family was not to be lightly named, every one was emphatic about that. My father suggested the name of Mildred Campbell, an ancestor whom he highly esteemed, and he declined to take any further part in the discussion. My mother solved the problem by giving it as her wish that I should be called after her mother, whose maiden name was Helen Everett. But in the excitement of carrying me to church my father lost the name on the way, very naturally, since it was one in which he had declined to have a part. When the minister asked him for it, he just remembered that it had been decided to call me after my grandmother, and he gave her name as Helen Adams.

I am told that while I was still in long dresses I showed many signs of an eager, self-asserting disposition. Everything that I saw other people do I insisted upon imitating. At six months I could pipe out "How d'ye," and one day I attracted every one's attention by saying "Tea, tea, tea" quite plainly. Even after my illness I remembered one of the words I had learned in these early months. It was the word "water," and I continued to make some sound for that word after all other speech was lost. I ceased making the sound "wah-wah" only when I learned to spell the word.

They tell me I walked the day I was a year old. My mother had just taken me out of the bathtub and was holding me in her lap, when I was suddenly attracted by the flickering shadows of leaves that danced in the sunlight on the smooth floor. I slipped from my mother's lap and almost ran toward them. The impulse gone, I fell down and cried for her to take me up in her arms.

These happy days did not last long. One brief spring,

musical with the song of robin and mockingbird, one summer rich in fruit and roses, one autumn of gold and crimson sped by and left their gifts at the feet of an eager, delighted child. Then, in the dreary month of February, came the illness which closed my eyes and ears and plunged me into the unconsciousness of a newborn baby. They called it acute congestion of the stomach and brain. The doctor thought I could not live. Early one morning, however, the fever left me as suddenly and mysteriously as it had come. There was great rejoicing in the family that morning, but no one, not even the doctor, knew that I should never see or hear again.

I fancy I still have confused recollections of that illness. I especially remember the tenderness with which my mother tried to soothe me in my waking hours of fret and pain, and the agony and bewilderment with which I awoke after a tossing half sleep, and turned my eyes, so dry and hot, to the wall, away from the once-loved light, which came to me dim and yet more dim each day. But, except for these fleeting memories, if, indeed, they be memories, it all seems very unreal, like a nightmare. Gradually I got used to the silence and darkness that surrounded me and forgot that it had ever been different, until she came—my teacher—who was to set my spirit free. But during the first nineteen months of my life I had caught glimpses of broad, green fields, a luminous sky, trees and flowers which the darkness that followed could not wholly blot out.

## CHAPTER TWO

I cannot recall what happened during the first months after my illness. I only know that I sat in my mother's lap or clung to her dress as she went about her household duties. My hands felt every object and observed every motion, and in this way I learned to know many things. Soon I felt the need of some communication with others and began to make crude signs. A shake of the head meant "No" and a nod, "Yes," a pull meant "Come" and a push, "Go." Was it bread that I wanted? Then I would imitate the acts of cutting the slices and buttering them. If I wanted my mother to make ice cream for dinner I made the sign for working the freezer and shivered, indicating cold. My mother, moreover, succeeded in making me understand a good deal. I always knew when she wished me to bring her something, and I would run upstairs or anywhere else she indicated. Indeed, I owe to her loving wisdom all that was bright and good in my long night.

I understood a good deal of what was going on about me. At five I learned to fold and put away the clean clothes when they were brought in from the laundry, and I distinguished my own from the rest. I knew by the way my mother and aunt dressed when they were going out, and I invariably begged to go with them. I was always sent for when there was company, and when the guests took their leave, I waved my hand to them, I think with a vague remembrance of the meaning of the gesture. One day some gentlemen called on my mother, and I felt the shutting of the front door and other sounds that indicated their arrival. On a sudden thought I ran upstairs before any one could stop me, to put on my idea of a company dress. Standing before the mirror, as I had seen others do, I anointed mine head with oil and covered my face thickly with powder. Then I pinned a veil over my head so that it covered my face and fell in folds down to my shoulders, and tied an enormous bustle round my small waist, so that it dangled behind, almost meeting the hem of my skirt. Thus attired I went down to help entertain the company.

I do not remember when I first realized that I was different from other people; but I knew it before my teacher came to me. I had noticed that my mother and my friends did not use signs as I did when they wanted anything done, but talked with their mouths. Sometimes I stood between two persons who were conversing and touched their lips. I could not understand and was vexed. I moved my lips and gesticulated frantically without result. This made me so angry at times that I kicked and screamed until I was exhausted.

I think I knew when I was naughty, for I knew that it hurt Ella, my nurse, to kick her, and when my fit of temper was over I had a feeling akin to regret. But I cannot remember any instance in which this feeling prevented me from repeating the naughtiness when I failed to get what I wanted.

In those days a little colored girl, Martha Washington, the child of our cook, and Belle, an old setter and a great hunter in her day, were my constant companions. Martha Washington understood my signs, and I seldom had any difficulty in making her do just as I wished. It pleased me to domineer over her, and she generally submitted to my tyranny rather than risk a hand-to-hand encounter. I was strong, active, indifferent to consequences. I knew my own mind well enough and always had my own way, even if I had to fight tooth and nail for it. We spent a great deal of time in the kitchen, kneading dough balls, helping make ice cream, grinding coffee, quarreling over the cake-bowl, and feeding the hens and turkeys that swarmed about the kitchen steps. Many of them were so tame that they would eat from my hand and let me feel them. One big gobbler snatched a tomato from me one day and ran away with it. Inspired, perhaps, by Master Gobbler's success, we carried off to the woodpile a cake which the cook had just frosted, and ate every bit of it. I was quite ill afterward, and I wonder if retribution also overtook the turkey.

The guinea-fowl likes to hide her nest in out-of-the-way places, and it was one of my greatest delights to hunt for the eggs in the long grass. I could not tell Martha Washington when I wanted to go egg-hunting, but I would double my hands and put them on the ground, which meant something round in the grass, and Martha always understood. When we were fortunate enough to find a nest I never allowed her to carry the eggs home, making her understand by emphatic signs that she might fall and break them.

The sheds where the corn was stored, the stable where the horses were kept, and the yard where the cows were milked morning and evening were unfailing sources of interest to Martha and me. The milkers would let me keep my hands on the cows while they milked, and I often got well switched by the cow for my curiosity.

The making ready for Christmas was always a delight to me. Of course I did not know what it was all about, but I enjoyed the pleasant odors that filled the house and the tidbits that were given to Martha Washington and me to keep us quiet. We were sadly in the way, but that did not interfere with our pleasure in the least. They allowed us to grind the spices, pick over the raisins and lick the stirring spoons. I hung my stocking because the others did; I cannot remember, however, that the ceremony interested me especially, nor did my curiosity cause me to wake before daylight to look for my gifts.

Martha Washington had as great a love of mischief as I. Two little children were seated on the veranda steps one hot July afternoon. One was black as ebony, with little bunches of fuzzy hair tied with shoestrings sticking out all over her head like corkscrews. The other was white, with long golden curls. One child was six years old, the other two or three years older. The younger child was blind—that was I—and the other was Martha Washington. We were busy cutting out paper dolls; but we soon wearied of this amusement, and after cutting up our shoestrings and clipping all the leaves off the honeysuckle that were within reach, I turned my attention to Martha's corkscrews. She objected at first, but finally submitted. Thinking that turn and turn about is fair play, she seized the scissors and cut off one of my curls, and would have cut them all off but for my mother's timely interference.

Belle, our dog, my other companion, was old and lazy and liked to sleep by the open fire rather than to romp with me. I tried hard to teach her my sign language, but she was dull and inattentive. She sometimes started and quivered with excitement, then she became perfectly rigid, as dogs do when they point a bird. I did not then know why Belle acted in this way; but I knew she was not doing as I wished. This vexed me and the lesson always ended in a one-sided boxing match. Belle would get up, stretch herself lazily, give one or two contemptuous sniffs, go to the opposite side of the hearth and lie down again, and I, wearied and disappointed, went off in search of Martha.

Many incidents of those early years are fixed in my memory, isolated, but dear and distinct, making the sense of that silent, aimless, dayless life all the more intense.

One day I happened to spill water on my apron, and I spread it out to dry before the fire which was flickering on the sitting-room hearth. The apron did not dry quickly enough to suit me, so I drew nearer and threw it right over the hot ashes. The fire leaped into life; the flames encircled me so that in a moment my clothes were blazing. I made a terrified noise that brought Viny, my old nurse, to the rescue. Throwing a blanket over me, she almost suffocated me, but she put out the fire. Except for my hands and hair I was not badly burned.

About this time I found out the use of a key. One morning I locked my mother up in the pantry, where she was obliged to remain three hours, as the servants were in a detached part of the house. She kept pounding on the door, while I sat outside on the porch steps and laughed with glee as I felt the jar of the pounding. This most naughty prank of mine convinced my parents that I must be taught as soon as possible. After my teacher, Miss Sullivan, came to me, I sought an early opportunity to lock her in her room. I went upstairs with something which my mother made me understand I was to give to Miss Sullivan; but no sooner had I given it to her than I slammed the door to, locked it, and hid the key under the wardrobe in the hall. I could not be induced to tell where the key was. My father was obliged to get a ladder and take Miss Sullivan out through the window—much to my delight. Months after I produced the key.

When I was about five years old we moved from the little vine-covered house to a large new one. The family consisted of my father and mother, two older half-brothers, and, afterward, a little sister, Mildred. My earliest distinct recollection of my father is making my way through great drifts of newspapers to his side and finding him alone, holding a sheet of paper before his face. I was greatly puzzled to know what he was doing. I imitated this action, even wearing his spectacles, thinking they might help solve the mystery. But I did not find out the secret for several years. Then I learned what those papers were, and that my father edited one of them.

My father was most loving and indulgent, devoted to his home, seldom leaving us, except in the hunting season. He was a great hunter, I have been told, and a celebrated shot. Next to his family he loved his dogs and gun. His hospitality was great, almost to a fault, and he seldom came home without bringing a guest. His special pride was the big garden where, it was said, he raised the finest watermelons and strawberries in the county; and to me he brought the first ripe grapes and the choicest berries. I remember his caressing touch as he led me from tree to tree, from vine to vine, and his eager delight in whatever pleased me.

He was a famous storyteller; after I had acquired language he used to spell clumsily into my hand his cleverest anecdotes, and nothing pleased him more than to have me repeat them at an opportune moment.

I was in the North, enjoying the last beautiful days of the summer of 1896, when I heard the news of my father's death. He had had a short illness, there had been a brief time of acute suffering, then all was over. This was my first great sorrow—my first personal experience with death.

How shall I write of my mother? She is so near to me that it almost seems indelicate to speak of her.

For a long time I regarded my little sister as an intruder. I knew that I had ceased to be my mother's only darling, and the thought filled me with jealousy. She sat in my mother's lap constantly, where I used to sit, and seemed to take up all her care and time. One day something happened which seemed to me to be adding insult to injury.

At that time I had a much-petted, much-abused doll, which I afterward named Nancy. She was, alas, the helpless victim of my outbursts of temper and of affection, so that she became much the worse for wear. I had dolls which talked, and cried, and opened and shut their eyes; yet I never loved one of them as I loved poor Nancy. She had a cradle, and I often spent an hour or more rocking her. I guarded both doll and cradle with the most jealous care; but once I discovered my little sister sleeping peacefully in the cradle. At this presumption on the part of one to whom as yet no tie of love bound me I grew angry. I rushed upon the cradle and overturned it, and the baby might have been killed had my mother not caught her as she fell. Thus it is that when we walk in the valley of twofold solitude we know little of the tender affections that grow out of endearing words and actions and companionship. But afterward, when I was restored to my human heritage, Mildred and I grew into each other's hearts, so that we were content to go hand-in-hand wherever caprice led us, although she could not understand my finger language, nor I her childish prattle.

## CHAPTER THREE

Meanwhile the desire to express myself grew. The few signs I used became less and less adequate, and my failures to make myself understood were invariably followed by outbursts of passion. I felt as if invisible hands were holding me, and I made frantic efforts to free myself. I struggled—not that struggling helped matters, but the spirit of resistance was strong within me; I generally broke down in tears and physical exhaustion. If my mother happened to be near I crept into her arms, too miserable even to remember the cause of the tempest. After awhile the need of some means of communication became so urgent that these outbursts occurred daily, sometimes hourly.

My parents were deeply grieved and perplexed. We lived a long way from any school for the blind or the deaf, and it seemed unlikely that any one would come to such an out-of-the-way place as Tuscumbia to teach a child who was both deaf and blind. Indeed, my friends and relatives sometimes doubted whether I could be taught. My mother's only ray of hope came from Dickens's *American Notes*. She had read his account of Laura Bridgman, and remembered vaguely that she was deaf and blind, yet had been educated. But she also remembered with a hopeless pang that Dr. Howe, who had discovered the way to teach the deaf and blind, had been dead many years. His methods had probably died with him; and if they had not, how was a little girl in a far-off town in Alabama to receive the benefit of them?

When I was about six years old, my father heard of an eminent oculist in Baltimore, who had been successful in many cases that had seemed hopeless. My parents at once determined to take me to Baltimore to see if anything could be done for my eyes.

The journey, which I remember well, was very pleasant. I made friends with many people on the train. One lady gave me a box of shells. My father made holes in these so that I could string them, and for a long time they kept me happy and contented. The conductor, too, was kind. Often when he went his rounds I clung to his coat tails while he collected and punched the tickets. His punch, with which he let me play, was a delightful toy. Curled up in a corner of the seat I amused myself for hours making funny little holes in bits of cardboard.

My aunt made me a big doll out of towels. It was the most comical, shapeless thing, this improvised doll, with no nose, mouth, ears or eyes—nothing that even the imagination of a child could convert into a face. Curiously enough, the absence of eyes struck me more than all the other defects put together. I pointed this out to everybody with provoking persistency, but no one seemed equal to the task of providing the doll with eyes. A bright idea, however, shot into my mind, and the problem was solved. I tumbled off the seat and searched under it until I found my aunt's cape, which was trimmed with large beads. I pulled two beads off and indicated to her that I wanted her to sew them on my doll. She raised my hand to her eyes in a questioning way, and I nodded energetically. The beads were sewed in the right place and I could not contain myself for joy; but immediately I lost all interest in the doll. During the whole trip I did not have one fit of temper, there were so many things to keep my mind and fingers busy.

When we arrived in Baltimore, Dr. Chisholm received us kindly, but he could do nothing. He said, however, that I could be educated, and advised my father to consult Dr. Alexander Graham Bell, of Washington, who would be able to give him information about schools and teachers of deaf or blind children. Acting on the doctor's advice, we went immediately to Washington to see Dr. Bell, my father with a sad heart and many misgivings, I wholly unconscious of his anguish, finding pleasure in the excitement of moving from place to place. Child as I was, I at once felt the tenderness and sympathy which endeared Dr. Bell to so many hearts, as his wonderful achievements enlist their admiration. He held me on his knee while I examined his watch, and he made it strike for me. He understood my signs, and I knew it and loved him at once. But I did not dream that that interview would be the door through which I should pass from darkness into light, from isolation to friendship, companionship, knowledge, love.

Dr. Bell advised my father to write to Mr. Anagnos, director of the Perkins Institution in Boston, the scene of Dr. Howe's great labors for the blind, and ask him if he had a teacher competent to begin my education. This my father did at once, and in a few weeks there came a kind letter from Mr. Anagnos with the comforting assurance that a teacher had been found. This was in the summer of 1886. But Miss Sullivan did not arrive until the following March.

Thus I came up **out of Egypt and stood before Sinai**, and a power divine touched my spirit and gave it sight, so that I beheld many wonders. And from the sacred mountain I heard a voice which said, "Knowledge is love and light and vision."

## CHAPTER FOUR

The most important day I remember in all my life is the one on which my teacher, Anne Mansfield Sullivan, came to me. I am filled with wonder when I consider the immeasurable contrasts between the two lives which it connects. It was the third of March, 1887, three months before I was seven years old.

On the afternoon of that eventful day, I stood on the porch, dumb, expectant. I guessed vaguely from my mother's signs and from the hurrying to and fro in the house that something unusual was about to happen, so I went to the door and waited on the steps. The afternoon sun penetrated the mass of honeysuckle that covered the porch, and fell on my upturned face. My fingers lingered almost unconsciously on the familiar leaves and blossoms which had just come forth to greet the sweet southern spring. I did not know what the future held of marvel or surprise for me. Anger and bitterness had preyed upon me continually for weeks and a deep languor had succeeded this passionate struggle.

Have you ever been at sea in a dense fog, when it seemed

---

**Out of Egypt... Sinai**: a reference to the mass departure of the Isrealites out of Egypt (Exodus 13-15), where they had been slaves of the Pharaohs for more than 400 years. Lead by Moses, they escaped the Pharaoh's soldiers when the Red Sea miraculously parted and went into the Sinai Peninsula, seeking the Promised Land.

as if a tangible white darkness shut you in, and the great ship, tense and anxious, groped her way toward the shore with plummet and sounding-line, and you waited with beating heart for something to happen? I was like that ship before my education began, only I was without compass or sounding-line, and had no way of knowing how near the harbor was. "Light! give me light!" was the wordless cry of my soul, and the light of love shone on me in that very hour.

I felt approaching footsteps. I stretched out my hand as I supposed to my mother. Some one took it, and I was caught up and held close in the arms of her who had come to reveal all things to me, and, more than all things else, to love me.

The morning after my teacher came she led me into her room and gave me a doll. The little blind children at the Perkins Institution had sent it and Laura Bridgman had dressed it; but I did not know this until afterward. When I had played with it a little while, Miss Sullivan slowly spelled into my hand the word "d-o-l-l." I was at once interested in this finger play and tried to imitate it. When I finally succeeded in making the letters correctly I was flushed with childish pleasure and pride. Running downstairs to my mother I held up my hand and made the letters for doll. I did not know that I was spelling a word or even that words existed; I was simply making my fingers go in monkey-like imitation. In the days that followed I learned to spell in this uncomprehending way a great many words, among them *pin*, *hat*, *cup* and a few verbs like *sit*, *stand* and *walk*. But my teacher had been with me several weeks before I understood that everything has a name.

One day, while I was playing with my new doll, Miss Sullivan put my big rag doll into my lap also, spelled "d-o-l-l" and tried to make me understand that "d-o-l-l" applied to both. Earlier in the day we had had a tussle over the words "m-u-g" and "w-a-t-e-r." Miss Sullivan had tried to impress it upon me that "m-u-g" is *mug* and that "w-a-t-e-r" is *water*, but I persisted in confounding the two. In despair she had dropped the subject for the time, only to renew it at the first opportunity. I became impatient at her repeated attempts and, seizing the new doll, I dashed it upon the floor. I was keenly delighted when I felt the fragments of the broken doll at my feet. Neither sorrow nor regret followed my passionate outburst. I had not loved the doll. In the still, dark world in which I lived there was no strong sentiment or tenderness. I felt my teacher sweep the fragments to one side of the hearth, and I had a sense of satisfaction that the cause of my discomfort was removed. She brought me my hat, and I knew I was going out into the warm sunshine. This thought, if a wordless sensation may be called a thought, made me hop and skip with pleasure.

We walked down the path to the well-house, attracted by the fragrance of the honeysuckle with which it was covered. Some one was drawing water and my teacher placed my hand under the spout. As the cool stream gushed over one hand she spelled into the other the word *water*, first slowly, then rapidly. I stood still, my whole attention fixed upon the motions of her fingers. Suddenly I felt a misty consciousness as of something forgotten—a thrill of returning thought; and somehow the mystery of language was revealed to me. I knew then that "w-a-t-e-r" meant the wonderful cool something that was flowing over my hand. That living word awakened my soul, gave it light, hope, joy, set it free! There were barriers still, it is true, but barriers that could in time he swept away.

I left the well-house eager to learn. Everything had a name, and each name gave birth to a new thought. As we returned to the house every object which I touched seemed to quiver with life. That was because I saw everything with the strange, new sight that had come to me. On entering the door I remembered the doll I had broken. I felt my way to the hearth and picked up the pieces. I tried vainly to put them together. Then my eyes filled with tears; for I realized what I had done, and for the first time I felt repentance and sorrow.

I learned a great many new words that day. I do not remember what they all were; but I do know that *mother, father, sister, teacher* were among them—words that were to make the world blossom for me, "like **Aaron's rod**, with flowers." It would have been difficult to find a happier child than I was as I lay in my crib at the close of that eventful day and lived over the joys it had brought me, and for the first time longed for a new day to come.

## CHAPTER FIVE

I recall many incidents of the summer of 1887 that followed my soul's sudden awakening. I did nothing but explore with my hands and learn the name of every object that I touched; and the more I handled things and learned their names and uses, the more joyous and confident grew my sense of kinship with the rest of the world.

When the time of daisies and buttercups came, Miss Sullivan took me by the hand across the fields, where men were preparing the earth for the seed, to the banks of the Tennessee River, and there, sitting on the warm grass, I had my first lessons in the beneficence of nature. I learned how

---

**Aaron's rod:** Aaron was the brother of Moses and a priest of the Hebrews in Egypt. He performed many signs of God, including turning his staff into a serpent and having it bud, blossom and bear almonds.

the sun and the rain make to grow out of the ground every tree that is pleasant to the sight and good for food, how birds build their nests and live and thrive from land to land, how the squirrel, the deer, the lion and every other creature finds food and shelter. As my knowledge of things grew I felt more and more the delight of the world I was in. Long before I learned to do a sum in arithmetic or describe the shape of the earth, Miss Sullivan had taught me to find beauty in the fragrant woods, in every blade of grass, and in the curves and dimples of my baby sister's hand. She linked my earliest thoughts with nature, and made me feel that "birds and flowers and I were happy peers."

But about this time I had an experience which taught me that nature is not always kind. One day my teacher and I were returning from a long ramble. The morning had been fine, but it was growing warm and sultry when at last we turned our faces homeward. Two or three times we stopped to rest under a tree by the wayside. Our last halt was under a wild cherry tree a short distance from the house. The shade was grateful, and the tree was so easy to climb that with my teacher's assistance I was able to scramble to a seat in the branches. It was so cool up in the tree that Miss Sullivan proposed that we have our luncheon there. I promised to keep still while she went to the house to fetch it.

Suddenly a change passed over the tree. All the sun's warmth left the air. I knew the sky was black, because all the heat, which meant light to me, had died out of the atmosphere. A strange odor came up from the earth. I knew it, it was the odor that always precedes a thunderstorm, and a nameless fear clutched at my heart. I felt absolutely alone, cut off from my friends and the firm earth. The immense, the unknown, enfolded me. I remained still and expectant; a chilling terror crept over me. I longed for my teacher's return;

but above all things I wanted to get down from that tree.

There was a moment of sinister silence, then a multitudinous stirring of the leaves. A shiver ran through the tree, and the wind sent forth a blast that would have knocked me off had I not clung to the branch with might and main. The tree swayed and strained. The small twigs snapped and fell about me in showers. A wild impulse to jump seized me, but terror held me fast. I crouched down in the fork of the tree. The branches lashed about me. I felt the intermittent jarring that came now and then, as if something heavy had fallen and the shock had traveled up till it reached the limb I sat on. It worked my suspense up to the highest point, and just as I was thinking the tree and I should fall together, my teacher seized my hand and helped me down. I clung to her, trembling with joy to feel the earth under my feet once more. I had learned a new lesson—that nature "wages open war against her children, and under softest touch hides treacherous claws."

After this experience it was a long time before I climbed another tree. The mere thought filled me with terror. It was the sweet allurement of the mimosa tree in full bloom that finally overcame my fears. One beautiful spring morning when I was alone in the summerhouse, reading, I became aware of a wonderful subtle fragrance in the air. I started up and instinctively stretched out my hands. It seemed as if the spirit of spring had passed through the summerhouse. "What is it?" I asked, and the next minute I recognized the odor of the mimosa blossoms. I felt my way to the end of the garden, knowing that the mimosa tree was near the fence, at the turn of the path. Yes, there it was, all quivering in the warm sunshine, its blossom-laden branches almost touching the long grass. Was there ever anything so exquisitely beautiful in the world before! Its delicate blossoms shrank from the slightest earthly touch; it seemed as if a tree of paradise had been transplanted to earth. I made my way through a shower of petals to the great trunk and for one minute stood irresolute; then, putting my foot in the broad space between the forked branches, I pulled myself up into the tree. I had some difficulty in holding on, for the branches were very large and the bark hurt my hands. But I had a delicious sense that I was doing something unusual and wonderful, so I kept on climbing higher and higher, until I reached a little seat which somebody had built there so long ago that it had grown part of the tree itself. I sat there for a long, long time, feeling like a fairy on a rosy cloud. After that I spent many happy hours in my tree of paradise, thinking fair thoughts and dreaming bright dreams.

## CHAPTER SIX

I had now the key to all language, and I was eager to learn to use it. Children who hear acquire language without any particular effort; the words that fall from others' lips they catch on the wing, as it were, delightedly, while the little deaf child must trap them by a slow and often painful process. But whatever the process, the result is wonderful. Gradually from naming an object we advance step by step until we have traversed the vast distance between our first stammered syllable and the sweep of thought in a line of Shakespeare.

At first, when my teacher told me about a new thing I asked very few questions. My ideas were vague, and my vocabulary was inadequate; but as my knowledge of things grew, and I learned more and more words, my field of inquiry broadened, and I would return again and again to the same subject, eager for further information. Sometimes a new word revived an image that some earlier experience had engraved on my brain.

I remember the morning that I first asked the meaning of the word "love." This was before I knew many words. I had found a few early violets in the garden and brought them to my teacher. She tried to kiss me: but at that time I did not like to have any one kiss me except my Mother. Miss Sullivan put her arm gently round me and spelled into my hand, "I love Helen."

"What is love?" I asked.

She drew me closer to her and said, "It is here," pointing to my heart, whose beats I was conscious of for the first time. Her words puzzled me very much because I did not then understand anything unless I touched it.

I smelt the violets in her hand and asked, half in words, half in signs, a question which meant, "Is love the sweetness of flowers?"

"No," said my teacher.

Again I thought. The warm sun was shining on us.

"Is this not love?" I asked, pointing in the direction from which the heat came. "Is this not love?"

It seemed to me that there could be nothing more beautiful than the sun, whose warmth makes all things grow. But Miss Sullivan shook her head, and I was greatly puzzled and disappointed. I thought it strange that my teacher could not show me love.

A day or two afterward I was stringing beads of different sizes in symmetrical groups—two large beads, three small ones, and so on. I had made many mistakes, and Miss Sullivan had pointed them out again and again with gentle patience. Finally I noticed a very obvious error in the sequence and for an instant I concentrated my attention on the lesson and tried to think how I should have arranged the beads. Miss Sullivan touched my forehead and spelled with decided emphasis, "Think."

In a flash I knew that the word was the name of the process that was going on in my head. This was my first conscious perception of an abstract idea.

For a long time I was still—I was not thinking of the beads in my lap, but trying to find a meaning for "love" in the light of this new idea. The sun had been under a cloud all day, and there had been brief showers; but suddenly the sun broke forth in all its southern splendor.

Again I asked my teacher, "Is this not love?"

"Love is something like the clouds that were in the sky before the sun came out," she replied. Then in simpler words than these, which at that time I could not have understood, she explained: "You cannot touch the clouds, you know; but you feel the rain and know how glad the flowers and the thirsty earth are to have it after a hot day. You cannot touch love either; but you feel the sweetness that it pours into everything. Without love you would not be happy or want to play."

The beautiful truth burst upon my mind—I felt that there were invisible lines stretched between my spirit and the spirits of others.

From the beginning of my education Miss Sullivan made it a practice to speak to me as she would speak to any hearing child; the only difference was that she spelled the sentences into my hand instead of speaking them. If I did not know the words and idioms necessary to express my thoughts she supplied them, even suggesting conversation when I was unable to keep up my end of the dialogue.

This process was continued for several years; for the deaf child does not learn in a month, or even in two or three years, the numberless idioms and expressions used in the simplest daily intercourse. The little hearing child learns these from constant repetition and imitation. The conversation he hears in his home stimulates his mind and suggests topics and calls forth the spontaneous expression of his own thoughts. This natural exchange of ideas is denied to the deaf child. My teacher, realizing this, determined to supply the kinds of stimulus I lacked. This she did by repeating to me as far as possible, verbatim, what she heard, and by showing me how I could take part in the conversation. But it was a long time before I ventured to take the initiative, and still longer before I could find something appropriate to say at the right time.

The deaf and the blind find it very difficult to acquire the amenities of conversation. How much more this difficulty must be augmented in the case of those who are both deaf and blind! They cannot distinguish the tone of the voice or, without assistance, go up and down the gamut of tones that give significance to words; nor can they watch the expression of the speaker's face, and a look is often the very soul of what one says.

## CHAPTER SEVEN

The next important step in my education was learning to read.

As soon as I could spell a few words my teacher gave me slips of cardboard on which were printed words in raised letters. I quickly learned that each printed word stood for an object, an act, or a quality. I had a frame in which I could arrange the words in little sentences; but before I ever put sentences in the frame I used to make them in objects. I found the slips of paper which represented, for example, "doll," "is," "on," "bed" and placed each name on its object;

then I put my doll on the bed with the words *is, on, bed* arranged beside the doll, thus making a sentence of the words, and at the same time carrying out the idea of the sentence with the things themselves.

One day, Miss Sullivan tells me, I pinned the word *girl* on my pinafore and stood in the wardrobe. On the shelf I arranged the words, *is, in, wardrobe*. Nothing delighted me so much as this game. My teacher and I played it for hours at a time. Often everything in the room was arranged in object sentences.

From the printed slip it was but a step to the printed book. I took my *Reader for Beginners* and hunted for the words I knew; when I found them my joy was like that of a game of hide-and-seek. Thus I began to read. Of the time when I began to read connected stories I shall speak later.

For a long time I had no regular lessons. Even when I studied most earnestly it seemed more like play than work. Everything Miss Sullivan taught me she illustrated by a beautiful story or a poem. Whenever anything delighted or interested me she talked it over with me just as if she were a little girl herself. What many children think of with dread, as a painful plodding through grammar, hard sums and harder definitions, is today one of my most precious memories.

I cannot explain the peculiar sympathy Miss Sullivan had with my pleasures and desires. Perhaps it was the result of long association with the blind. Added to this she had a wonderful faculty for description. She went quickly over uninteresting details, and never nagged me with questions to see if I remembered the day-before-yesterday's lesson. She introduced dry technicalities of science little by little, making every subject so real that I could not help remembering what she taught.

We read and studied out of doors, preferring the sunlit

woods to the house. All my early lessons have in them the breath of the woods—the fine, resinous odor of pine needles, blended with the perfume of wild grapes. Seated in the gracious shade of a wild tulip tree, I learned to think that everything has a lesson and a suggestion. "The loveliness of things taught me all their use." Indeed, everything that could hum, or buzz, or sing, or bloom, had a part in my education—noisy-throated frogs, katydids and crickets held in my hand until, forgetting their embarrassment, they trilled their reedy note; little downy chickens and wildflowers, the dogwood blossoms, meadow-violets and budding fruit trees. I felt the bursting cotton-bolls and fingered their soft fiber and fuzzy seeds; I felt the low soughing of the wind through the cornstalks, the silky rustling of the long leaves, and the indignant snort of my pony, as we caught him in the pasture and put the bit in his mouth—ah me! How well I remember the spicy, clovery smell of his breath!

Sometimes I rose at dawn and stole into the garden while the heavy dew lay on the grass and flowers. Few know what joy it is to feel the roses pressing softly into the hand, or the beautiful motion of the lilies as they sway in the morning breeze. Sometimes I caught an insect in the flower I was plucking, and I felt the faint noise of a pair of wings rubbed together in a sudden terror, as the little creature became aware of a pressure from without.

Another favorite haunt of mine was the orchard, where the fruit ripened early in July. The large, downy peaches would reach themselves into my hand, and as the joyous breezes flew about the trees the apples tumbled at my feet. Oh, the delight with which I gathered up the fruit in my pinafore, pressed my face against the smooth cheeks of the apples, still warm from the sun, and skipped back to the house!

Our favorite walk was to Keller's Landing, an old tumbledown lumber-wharf on the Tennessee River, used during the Civil War to land soldiers. There we spent many happy hours and played at learning geography. I built dams of pebbles, made islands and lakes, and dug river-beds, all for fun, and never dreamed that I was learning a lesson. I listened with increasing wonder to Miss Sullivan's descriptions of the great round world with its burning mountains, buried cities, moving rivers of ice, and many other things as strange. She made raised maps in clay, so that I could feel the mountain ridges and valleys, and follow with my fingers the devious course of rivers. I liked this, too; but the division of the earth into zones and poles confused and teased my mind. The illustrative strings and the orange stick representing the poles seemed so real that even to this day the mere mention of temperate zone suggests a series of twine circles; and I believe that if any one should set about it he could convince me that white bears actually climb the North Pole.

Arithmetic seems to have been the only study I did not like. From the first I was not interested in the science of numbers. Miss Sullivan tried to teach me to count by stringing beads in groups, and by arranging kindergarten straws I learned to add and subtract. I never had patience to arrange more than five or six groups at a time. When I had accomplished this my conscience was at rest for the day, and I went out quickly to find my playmates.

In this same leisurely manner I studied zoology and botany.

Once a gentleman, whose name I have forgotten, sent me a collection of fossils—tiny mollusk shells beautifully marked, and bits of sandstone with the print of birds' claws, and a lovely fern in bas-relief. These were the keys which unlocked the treasures of the antediluvian world for me.

With trembling fingers I listened to Miss Sullivan's descriptions of the terrible beasts, with uncouth, unpronounceable names, which once went tramping through the primeval forests, tearing down the branches of gigantic trees for food, and died in the dismal swamps of an unknown age. For a long time these strange creatures haunted my dreams, and this gloomy period formed a somber background to the joyous Now, filled with sunshine and roses and echoing with the gentle beat of my pony's hoof.

Another time a beautiful shell was given me, and with a child's surprise and delight I learned how a tiny mollusk had built the lustrous coil for his dwelling place, and how on still nights, when there is no breeze stirring the waves, the Nautilus sails on the blue waters of the Indian Ocean in his "ship of pearl." After I had learned a great many interesting things about the life and habits of the children of the sea—how in the midst of dashing waves the little polyps build the beautiful coral isles of the Pacific, and the foraminifera have made the chalk-hills of many a land—my teacher read me "The Chambered Nautilus," and showed me that the shell-building process of the mollusks is symbolical of the development of the mind. Just as the wonder-working mantle of the Nautilus changes the material it absorbs from the water and makes it a part of itself, so the bits of knowledge one gathers undergo a similar change and become pearls of thought.

Again, it was the growth of a plant that furnished the text for a lesson. We bought a lily and set it in a sunny window. Very soon the green, pointed buds showed signs of opening. The slender, fingerlike leaves on the outside opened slowly, reluctant, I thought, to reveal the loveliness they hid; once having made a start, however, the opening process went on rapidly, but in order and systematically. There was always one bud larger and more beautiful than the rest, which pushed her outer covering back with more pomp, as if the beauty in soft, silky robes knew that she was the lily-queen by right divine, while her more timid sisters doffed their green hoods shyly, until the whole plant was one nodding bough of loveliness and fragrance.

Once there were eleven tadpoles in a glass globe set in a window full of plants. I remember the eagerness with which I made discoveries about them. It was great fun to plunge my hand into the bowl and feel the tadpoles frisk about, and to let them slip and slide between my fingers. One day a more ambitious fellow leaped beyond the edge of the bowl and fell on the floor, where I found him to all appearance more dead than alive. The only sign of life was a slight wriggling of his tail. But no sooner had he returned to his element than he darted to the bottom, swimming round and round in joyous activity. He had made his leap, he had seen the great world, and was content to stay in his pretty glass house under the big fuchsia tree until he attained the dignity of froghood. Then he went to live in the leafy pool at the end of the garden, where he made the summer nights musical with his quaint love-song.

Thus I learned from life itself. At the beginning I was only a little mass of possibilities. It was my teacher who unfolded and developed them. When she came, everything about me breathed of love and joy and was full of meaning. She has never since let pass an opportunity to point out the beauty that is in everything, nor has she ceased trying in thought and action and example to make my life sweet and useful.

It was my teacher's genius, her quick sympathy, her loving tact which made the first years of my education so beautiful It was because she seized the right moment to impart knowledge that made it so pleasant and acceptable to me. She realized that a child's mind is like a shallow brook which ripples and dances merrily over the stony course of its education and reflects here a flower, there a bush, yonder a fleecy cloud; and she attempted to guide my mind on its way, knowing that like a brook it should be fed by mountain streams and hidden springs, until it broadened out into a deep river, capable of reflecting in its placid surface, billowy hills, the luminous shadows of trees and the blue heavens, as well as the sweet face of a little flower.

Any teacher can take a child to the classroom, but not every teacher can make him learn. He will not work joyously unless he feels that liberty is his, whether he is busy or at rest; he must feel the flush of victory and the heart-sinking of disappointment before he takes with a will the tasks distasteful to him and resolves to dance his way bravely through a dull routine of textbooks.

My teacher is so near to me that I scarcely think of myself apart from her. How much of my delight in all beautiful things is innate, and how much is due to her influence, I can never tell. I feel that her being is inseparable from my own, and that the footsteps of my life are in hers. All the best of me belongs to her—there is not a talent, or an aspiration or a joy in me that has not been awakened by her loving touch.

# ACKNOWLEDGMENTS

COVER

MAXFIELD PARRISH. *The Milkmaid*, 1901. Oil on paper. 25' x 18'. Private collection. Photo detail from the archives of Alma Gilbert, Cornish, NH.

W.H. AUDEN. "The Unknown Citizen," from W.H. Auden: Collected Poems, edited by Edward Mendelson. Copyright © 1940 and renewed 1968 by W. H. Auden. Reprinted by permission of Random House, Inc.

COUNTEE CULLEN. "Heritage" from Color, copyright © 1925 by Harper & Brothers; copyright renewed 1953 by Ida M. Cullen. Reprinted by permission of GRM Associates, Inc., agents for the estate of Ida M. Cullen.

E.E. CUMMINGS. "next to of course god america i" copyright 1926, 1954, © 1991 by the Trustees for the E. E. Cummings Trust. Copyright © 1985 by George James Firmage, from Complete Poems: 1904-1962 by E.E. Cummings, edited by George J. Firmage. Reprinted by permission of Liveright Publishing Corporation.

EMILY DICKINSON. "Because I Could Not Stop For Death." Reprinted by permission of the publishers and Trustees of Amherst College from The Poems of Emily Dickinson, Thomas H. Johnson, ed. Cambridge, Mass.: The Belknap Press of Harvard University Press © 1951, © 1955, 1979, 1983 by the President and Fellows of Harvard College.

T.S. ELIOT. "Macavity: The Mystery Cat," from Old Possum's Book of Practical Cats. Copyright © 1939 and renewed 1967 by Esme Valerie Eliot. Reprinted by permission of Harcourt, Inc. and Faber and Faber, Ltd.

WILLIAM FAULKNER. "Barn Burning," from The Country, in Collected Stories of William Faulkner. Copyright © 1950 by Random House and renewed 1977 by Jill Faulkner Summers. Reprinted by permission of Random House, Inc.

ROBERT FROST. "Fire and Ice" From The Poetry of Robert Frost, edited by Edward Connery Lathem. Copyright Henry Holt and Co. 1923, © 1969 copyright 1936, 1942, 1951 by Robert

Frost, copyright © 1964, 1970 by Lesley Frost Ballantine. Reprinted by permission of Henry Holt and Company, LLC

ROBERT FROST. "Nothing Gold Can Stay" From The Poetry of Robert Frost, edited by Edward Connery Lathem. Copyright Henry Holt and Co. 1923, © 1969 copyright 1936, 1942, 1951 by Robert Frost, copyright © 1964, 1970 by Lesley Frost Ballantine. Reprinted by permission of Henry Holt and Company, LLC.

ROBERT FROST. "Design" From The Poetry of Robert Frost, edited by Edward Connery Lathem. Copyright Henry Holt and Co. 1923, © 1969 copyright 1936, 1942, 1951 by Robert Frost, copyright © 1964, 1970 by Lesley Frost Ballantine. Reprinted by permission of Henry Holt and Company, LLC.

THOMAS HARDY. "Channel Firing," from The Complete Poems of Thomas Hardy, 1948. Edited by James Gibson (New York: Scribner, 1978).

LANGSTON HUGHES. "The Negro Speaks of Rivers," from Collected Poems. Copyright © 1994 by the Estate of Langston Hughes. Reprinted by permission of Alfred A. Knopf, Inc.

LANGSTON HUGHES. "Harlem," from Collected Poems. Copyright © 1994 by the Estate of Langston Hughes. Reprinted by permission of Alfred A. Knopf, Inc.

LANGSTON HUGHES. "Life is Fine," from Collected Poems. Copyright © 1994 by the Estate of Langston Hughes. Reprinted by permission of Alfred A. Knopf, Inc.

FRANK O'CONNOR. "My Oedipus Complex," from Collected Stories. Copyright © 1950 by Frank O'Connor. Reprinted by permission of Alfred A. Knopf, Inc. and the Joan Daves Agency on behalf of the estate of Frank O'Connor.

GEORGE ORWELL. "Shooting an Elephant," from Shooting and Elephant and Other Essays. Copyright © 1950 by Sonia Brownell Orwell and renewed 1978 Sonia Pitt- Rivers. Reprinted with permission of Harcourt, Inc. and Bill Hamilton as the Literary Executor of the Estate of the Late Sonia Brownell Orwell and Martin Secker & Warburg Ltd.

WILFRED OWEN. "Anthem for Doomed Youth," from The Collected Poems of Wilfred Owen. Copyright © 1963 by Chatto & Windus, Ltd. Reprinted by permission of New Directions Publishing Corp.

WILFRED OWEN. "Dulce et Decorum Est," from The Collected Poems of Wilfred Owen. Copyright © 1963 by Chatto & Windus, Ltd. Reprinted by permission of New Directions Publishing Corp.

KATHERINE ANN PORTER. "The Jilting of Granny Weatherall," from Flowering Judas and Other Stories. Copyright © 1930 and renewed 1958 by Katherine Anne Porter. Reprinted by permission of Harcourt, Inc.

THEODORE ROETHKE. "My Papa's Waltz," from The Collected Poems of Theodore Roethke. Copyright 1942 by Hearst Magazines, Inc. Used by permission of Doubleday, a division of Random House, Inc.

JAMES THURBER. "The Night the Bed Fell," from My Life and Hard Times. Copyright © 1933, 1961 by James Thurber. Reprinted by arrangement with Rosemary A. Thurber and the Barbara Hogenson Agency.

JAMES THURBER. "The Secret Life of Walter Mitty" From My World and Welcome To It, Coprright © 1942 by James Thurber. Copyright renewed 1970 by Helen and Rosemary A. Thurber. Reprinted by arrangement with Rosemary A. Thurber and the Barbara Hogenson Agency.

WALLACE STEVENS. "Anecdote of the Jar," from Collected Poems. Copyright ©1923, renewed 1951 by Wallace Stevens. Reprinted by permission Alfred A. Knopf, Inc.

WILLIAM CARLOS WILLIAMS. "This Is Just to Say," from Collected Poems: 1909-1939, Volume. 1 Copyright © 1938 by New Directions Publishing Corporation. Reprinted by permission of New Directions Publishing Corp.

WILLIAM CARLOS WILLIAMS. "The Red Wheelbarrow," from Collected Poems: 1909- 1939, Volume. 1 © 1938 by New Directions Publishing Corporation. Reprinted by permission of New Directions Publishing Corp.